THE GANGSTER'S WIFE

David Leslie is the author of the bestselling *Crimelord*, about Tam McGraw, as well as *The Happy Dust Gang*, *Bible John's Secret Daughter* and *Mummy, Take Me Home*.

THE GANGSTER'S WIFE

LIFE WITH A NOTORIOUS CRIME BOSS

DAVID LESLIE

MAINSTREAM
PUBLISHING

EDINBURGH AND LONDON

This edition, 2013

First published in Great Britain in 2009 by
MAINSTREAM PUBLISHING COMPANY
(EDINBURGH) LTD
7 Albany Street
Edinburgh EH1 3UG

ISBN 9781845967307

This book is a work of non-fiction. In some cases, names of people have
been changed to protect the privacy of others. The author has stated
to the publishers, except in such respects not affecting the substantial
accuracy of the work, the contents of this book are true

A catalogue record for this book is available
from the British Library

Typeset in Optima and Sabon

Printed and bound by
CPI Group (UK) Ltd, Croydon, CR0 4YY

1 3 5 7 9 10 8 6 4 2

ACKNOWLEDGEMENTS

MANY MONTHS BEFORE THE SUDDEN DEATH OF MY FRIEND TAM McGraw, I had decided to ask Margaret – Mags – if she would be willing to tell me her story. After his passing, we chatted occasionally at her home, and it was there that I met Jim McMinimee for the first time. Eventually, I broached the subject of a book, and Margaret, encouraged by Jim, was all for it. We met regularly, sitting around her table drinking a seemingly endless supply of tea and coffee, and I was enthralled by her anecdotes and memories of life in Glasgow's East End. On occasions, her friends would join us, some to contribute, others simply to listen. Some I have mentioned by name, while I have respected that others wished to remain anonymous. My genuine thanks go to them all for their candour and help. Brian Anderson, the very talented cameraman, was so trusted by Margaret and Tam that they not only allowed him into their home, but posed for photographs. I am indebted to Brian, to our colleagues at the *News of the World* George Wright and Gary Jamieson for their particularly generous help, and to Ciaran Donnelly. Once again, I have been fortunate to have worked with and benefited from the patience and guidance of Paul Murphy, my editor at Mainstream. But this book would not have been possible without Mags McGraw. I am very fortunate to have shared her friendship and kindness, and I wish her and Jim a long life together and much happiness.

CONTENTS

1

HEARTS AND SWORDS

Sitting quietly, calmly and alone at a round glass-topped table in her favourite living room, a slim, attractive, dark-haired woman is laying cards. She is no gambler, and this is no ordinary deck. No king of hearts, queen of diamonds, jack of clubs or ace of spades will appear from her hand. No money is before her, but the stakes are greater than those bet by any high roller. This pack, not of the customary 52 but of 78, holds the key to a fortune, but not in the material sense. This is a fortune with consequences far beyond those earned by the poker or blackjack player. For she is, quite simply, playing a game of life and death.

At her side is a small booklet no bigger than a postcard. It gives the meaning of each card, but she is an experienced player and needs no guidance, because for three decades she has sat at a table and dealt the future. Over the years, she has patiently watched the cards, not challenging them to show her favour, but rather acknowledging their meaning. She knows that what they foretell cannot be amended and must be accepted as fate.

So, what do these cards show? The wheel of fortune, for example, indicates helpful or destructive periods in the journey through life; the emperor reveals man's qualities and quirks; the devil means misguided self-judgement; and the lovers promises inescapable seduction and sexual attraction. There are cards from four unlikely sounding suits, named wands, cups, swords and pentangles, each with its own meaning; for instance, sorrow, success, trouble or victory. She knows they must be interpreted not as individuals, but rather as the letters of a code that singly mean nothing but when examined as a group make sense to the player who has studied and thus understands the make-up of the cipher.

For six centuries, men and women have sat at tables and laid down cards just like these. Their name? Tarot cards. Used to give predictions as to what the future may bring, they are revered by experienced players but often feared by those who do not take time to understand the meanings of the various cards. Our player is of the former kind. She knows the pack holds secrets and how these must be interpreted.

Her name is Margaret McGraw – 'Mags' to those who know her well – and she is about to deal herself a wicked hand. The order and pattern in which two cards in particular appear leave her in no doubt that tragedy has appeared on the skyline. It is as if the grim reaper himself is the dealer, because the cards tell Margaret that her husband of 36 years Thomas – 'Tam' – is to die. This news would not come as a shock to many people. For Tam McGraw, known to his enemies and rivals as 'The Licensee', is widely accepted to be the most successful and hence the richest criminal of his generation. And in his world, success and wealth are looked on with jealousy and malice.

In gangland, it does not pay to win. To the victor there may be spoils, but losers hold knives and guns. Tam has a favourite saying about his home town of Glasgow: 'Here they will spend a pound to stop you making 50 pence.' And few would disagree. For 30 years, he has been linked to major crimes galore. Murder, arson, safecracking, intimidation, theft and drugs smuggling on an enormous scale have all been laid at his door. Police, even specially formed teams of highly trained experts in tackling serious and organised crime, have tried and failed to rid society of this scourge of the forces of law and order.

If a man is murdered anywhere in Scotland, the rumour mill will have it that an associate of Tam McGraw has been responsible and has been acting on his boss's orders. If the killing is in Glasgow or its environs, then undoubtedly the man himself must have been the assassin. It is said that his enemies prefer to come out only at night to avoid him seeing them, and that his cronies use his name to achieve status and safety usually without first enquiring whether he has given permission.

However, there are many people who believe that it is Margaret who has guided him in relative safety away from being forced to spend many years in grim prison cells, with just a slop bucket for company. Rivals concede it is her wisdom and sound advice that have brought Tam material security and comfort – and a nest egg variously, although optimistically, estimated to be somewhere between £5 million and £30 million. He himself concedes it is Mags who has made him the happy man he is. 'She is my rock,' he cheerfully admits, at the same time meaning his words to be taken seriously. 'Without her I would be nothing.'

Death is life's only certainty. Tam's friends believe it will come to him not as a result of a knife or bullet, but as a consequence of the 60-plus cigarettes he lights each and every day, pledging with each draw that he will listen to their pleas for him to kick the habit and will give up 'tomorrow'. But Tam seems indestructible. Margaret's husband is approaching his 55th birthday. He is slim, muscled and deceptively tall, although less than six feet. He looks fit and healthy. And yet Margaret McGraw is in no doubt that he is doomed for the simple reason that her cards say he is. Her interpretation of the hand she has dealt even predicts that death will come in a matter of months.

You might expect the normal reaction in such bizarre and terrifying circumstances would be for a wife to rush to her husband and beg him to alter his lifestyle drastically, to cease smoking and drinking endless cups of tea, to eat regular meals and to consult his doctor. But shocked and distressed though she may be, Margaret faces no dilemma over what action to take. She does nothing. She is convinced that there would be no point, because she is in no doubt whatsoever that her interpretation of what the cards say is correct. She knows her husband is going to die soon, and that is a fact that cannot be changed. So why tell him?

Tam might say to those close to him that he is not interested in his wife's investigations into what awaits. But privately he is her most avid dependant. There have been many instances when he and others have apparently in all innocence enquired of her whether the cards suggest fortune favours them and have then used her answers to dictate their ensuing actions. If Margaret tells him he is to die, he will undoubtedly accept her forecast and be doomed to spending the next weeks and months as a man awaiting a meeting with the hangman at a set time on a particular day. To expose him to such misery is, she reasons, cruel and unfair. And so she will not tell him. In her eyes, his death sentence is as inevitable as night following day, and she will carry the awful knowledge for them both, although she will share it with the very closest of her friends, knowing that it will remain a secret with them.

Is there any possibility her diagnosis of the Tarot cards is wrong? Margaret can recall instances in the past when a card reader has misread a message. In one especially distressing example, she prevented severe embarrassment for another reader and a nightmare for a family friend. But this time she is the reader, and she is wholly convinced that there can be no mistake. She recalls occasions in the past when the cards have foretold of other deaths that have come to pass. Deaths of friends, men younger than Tam, with no health concerns. What has made the predictions of these deaths all the more terrible is that the dead have been the victims of sudden, unpredictable murder. They did not know they were about to die. Margaret did. She will, of course, as the days and weeks pass, continue to consult her Tarot cards to see whether by some miracle the course of the future has changed. But the outcome is always the same. Tam is a dead man walking.

And she will consult another, highly personal, pack of Russian gypsy fortune-telling cards, bought for her during a trip to London many years earlier by her husband. This unique set consists of colourful cards divided into quarters, each segment showing half of various illustrations, such as those of a hearse or mountain. The cards can be turned about on their positions to link the illustrations and thus give pictures of how the future appears. As the result of a session with these cards at her round table one day, Margaret will learn that her husband shall not die as a result of violence but of an illness, and later that that illness is of the heart and is unavoidable.

How does she remain so calm? Perhaps it is a consequence of having lived her entire married life on the fringes of uncertainty and unpredictability. How often in days gone by has she wondered when her husband has gone out whether he would return or if there would be a call to say he was in police hands? In earlier times, when she was younger, she would worry about his whereabouts, but as time passed she accepted the presence of police in their lives as inevitable. He is a criminal, crime is his chosen career, and criminals attract police interest in themselves, their homes and their families.

Over time and as a result of his lifestyle, the passion of their marriage has seeped away. But while she has discovered new love, she has remained loyal and supportive to her Tam. Others might have sought relief in the divorce courts from such stresses. This is one alternative she has never considered, and now she knows that she will stay with him until the end, when she will no longer be his wife but his widow.

She has carried so many of his burdens and worries. Now this, the news of the ultimate sanction, she decides to keep within her. And so, as the fatal swords cards lie in their mute guilt, Margaret reaches for a cigarette and begins to remember.

She has known so much death and sorrow and sadness. Friends and enemies alike slain. Allies turned traitor. Bloodshed and beatings. Good times, too. Laughter echoing through ruins. Men on the run. Burning cars. Blazing-hot island beaches. Ghosts peeking through smoke. Being poor. Being rich. Being young and in love. It is an odd thing, she thinks, how so many people think about the beginning of a journey when nearing its end.

2

DEATH IN THE FAMILY

JUST AS FATE PREDICTED THE END OF MARGARET'S LIFE WITH TAM, it had intervened years before to bring about her first meeting with the man who would become her husband. Born in Glasgow's East End in January 1952, she had a happy childhood, marred only by a death that remains a mystery to her to this day. Deaths of those close to her have dogged her throughout her life, and it may be that this early tragedy helped prepare her for the many that have followed, although she was not aware of this at the time.

Her mum, Jessie, was born in Forth, Lanarkshire, while her bricklayer dad, William, was from Carnwadric in Glasgow. From their first meeting, Margaret's parents were devoted to one another, and their love would produce seven children. Six months after Margaret was born, the family went to live in a three-bedroom tenement in Barlanark in the East End of Glasgow. It was a move that would have profound consequences for Margaret.

Barlanark has a reputation as being a spawning ground for many of the city's criminals. But it is true that while many of the area's residents opted to become apprenticed in various forms of dishonesty, the streets did not suffer the appalling violence that was associated with the Gorbals, which provided the background for the novel *No Mean City*, telling of bloodthirsty razor gangs, poverty and misery. It is not to say that rough justice was not meted out on occasions, but Barlanark nurtured a community spirit, a sense of 'them and us' when applied to the police in particular and officialdom in general.

There were genuine friendships within the closes of the grey blocks of flats where William and Jessie Adams took their furniture and children. The sense of camaraderie was helped by the fact that the vast majority of those living in Barlanark survived on or just above the breadline. The men who could afford to do so drank in the same public houses, housewives bought from and gossiped at the same shops, and children attended the same schools. In Margaret's case, her encounter with schooling began in Barlanark Primary, just a few yards from her home.

These were joyous days indeed. 'I was very, very happy,' she remembers. 'We all got on well together and had lots of friends. There was always somebody to play with. And I liked school. My favourite lesson was art, probably because it seemed to me to be the easiest thing to do. Did I have any special pals? Well, I knew everybody, because everybody at school was from the tenements, and we were all already friends with each other. I had two special friends: Debbie, who went to St Jude's, and Alice, who went to the same school as me. I was at that age when you don't think about what the future holds. You live for each day and for the next playtime. There was no such thing as worry.'

Then, out of the blue, tragedy struck, although Margaret, then aged ten, was not aware of the extent of the trauma that brought heartbreak to her parents. She does recall being saddened and bewildered. Coming home from school one day, she realised that her sister, Jessie, five years younger, was missing. So were her parents, and her grandmother was in their place. 'In those days,' she says, 'ten year olds weren't as intelligent as ten year olds are now. My ma and da were lovely, but suddenly Gran was there, and she was dead strict. We had to do exactly as we were told. While we knew that Jessie was no longer with us, we didn't know why or what had happened to her. We didn't even know where our parents had gone.

'It was an awful time, probably made even worse because we'd been so happy and carefree up until then. The disappearance of Jessie was the only sad thing I can remember from my childhood. Looking back, I think if it had been explained – although this was not what adults did with children then – what was a pretty frightening mystery might have been understood, and we would not have been so unhappy. Of course, we would have been sad, but not frightened.'

In fact, little Jessie was in hospital, dying as the result of a kidney disease while her helpless parents sat at her bedside until the end. 'Nobody came into the house to tell us our sister had died and that we were never going to see her again,' Margaret says. 'All that happened was that Gran went away, and then Ma's back in the house and Da's back at work, and we all went on wondering.' Even to this day, the enigma of precisely what happened to her sister remains.

Moving up the school ladder, Margaret found herself at secondary school in Cranhill, another East End scheme on the other side of Edinburgh Road from Barlanark. It was there that Margaret had her first experience of vying with authority: 'I liked the school, but there were days when it seemed very tedious, boring even. My pal Janice lived in Starpoint Street across the road from the back of the school, and she and I would sometimes go to her house during the dinner hour. Her ma and da both worked, and the house was empty. From time to time, we'd decide we couldn't be bothered to go back in the afternoon for lessons. My ma didn't work, so there was no way we could go to my house, and we just stayed at Janice's, talking and playing music. Then when it was time for school to come out, we'd cross the road and hang about and mingle with everybody else before going home for tea at the normal time. I did that a few times, and nobody seemed to miss us, because we never got caught.'

Before leaving school, Margaret found herself, as many of her friends had managed to do, a part-time evening job, in her case working for a catering company. The money came in useful for a girl reaching womanhood and beginning to put behind her childhood games for interests that seemed so much more grown up and exciting. For it was the swinging '60s, and the rigours and hardships of the post-war years were now well in the past. Entertainment on an astonishing scale and variety was now available.

Almost overnight, it seemed, every family had acquired a black-and-white television set, although in Glasgow not every family had actually bought one. Like other commodities, sets frequently disappeared from stores and delivery lorries, and if they found themselves in flats in Barlanark, nobody was complaining or inviting the police around to share in the fun. In 1967, colour sets appeared for the first time. The television boom encouraged a thirst for knowledge among the young, and suddenly the world seemed small.

Events thousands of miles away could be flashed into Barlanark homes within hours. Adolescent Margaret learned of flower power in San Francisco, had the space race explained to her and began to hear a word that meant little to her then but which much later would bring about a huge change in her life and lifestyle. The word was 'drugs'.

Others might have experimented with this alternative to drink, but Margaret saw the perils and potential for destruction in drugs. Instead, she concentrated on music. Music and dancing were hugely popular pastimes everywhere, but no more so than in Glasgow. The city had a formidable reputation as the ballroom capital of Britain. It attracted the best bands and dancers from all over central Scotland. So many people wanted to tread the light fantastic that the local corporation opened a series of wash houses – 'steamies' – where young men and women could get a wash and brush up after work then head to the nearest dance hall without the nuisance of first taking a trip home to prepare.

Of course, the dancing brought with it its share of trouble. Drink-fuelled fights were frequent. But there was worse. In 1968 and '69, three women were brutally murdered after being picked up at the Barrowland Ballroom in the East End. The killer of Patricia Docker, Jemima McDonald and Helen Puttock would become known as 'Bible John', but his identity is still a mystery. One of the dancers who escaped the killer's clutches, although not without lasting cost, was a young factory worker named Hannah Martin. Of course, no one could know it then, but nearly 30 years later Hannah would play a major role in the story of the McGraws.

Despite these tragedies, Glasgow swung on. Everyone, it seemed, regardless of age, was humming a Beatles or Rolling Stones number or taking sides in the great transatlantic battle for supremacy between Elvis Presley and Cliff Richard. Margaret was for Cliff, singing happily as she picked up extra pocket money from her night job with the local catering company. Leaving school and job prospects held no fears for her. This was an era when teenagers were faced not with the quandary of whether they would be able to find a career, but of choosing from the variety of prospects that were on offer. In fact, Margaret did a variety of jobs. Her first was in a grocery store before a move to the Yellow Bird, a fish-and-chip shop in Buchanan

Street in Glasgow. For some time, she also retained her part-time catering work.

Like most of her pals, Margaret had a boyfriend. In fact, it was understood by those in her wide circle of friends that she had found a young man with whom she would in the not too distant future settle down and marry. Her life, it seemed, was already mapped out to parallel that of so many of her generation: leave school, work for a short time then raise a family with a husband who had steady work. She had given the prospect considerable thought but had concluded that she was too young for a public declaration and making the relationship permanent by becoming engaged.

Growing up in Barlanark, it was difficult, maybe impossible, not to know someone who had had some brush or other with the police. It might have been for something minor – riding a bicycle with no lights, for instance – but the feeling among many families was that the police picked on youngsters simply because they came from the scheme. Of course, there were those who gave the impression of being hell-bent on a career in crime even while they were still at school, on the rare days, that was, when they observed the niceties and actually turned up for lessons. Units of like-minded teenage boys were already forming into groups that would remain friends for years. It was these gangs that the police really wanted to target, the theory being that giving them a rough time at an early age would discourage them from graduating into more serious crime later on.

Margaret watched as the brothers of her friends were marched off to approved school for short spells, during which the intention was to punish offenders with treatment so harsh that it would guarantee their determining never to go back for a second dose. Like the traditional clip round the ear from a policeman's glove, that might have worked for some. For others, it simply bonded the young men more closely and encouraged a belief that by sticking together they could absorb punishment more easily and with less pain than by taking on the establishment as individuals. Many of the gangs who controlled the underworld would agree that their formation came about in this way.

Margaret was appalled to watch married women or even old school friends regularly troop off to Barlinnie Prison in Glasgow or to approved schools to visit sons or boyfriends. She abhorred the prospect of becoming caught up in such misery herself. One of the attractions of her 'steady' was that he appeared set on living a life of relative respectability and was certainly no miscreant.

She was especially saddened when her brother, John Adams, was caught up in the web of lawlessness and ended up in an approved school. The siblings had always been close and still are. John had acquired the tag 'Snads' during a childhood game when friends decided to rechristen each other by creating names from the jumbled letters of their surnames. In his case, it was decided that slight leeway with one letter was permissible, and the nickname has stuck to this day. John was a likeable young man who made friends easily. He had a reputation for sticking his neck out to help his comrades, even to the extent of taking the blame to protect others. It is a trait he has never lost, but Margaret despaired as she saw the inevitable consequence of his actions.

Of his many friends, two were looked on as being particular: Andrew 'Drew' Drummond and Thomas McGraw. Drew, tall and cheerful, was fascinated with cars, regarding a driving licence as an advantage, not a necessity. Tam was outgoing and occasionally tempestuous. Smaller then for his age, he was a target for bullies, some of whom later came to regret their audacity. Although Margaret saw Tam from time to time, she took little notice of him until one evening a breathless Snads arrived home with his two friends and shouted to her for help.

The trio had established themselves as the core of a gang that committed fairly minor larcenies in the East End. They called themselves the 'Barlanark Team' and set about building their criminal empire by graduating from stealing clothes from washing lines to car hubcaps and then to the vehicles themselves. Such enterprise occasionally attracted attention from the legitimate owners, some of whom were sufficiently enraged to give chase. During one such flight, Tam badly scraped his arm, leaving gravel and dirt embedded in his skin. Hospital was not an option, because too many questions as to the cause of the injury would have been asked. Snads had a solution. 'Come on home, and I'll get Margaret to patch you up,' he told his friend. And so irony decreed that just as an issue of Tam's health brought him and Margaret together, it would part them nearly four decades later.

3

WEDDING BLUES

MARGARET WAS NOT ESPECIALLY IMPRESSED BY A BLOODSTAINED TAM at their first meeting. 'I didn't particularly like him,' she admits now. 'I don't really know why. I think it was mainly because he was John's pal, and I knew fine well he was going to be in and out of jail all the time.'

By the time of that initial introduction, Margaret had again switched jobs and worked as a linker with Kenspeckle, a Glasgow rag-trade company based on the Queenslie Industrial Estate. Her work involved fixing collars to jumpers. She enjoyed the job and the pleasant, friendly surroundings. And on occasions she could still pick up an extra few pounds doing an additional shift with the catering company.

The night Snads and Drew arrived with Tam, she was making ready to go to bed. 'I didn't know what they'd been doing when they came, but I bet they had been up to no good, breaking in somewhere probably,' she says. 'John wanted me to tend to Tam's arm, which looked as though it had been scraped along gravel. His skin was heavily stained and marked. John said, "Go on, Margaret, do us a favour and scrub his arm." I said, "I'm away to my bed. I've got work in the morning." But John persisted: "Come on. Just take out these stains." And that's what I did.'

Tam said little while Margaret performed her Florence Nightingale act, but there was never any doubt about the impression she made on him. That night, when he left her home in Barlanark, he was already in love.

Although he was a regular about the scheme, Tam was not a Barlanark native. In February 1952, Janet McGrow, holidaying in Lennoxtown, realised that she was about to give birth earlier than expected. And so her son Thomas was delivered in the local hospital. The family lived in the Calton, still in Glasgow's East End but nearer the city centre than Barlanark. At some stage, possibly due to a school spelling error, Tam McGrow became 'McGraw'. At around the same time, Tam regularly stayed with his grandparents in Barlanark. As far as locals there were concerned, he was Tam McGraw. Soon he was friends with Drew and Snads, so it was inevitable that at some stage he would come into contact with Margaret. Struck by her good looks and calmness, he set about seeking excuses to see her again. A second meeting was followed by others that encouraged him to ask her for a date.

During Tam's first visits to her home, Margaret found him irritating, nervous and jumpy. In spite of this, she discovered that she was developing a liking for him. He could make her laugh, he was kind and he was good-looking. But she knew that as her affection grew so would the consequent problems: 'I'd been going with the other guy for a long time, around two and a half years. We weren't engaged, because I'd always thought I was too young to think about marriage. My boyfriend's ma gave out the work for the catering firm, making sure I got all the best jobs, so I wasn't really for falling out with him by announcing that I was breaking up with him and going out with Tam. But Tam persisted in asking me out, even though he knew about the other guy. He actually liked my boyfriend, who was a wee bit older than me.

'I eventually gave in. I don't know why, because he'd asked me loads of times. I almost got fed up and would say to him, "Get away. Fuck off." But finally I relented. Our first date was to the cinema to see *The Exorcist*. It was so scary and gruesome that I vomited. There were loads of weans in the audience, and they must have been from the East End, because they thought it was funny.

'My ma liked my boyfriend – she thought he was really nice – but she didn't take to Tam when I took him home to meet her for the first time. At the start, she definitely did not like him, yet she ended up being mad about Tam, adored him. She used to say to me, "Have nothing to do with him. He's the same as your brother John. You'll spend your life running up and down to jails to see him." And how right she was. But I realised I was falling in love with Tam. I couldn't stop myself. In the end, I suppose it was always Tam and only Tam.

'Did he have a chat-up line? Not Tam. We knocked about together in a group, his friends and mine, and we talked about clothes, not about love – going to Arthur Black's store in the city to buy a suit or trousers, what was in the shop, about maybe getting a pair of made-to-measure trousers there or going to Skint in Queen Street to buy a leather jacket, or even splashing out and having one made.

'Tam was hardly a romantic, but then he started proposing. He begged me stacks of times to marry him, but I kept insisting that we were too young. Eventually, though, just as I had when he'd pestered me for a date, I gave in.

'When I told my ma I'd decided it was Tam I was going to marry, she went mental, and the first thing she said to me was, "Margaret, you've got to be joking." I knew she probably wouldn't approve but hadn't realised how strongly she felt. She said, "Do you know what your life is going to be like? Well, I'll tell you. A total misery. It's going to consist of jails, of police and jails, and police and more jails, and more police. Don't even think about getting married, Margaret. You'll not like it. You can't just go and do what you want. You won't be able to telephone me and say, "Get this dress ironed because I've only got an hour for a shower and to get ready. You won't be able to do that any longer, Margaret." I said, "Oh no?" but still went ahead and did it.

'One of our closest friends was Colin Campbell, and his mum was just as surprised. "We are totally shocked that you would even consider marrying a person like that," she told me. "The whole of Barlanark is amazed by what you're doing."

'I'd never had any real intentions of marrying the other guy, even though I really liked him. But, then, I never had any intentions of marrying full stop. Then, when we'd only been going out for a few months, Tam took me to one side one night and proposed. I can't even remember what he said, but I do recall replying, "Oh, I don't think so. I don't really want to get married. Why should we get married?" But all our pals seemed to be getting married, and maybe that had something to do with us doing the same. I certainly think it was what put the idea of a wedding into Tam's mind.'

For all his brash toughness, Tam McGraw had a romantic streak when it came to Margaret. Like his bride to be, he wanted to marry on Valentine's Day. Yet so many couples had the same thought that when he went to the main Glasgow registry office in Martha Street to book the date, he was told it was already full up. So Tam did what he thought was the sensible thing and booked an alternative day. Then he went off to see his bride to be.

'You've what?' his astonished fiancée gasped when he broke the news to her. 'You've booked it for when?'

'The 13th.'

'The 13th? I don't believe it.'

'It was all they had, Margaret.'

'We're getting married on the 13th?'

'They said we could have any time we wanted, because nobody else was getting married that day.'

'Didn't you wonder why?'

'No, I just wanted to marry you.'

And so they were married on 13 February 1971. Tam was 18 and his bride 19. Margaret's mother was so set against the marriage that she did not go. Just her older brother William, his wife Shirley and another friend went along as witnesses to the great occasion. Margaret had met her new husband just nine months previously, but even now she does not think that her courtship was a whirlwind romance: 'Once we started going out, I felt as if I'd always known Tam. There was no sense of rushing into or being rushed into marriage. It just seemed a natural thing to do.'

The wedding was early in the day, and the wedding party went to a Glasgow restaurant for lunch before returning for a quiet afternoon at the home of William and Shirley. They had planned to go back into town that night for a meal, a few drinks and a spot of dancing. Times were hard, and they could not afford a honeymoon, but a night spent with a host of pals promised much.

However, it was not to be. That afternoon, William and Shirley's infant son became ill after his natural curiosity got the better of him and he began hunting around in the house while the adults talked. Discovering a number of bottles under the kitchen sink, he took a swig from one, and minutes later was in the world-renowned Yorkhill Children's Hospital in Glasgow, his anxious parents at his bedside together with the newly weds. Happily, the youngster made a full and speedy recovery. But not soon enough to prevent a cancellation of the planned night out. In later life, when attending the unions of friends and the conversation made its inevitable way round to unusual stories of marriage-day mayhem and disaster, Margaret would tell how she and Tam spent their wedding night sitting in a hospital at a child's bedside.

Earlier that day when he was asked by the registrar for details of his occupation, the young bridegroom asserted that he was employed as a bus conductor. In fact, it was true that his occupation involved travel, although not generally during the periods when buses operated. Tam and the others were forever on the move. By day, they'd look for potential targets, at first around Glasgow before they extended their range to central Scotland as a whole. The work was then mainly carried out at night or in the hours of darkness, and soon the fledgling Barlanark Team gained a reputation for astuteness and daring. Sadly for the three founding members, police investigating a number of thefts from stores in the Glasgow area began hearing the names of McGraw, Drummond and Adams ever more frequently.

For the most part, they stayed clear of the clutches of the law. But while police had difficulty in proving the trio were the culprits, word on the streets reached their ears that their days of freedom were numbered. They began to wonder whether a new hunting ground or even a change of career might be needed.

It was not long after Tam and Margaret's wedding that a further complication arose – Margaret discovered that she was expecting a baby. As the signs of her pregnancy became increasingly obvious, she tried desperately to help her husband find legitimate work. An uncle agreed to her suggestion that Tam be employed on his construction site near Johnstone in Renfrewshire. Each morning before setting off to her own job, she would contentedly rise early to make his lunchtime piece: wedges of brown bread with jam and Cadbury Flake in between. At first, all went well. But Tam, as his wife had discovered, had a rebellious, independent streak. One day, following a ticking off by the site fireman, he pushed a dumper truck into a deep, water-filled pit. Vandals were blamed, but Tam had had enough. He quit.

These were difficult times for many young couples – money was tight and setting up home difficult. After their wedding, Margaret and Tam had initially settled in a single-end flat in Shettleston, but they wanted to be near their friends and Margaret's family in Barlanark. So it was that they made themselves technically homeless. They further improved their chances of being given a council house in the area by moving in with Margaret's mum, Jessie, because she could claim that her house was overcrowded. Now they had no home of their own, and Tam had no job and owed money. Then, in November 1971, Margaret was rushed into hospital in Bellshill, a few miles from Jessie's home, and gave birth to their son William.

It was a happy time, but the parents of the new baby realised that difficult decisions had to be made. They wanted their own home and enough money in their pockets and purse to provide for their son. They wanted a car and the independence that came with having cash. Meanwhile, Tam's brushes with the police had left him with fines that he just could not pay. Prison was looming. Tam and Margaret talked matters over with Drew and Snads, and, having come to a decision, asked Jessie for help.

Margaret knew that her mother, despite her disappointment about her choice of husband, would help. She always did in times of need. It was decided that William would stay with his grandmother while his parents, along with Drew and Snads, would leave Glasgow in search of work. They decided on London, having seen many Scots, including some of their friends, go south and report back tales of prosperity and contentment. It was, of course, a gamble. Nothing could be certain. But Tam had a relative who was already in the capital, and he agreed to look for accommodation for all four. For Margaret, leaving her baby was a huge wrench. But she saw that her mother doted on William and made it clear to Tam and the others that she wanted to return home to her son every weekend. Christmas came and went. Then Hogmanay. A new year promised a new start. The great adventure came at the onset of 1972. London beckoned.

4

ON THE BUSES

THE FOUR ARRIVED AT VICTORIA COACH STATION AFTER WHAT FELT like an endless journey from Glasgow. They had little money, it was late and they did not have enough time to find somewhere to stay. And so Tam and Margaret spent their first night in London huddled together under the warmth of the lighting from advertising displays, with Drew and Snads nearby. Studying one of the signs, they read that London Transport was recruiting staff, in particular conductors, to work on its bus fleet. Tam had briefly flirted with this work in Glasgow, where crafty veterans of the job had tipped him off about a neat little scam that was worth a few extra pounds when operated discreetly. It involved reselling, as new, discarded journey tickets, and this small perk was a factor in his decision to answer the advertisement. It was not one that he passed to Margaret, admitting in later life that he could never have forgiven himself had his young wife found herself in trouble.

The immediate priority was to find a home, somewhere to stay during the week before they headed back to Glasgow for the weekend so that Tam and Margaret could see their baby son. All four would quickly come to accept the routine of the weekly trek back and forth, but on that first morning they had lots to do. Much as they had enjoyed the warmth and intimacy of squeezing together beneath the lights, it was hardly a permanent alternative to bricks and mortar. Once they had breakfasted, Tam phoned his relative. He came back with good news for the others that a prospective landlord awaited them. It meant a journey to Worple Road, Wimbledon, where they were introduced to an Asian businessman who had converted a sizeable house into flats. Tam and Margaret would share one, with Snads and Drew on the floor below. All were happy with the arrangement and agreed to move in immediately. It meant that they could now concentrate on finding work, and they wasted no time in doing so.

Margaret has mixed memories of the time that she and Tam spent in the capital: 'London was all right, I suppose. Some of the people were OK, but they were not so nice or as friendly as those we'd left behind in Glasgow. I think I found them kind of heartless.

'We applied for work as bus conductors and spent a few days being trained how to work the ticket machines, learning about routes, making sure we were confident when it came to the safety of passengers and being advised on how to deal with the public. After the training was completed, all of us were ushered into a small room to be given our identification badges. A man shouted "McGraw", and I automatically stood up, went forward and was given my badge. Even before I'd sat down, "McGraw" was shouted out again, and it was Tam's turn.

'They had an expression on the buses when they teamed you up with your driver – it was that the conductor was "married" to him. It seemed only appropriate that because we were husband and wife, Tam and I would work similar shifts and begin and end our days together, so they tried to arrange for us to be married to two drivers doing the same hours. It didn't always work out that we worked identical shifts, but the depot manager did his best to ensure we finished at roughly the same time.

'I loved working on the buses, especially the banter with kids. They used to crack jokes about Scotland and call me "Scotty". I'd tell them, "Scotty, fuck all. You stand in the queue like everybody else." They were a good laugh and no trouble.'

Maybe it was because in Glasgow she knew that it paid to be wary of strangers who asked questions, Margaret found herself one day showing the door to a pair of unexpected visitors. Tam, Drew and Snads were out at work, and she had just ended a shift with London Transport when she answered a knock at the door. She takes up the story: 'A man and a woman are standing there, and the man asks, "Is Drew Drummond there?" I don't know who they are, so I tell him, "No." He goes, "Well, does he live here?" I say, "Who's asking?" And he says, "His brother." I say, "You're no his brother."

And he goes, "But I am his brother." I'm thinking to myself that to be who he claims he is, he must have been a good bit older than Drew, married and away from home before I even knew Drew's mum and family. Should I believe him? I decide not to and say, "No chance. I know his brothers, and you're not one of them." He insists: "I am. I'm his brother James." And I say, "That makes no difference. You're not getting in. You'll just have to come back when he comes in from work." He gave me a funny look and didn't look too chuffed, but off he and the lassie went.

'So, Drew eventually comes back from work, and I say, "There was a guy and a lassie at the door, and he said he was your brother." Drew says, "My brother?" And I go, "Aye, what a load of shite. I know your brothers." So that was that.

'Later on that night, I hear a knock at the door. I'm upstairs, and I've been looking out of the window and have seen the same couple who had been there earlier coming to the house. So I go down and chap at Drew's door and say, "That guy's coming. He'll be chapping at the door now. The one who said he was your brother." At that, there is a chap at Drew's door, and I hear Drew saying, "Oh Christ, James. What are you doing down here?" He brings the couple through, and I ask Drew, "Well, who is he?" Drew replies, "He's my brother." I say, "Oh fuck. I tossed him out this afternoon. I didn't know he was your brother." Drew says, "Yes, he's my older brother." I say, "But I didn't know you had an older brother. You never spoke about him." James is standing there, and he says to Drew, "Aye, that woman wouldn't even let me in." So I tell him, "Well, you could have been anybody – the police, social security or anybody at all." Happily, it ended up with us all having a good laugh about it. It turned out that James and his wife had come down to London for a fortnight's holiday and had decided to look Drew up.

'After I'd been working with London Transport for four months, the manager at our Morden depot pulled me in one day and said, "Margaret, I have a letter of complaint here that you put somebody off the bus." I said, "Me? No way. Apart from the weans when they climb all over me – but even that's in fun – I've not put anyone off a bus." The manager insisted I had. "Margaret, there it is," he said and handed over the letter of complaint. I was horrified when I read it, because it accused me of using offensive language. It was hard to take in, and after I read it a second time, I told the boss, "That's just not true. It never happened." But the manager insisted: "Margaret, it must have happened, because that's your badge number on the complaint." I continued to argue with him, saying, "Look, I'm telling you this didn't happen. If it had happened, you know I'd tell you." By this time, he was shouting: "Margaret, it must have happened." And I was yelling back at him: 'I'm telling you, it didn't fucking happen." We got absolutely nowhere, and he said he was going to investigate further.

'I was desperately upset, but it was some time before they discovered what had happened. Somebody had been thrown off a bus, but by Tam. In that wee room, at the end of our training, they'd given me Tam's badge, and I had his. Tam admitted that he'd tossed a rude passenger off a bus, all right, and that he'd given him a bit of choice Glaswegian language as he did so. The result was that Tam was sacked, so I left as well.'

Throughout their stay in London, the newly weds strove to return home to Glasgow at every opportunity. Irregular hours on the buses made the visits home more difficult, but they made it back most weekends, depending on their shift patterns. After quitting as conductors, Tam and Margaret both found work in factories close to one another. The settled work arrangements meant that most Friday evenings they were able to catch a train heading north, returning late on Sundays. There was no doubt that they missed their friends in Scotland, but worst of all for Margaret was the heart-wrenching Sunday ordeal of kissing her son goodbye. It was a nightmare with which she never came to terms. She had come from a close-knit family, one in which the absence of any member affected the others deeply. Now she was discovering the emotions through which her own mother went when Margaret had announced that she was leaving the fold to marry and then to live in London. She describes the bond with her family as 'dead close'. Friends remember her as being happy in London, because it meant being close to Tam, but that she left her heart with William in Glasgow.

Tam, Drew and Snads had an additional motive for returning home regularly. Despite its occasional encounters with the police, the Barlanark Team had been reasonably successful before they left for England. They saw no reason to abandon the enterprise. It meant sizing up likely targets one weekend and hitting them a week later. There was an added advantage to this arrangement. It was well known that the three men were now working in London, and the fact that their once-familiar faces were hardly to be seen on the streets of Barlanark tended to discount them as potential suspects in the eyes of the police.

There was no shortage of jobs in London. Margaret worked alongside Drew, albeit briefly, for Decca Records, helping to churn out millions of discs, some of which no doubt found their way into the homes of pop-music fans back in Barlanark, while Snads found employment with a company manufacturing vehicle tyres. It was, for Margaret, only a brief flirtation with the industry, because while Tam had found employment with Changewear, an electroplating company at North Cheam, she discovered that a firm close by in Morden, which manufactured parts for Concorde, was taking on workers. She had no difficulty in being taken on. In both cases, the money was good, enabling them to upgrade their accommodation and move into another rented property on Worple Road, not far from the singing star Tommy Steele.

Margaret and Tam were still regularly commuting to Glasgow, although Snads and Drew had decided to return to Barlanark for good. Margaret was happy. She found her workmates to be friendly and interested in her, and they even demonstrated genuine pleasure in showing her around their city. But then two incidents soured her view of life down south. Returning home from work one evening, she discovered a child of about eight lying on the pavement. The young girl had clearly been knocked down and, while not at death's door, was hurt and crying. What appalled Margaret most was the sight of other pedestrians simply walking around the helpless child or even stepping over her so as not to get involved and interrupt or delay their return home. 'The wee lassie was lying there, crying and frightened,' Margaret remembers. 'Somebody had lifted her from the road onto the pavement but had then just left her. She wasn't desperately ill, but her leg was definitely broken. I went hysterical, shouting, "Somebody phone the fucking ambulance." It transpired that someone already had, although they hadn't stayed around. I'd got on fine with the people in London and had lots of pals at work. But this made me think how different they were to us. I'd met some smashing people, but I really didn't know them. As I waited with the wean for the ambulance, people stepped over her, and I kept thinking, "How could you do that to a wean?" It would never have happened in Glasgow.'

Not long after the incident, Margaret found herself facing another near tragedy. This time the victim was Tam. Attempting to free jammed machinery at work, he fell into a vat of chemicals that included caustic soda. Within seconds, workmates had hauled him clear, but the damage had been done. His legs had come into contact with the liquids, burning one to the bone. Tam recovered, but not before he had spent three months in hospital.

Margaret rang Jessie to break the news. 'Oh Jesus. You're there by yourself. I'm not having that,' Jessie told her daughter and promptly despatched Margaret's brother Robert to stay with her until Tam was well enough to be discharged. When they judged that he was well enough, Tam and Margaret headed back home to William and Barlanark for good, leaving behind a lawyer to negotiate compensation for what had happened and Robert to fall in love and marry an English girl. He never returned to Glasgow, and died 25 years later at a time when Tam was finding himself in more trouble.

5

THE MOHICAN ENCOUNTER

As much as they had enjoyed working and living in London, Margaret and Tam were glad to be back among their own kind in Glasgow. They had found most cockneys to be friendly enough, although perhaps more introverted than Glaswegians, and there was no doubt that the couple missed the friendliness of the tenement closes that were, and still are, such a big part of domestic life in Scotland. Families who shared these closes and took their turns on the voluntary cleaning rota became more than mere neighbours, as the years of borrowing and gossiping invariably developed a warmth and closeness that was rarely, if ever, found among the sprawling estates of semi-detached houses. And the schemes that dominated working-class Glasgow had not witnessed the establishment of the kinds of immigrant communities that were beginning to dominate many of the poorer areas of London. Admittedly, there were occasional fallouts, but by and large the families who lived in Barlanark got on well, while most of those who did not at least tolerated one another, because they had lived cheek by jowl for many years.

Margaret and Tam knew the strengths and weaknesses of their neighbours: who were in debt and to whom, who were having affairs and who were the culprits when it came to crime. Yet this was information reserved for the community and not to be shared with outsiders. And the police were outsiders. Of course, the boys in blue liked to think that they had friends among the scheme dwellers. And it was true that they did occasionally get information from those whom they were convinced were their friends. But the scraps given to the police were strictly rationed to material that when analysed came down to little or nothing.

Thus it was that gangs such as the Barlanark Team were able to function so successfully for so long. The police knew the names of the members. They could almost pinpoint exactly who had taken part in any particular raid. Intelligence reports would reveal who had driven, who had cut telephone wires, who had been lookouts, who had forced open safes, who had shared the night's loot. But knowing it was one matter, proving it to a judge or sheriff another. And the likelihood of actually finding someone willing and brave enough to stand in a witness box and point the finger at one of the miscreants was so remote as to be out of the question. Grasses did not survive for long in Barlanark.

Tam was sure a bright future lay ahead for him, Drew, Snads and the others who would from time to time be brought in to bolster the team when he and Margaret decided to head back north for the last time. He was aware that the opportunities were manifold. And in Drew and John Adams, he had two friends he could trust with his life. They would stick to depriving stores, clubs and sub-post offices throughout central Scotland of the contents of their safes. It was potentially lucrative and relatively easy, although it was risky. Never would they target the homes of ordinary folk such as themselves. And the golden rule was that violence was forbidden.

Things seemed rosy, but the fact was that the warnings Margaret had been given by her mother and others that marriage to Tam would see her trooping between home and prisons, generally Barlinnie, would come to fruition. There would be many times when she would discover that her life revolved around prison routine. But that was a penance of marrying a man whom she knew to have set upon a career in crime. There is a misconception that the life of a criminal, and even more so that of the wife of a criminal, is one steeped in glamour – a life of big houses, fast cars, racy clubs and bulging wallets. And for a few, that is the case, although the glitz and wealth usually come in short phases. The reality is that most criminals spend much of their lives in prison, and the periods when they are not in custody are usually spent worrying about the probability of detection and the next long stretch.

Tam McGraw hated jail. He loathed the food and missed the

comforts of home. Yet he was confident he was clever enough and could plan sufficiently skilfully to stay one step ahead of the law. Margaret was wiser. She simply resigned herself to the fact that there would be many occasions when her conversations with Tam would be in the Barlinnie visiting room. One of her closest friends summed up her situation: 'Tam was a criminal, no arguing about it. He spent most of his life breaking the law. People judge by what they see on television and imagine a criminal's wife just sits back and gets her nails done and her body tanned. It's true that some are like that. But never Margaret. She got on with the business of running her family, including Tam.'

While short spells for Tam in a prison cell loomed, their abode in 1974, on their return to Glasgow, was once again with Jessie. As far as the rules were concerned, the young couple were still homeless and therefore entitled to priority on the council's housing list. Even more in their favour was the fact that they had a son, now approaching his third birthday. Consequently, it was not long before a letter arrived, offering them the keys to an apartment at 20 Burnett Road, Barlanark. Both had wanted to live there, because the area was home to most of their friends. They would have the address for 19 years.

After the explosion in freedoms of the '60s, when young people broke from the shackles of discipline instilled by enforced conscription into the armed forces, the '70s steered towards a more sinister form of entertainment. In Glasgow, they still talked about Bible John and the ceaseless search for the triple killer. It has been suggested that his actions and the failure of the police to identify and capture him were instrumental in the falling off of the once thriving ballroom-dance scene as venues became home to rock bands. The truth is more likely to be that as television sets increasingly came within the budgets of most families, once avid dancers simply decided that they preferred sitting in an armchair, watching the exertions of others. Ballrooms gave way to clubs, where young people drank and went through motions said to be new-style dances, but which were more akin to those performed by jungle dwellers. A few of the more affluent found that they could gain added excitement by the acquisition of an increasingly popular stimulant.

Drugs were not new, but because few were smuggled into Britain, they were expensive and largely confined to the comparatively well-off middle classes. Gradually, their popularity spread north. In Glasgow, cocaine – 'Happy Dust' – eventually made its limited mark. It was too costly for most Scots, some of whom would instead settle for cannabis, a drug that would much later dramatically affect the lives of the McGraws and some of Tam's closest friends. But as they prepared for the move to Burnett Road, the McGraws had no interest in drugs, especially after hearing the remarkable tale of one of their friends.

The friend and his young wife had gone clubbing in Glasgow city centre one night. When the time came for them to return to the East End, they had waited patiently, with many others, in a queue for taxis. There was the usual good-natured, occasionally drink-inspired banter in the crowd, which grew and diminished as a steady stream of cabs arrived and departed. Nearing the head of the queue, the young man discovered that a small knot of interlopers had decided to cut in. Their nerve appeared to be bolstered by the passing around of a joint. The appearance of the one who was evidently the leader, and in particular his hair, drew the attention of the people patiently waiting. Gaily coloured in a variety of reds, blues and yellows, his hair stuck stark upright, stiff and pointed, in what was termed a Mohican style. This was a fashion most Glaswegians had previously seen only on television or in newspapers, and it became the butt of a series of typically cutting wisecracks.

The ringleader was clearly unhappy at constant references to him as 'Billy' and 'Two Rivers', the nickname of a popular television all-in wrestler from some years earlier. He was even more disturbed at being informed in no uncertain terms by the young friend of Tam and Margaret that he should, without delay, 'get to fuck' to the back of the taxi queue, where he could await the arrival of a wagon train. This advice was not welcomed. Words of increasing bitterness were exchanged, which led to threats, followed by pushing. It was handbags-at-ten-paces stuff compared to a typical Glasgow rammy, but during a scuffle between the men, rainbow bonce made the mistake of head-butting his opponent several times. The blows were intended for the nose, but because Tam and Margaret's friend was smaller, they landed on his forehead. These having failed, the punk was appalled to find himself on the receiving end of a series of heavy blows to the face, which knocked him to the pavement. As the people in the taxi queue cheered, he was further punched and kicked before being dragged away to safety by his comrades. The victor, who had admittedly earlier imbibed enthusiastically, and his wife duly went home by taxi and retired to bed.

The next morning, they awoke to the horrific discovery that the bedding and his pyjamas were soaked in blood. An ambulance was called to take him to hospital, where a series of tiny holes were found in his forehead and on the top of his head. When doctors who curtailed the bleeding asked about the possible cause, none seemed surprised to learn of the altercation with the man with the Mohican haircut. 'They put all sorts of stiffeners, even glue, in the paint,' said one. 'Coming into contact with one is the equivalent of falling on a bed of nails. We've even tried to convince the police these people should be arrested for wearing offensive weapons.'

Tam roared with unsympathetic laughter when he heard the story. But then he and Margaret had much to smile about at that time. Their son was thriving, Tam's nightly excursions with the Barlanark Team were bearing fruit and Margaret was especially contented in her new home in Burnett Road. She loved her surroundings, and got on well with all the families around her, one of which was the McPhees. They lived on the top floor, and young Billy McPhee would come to play a significant part in their lives. Close by lived another young man, Jonah McKenzie, who had relations in Burnett Road. Jonah, who always seemed to be smiling, was a frequent visitor to the McGraw home, where he was welcomed. He was, after all, one of the gang. But Jonah would discover the cost of turning his back on his friends.

Tam's activities with the Barlanark Team meant he frequently left home at a time when many other men were returning from a night's drinking. He would give Margaret his destination but no other details of what he and the others intended. Should something go wrong and the police come knocking, she could tell them in all honesty that she was not party to what her man did outside the family home. She was confident that she always knew where he was – a certainty she retained until his dying day – but not necessarily what he was doing. And while some of those around him might disappear for days on end, leaving wives or girlfriends to wonder and worry over their whereabouts, Tam always returned to his wife, provided that the police had not got to him first. But his prolonged absence one winter night caused her to worry.

The couple had only just taken possession of 20 Burnett Road, and Margaret was still arranging and rearranging furniture, choosing curtains, and working out the best combinations of wall coverings. Throughout the flat, there were huge rolls of carpet and undercover lying about. At times, tricky footwork was needed to step over and between them without toppling. It was only a temporary inconvenience, because a carpet fitter was due the next day. A friend called Sean was visiting, and Tam asked Margaret to make an umpteenth cup of tea, a choice of beverage taken by him in prolific quantities and which would remain his favourite tipple for the whole of his life. She discovered that they were out of milk and asked her husband to briefly nip out for a bottle. It was a freezing-cold night, and snow had fallen during the day. The ground was white and icy, treacherous for walking, and only a couple of hours earlier the last of the children, shouting and laughing at the thrill of running and slipping along the roads and pavements, had been called in by their mothers. The hour was late, and the local corner shop was closed, but Sean announced that he had a surplus of milk at home, and it was to there that he and Tam headed, promising they would return in only a few minutes. Two hours later, Margaret was still waiting, worrying that Tam had fallen victim to the police, who frequently stopped him in the hope of finding him carrying something that would provide them with the cause they wanted to arrest him and cart him off to the nearest station.

'Bugger's in jail. Something's wrong. It only takes ten minutes to get there and back,' she kept telling herself. Margaret did not know it, but Sean's visit was fortuitous, as he had discovered that an opportunity was at hand. He had heard of a long-distance lorry driver who was having an affair with a pretty woman from the East End. Her husband also drove lorries, mainly to the Continent, a task taking him away from home for days on end. The woman lived in Barlanark and had persuaded her lover to spend the night with her, and he had parked his lorry close by in Edinburgh Road.

Hours after leaving, a breathless Tam and Sean returned and were confronted by Margaret, who demanded, 'Where the fuck have you been?' A remarkable story unfolded. According to the pair, they had gone off fully intending to visit Sean's home, collect milk and head back immediately to Burnett Road. On the outward journey, they'd come across the deserted lorry. Realising where the driver would be, they had the rear doors opened in no time at all. They were met by the ends of giant rolls of carpets. They began dragging them out, an experience they likened to watching seemingly endlessly long strips of spaghetti emerging from a plate of pasta. They had no idea where to take the rolls or how to move them, but they soon discovered that there was no need to worry. The icy roads and pavements made it relatively easy to drag the mountainous rolls to a temporary hiding place in a flat in Barlanark. The rolls were so long that they had to remove some of the doors in the flat to accommodate them.

When the carpet fitter arrived the next day, Margaret told him that Tam wanted a quick word. As a result, a number of flats in Barlanark were sporting brand-new wall-to-wall carpets by the end of the week, and neighbours could hear the sound of sawing as doors were shortened. Anyone who wanted new floor covering was offered it without charge – the only cost was that of hiring the fitter, who knew better than to ask questions as to the source of so much high-quality material. Margaret would later confide to one of her friends: 'One of the houses to which they took some carpet was at the foot of a sloping street. Tam and Sean said they just sat on the roll and sledged to the front door. We were the only ones to lose out. The carpets we had ordered had been delivered that day, and we had paid for them. Everybody else got theirs for free.' Margaret never begrudged Tam his generosity to others, although she would increasingly wonder whether that gratitude was reciprocated as the years slipped by.

Although he constantly sought her advice and guidance throughout their life together, she would always maintain to friends, 'How he earns his money is his business. We have a simple rule. He makes it, and I spend it.' In fact, that was not quite true. She was a woman who valued and guarded her independence. She realised that while the Barlanark Team's success continued, her husband would always be sufficiently cunning and skilled to put food on the table. But word on the street was that the police were increasingly asking questions about Tam and the others. If he were caught and jailed, how would she provide for her son in his father's absence? The answer had been mulling around in her mind since their return from London. She decided that the time had come to go into business.

6

WANDERING GNOMES

At that time, every street on every scheme in Glasgow was serviced by an ice-cream van that drove by up to four times a night, stopping every fifty yards or so. Provided the hour was not late, vans would play a tune that was hoped to be easily recognisable and therefore attractive to children. Each van had its own musical signature, such as 'The Happy Wanderer' or 'Jingle Bells' (even in summer), and produced a cacophony not unlike the sounds that emanate from modern-day mobile telephones to signal an incoming call. However, the term 'ice-cream van' was something of a misnomer. Often ice cream was not the principal product on board. Vans carried supplies of sweets, soft drinks, cigarettes and crisps, and they tried to accommodate the requests of most customers. Like all her contemporaries, Margaret had grown up to the sound of the chimes. The vans were a way of life and in many cases a necessity for families without the means or the desire to travel to the nearest available shops.

Satisfying the demands of her baby meant that after returning from London Margaret had little time to think about her future. But the constant chimes gave her the idea of running her own van. She had little or no money at this time, relying on whatever Tam was able to give her. While she could never be sure of its source, she assumed this was from the proceeds of the regular excursions of the Barlanark Team. The money they had saved in London, together with generous compensation received by Tam resulting from his accident, had soon gone. Some of it was used to pay the outstanding fines that he had run up and thus kept him out of jail. What remained paid for the furnishing of 20 Burnett Road. Margaret hated the idea of hire purchase, of being in debt. But there was simply not enough to go round, and she was forced to buy their first three-piece suite 'on tick', while the new cooker meant £2 a quarter being added to their electricity bill.

She had always been industrious and abhorred the prospect of spending the rest of her married life surviving on a hand-to-mouth basis. Additionally, there was the worry of managing if her man was locked up. The idea of having her own van came almost by accident. Margaret remembers, 'Somebody in almost every area had a van that serviced a few streets. You came to rely on the vans, particularly when you had a young family. But sometimes you'd sit waiting and waiting for the ice-cream van to arrive so you could buy cigarettes, and then it would never turn up. Any smoker knows what that is like. Tam would moan, "Fuck this, they're not here tonight again," and he'd have to troop off down to the nearest garage for cigarettes.

'One night I said to him, "Fuck it, I'll get one of my own and supply ours and the next street. At least we'll always have fags." We decided we'd had enough of hanging around watching for the van and listening for the chimes.'

They knew they did not have enough money to buy their own van. Initially, it would mean hiring one, or even two, but the plan was to save as high a proportion of their profits as possible in order to then become owners. Some of those people operating vans had gone into the business because they found themselves being offered vehicles at prices so low that it was impossible to reject them. A clapped-out ice-cream van is primarily limited to use as an ice-cream van. Owners of vehicles long past their sell-by dates and anxious to get them off their hands offered them at extremely low prices, concluding that it was better to get a few pounds than fork out to have the van scrapped. After all, no garage was going to accept a dilapidated ice-cream van in part exchange for a replacement or for some other vehicle, because the resale value would be less than nil. But the cheap vans that came onto the market were an incentive for newcomers to try their hands, which led to competition for routes.

Margaret had no intention of buying a worn-out vehicle or scrapping over a route. She wanted a van that was clean and reliable, and had already worked out that her intended route was available – the volume of complaints by those living along it about the unpredictability of the previous incumbent were enough to tell her that the way was clear. And so Tam went off to meet a pleasant family who ran a company named Marchetti Brothers based in Bishopbriggs that specialised in the hiring and selling of ice-cream vans and the supply of stock. A deal was reached for the hire of a van – Margaret would pay a weekly rent – and soon after she leased a second. By 1976, a year after going into business, Margaret had bought her own van. She ran the little company, and everything was in her name: she ordered supplies, did the books and served her customers. 'I loved the van,' she says. 'It was a laugh, and you heard all the gossip. You got to know everyone on your round and, as a result, everything that went on. If you stopped somewhere and spotted a police car parked near a close and wondered what it was doing there, you could be sure that somebody knew the reason. And if they didn't, they'd find out. "Tell you when you come around next time, Margaret," they would say, and you can bet they did. There were no secrets.'

She worked out a simple route around the streets near her own: Barlanark Road, Bressay Road, Barlanark Place, Garvel Crescent, Kentallen Road, Blythe Road, Kerrera Road, Hallhill Road, Hallhill Crescent and, of course, Burnett Road. 'I knew everybody, because we'd always stayed in Barlanark,' she says. 'If I went to Barlanark now, it would be entirely different, because all the people I knew have left or moved, so those living there would mostly be strangers to me. But when we were there, you really didn't move. Once you got a home in Barlanark, you were usually there for always and ever.

'We would go around the streets in the van three or four times during a shift, depending on how busy it was and how long each stop took, finishing at eleven, or just after eleven, at night. There were never any threats or nastiness then. And the vans gave us a very good income. After a year, we'd worked very hard and saved £1,500, enough to buy our own second-hand van.'

A condition of hiring from Marchetti Brothers was that stock also had to be bought from the company. Because the Marchetti garage was some miles from Barlanark, this inevitably added time to her daily routine. But once she freed herself from ties with the firm by becoming an owner, this commitment no longer existed, and she could purchase stock from another company called Fifti, much nearer to home.

Many people believe that ice-cream vans were a front for selling drugs, but this was not the case at the time Margaret was in business. She had heard rumours that others might have gone down this path but never witnessed evidence to back up these stories. It is true that as time passed the vans would become the cause of considerable aggravation and trouble for some of those operating them. There would be threats and fights over who had the right to a particular route, but not because the greater the number of areas a van operator served the more opportunity there was to deal drugs. The cause was much simpler. The routes themselves were so lucrative without the involvement of drugs that they became prized possessions. Ultimately, with the advent of superstores and car ownership, families would desert the vans. But not before an undercurrent of violence had led to the infamous 'Ice Cream Wars' of the early 1980s, culminating in the burning of a flat in Ruchazie, Glasgow, in 1984, and resulting in the deaths of six members of the Doyle family, one of them a baby just eighteen months old. Margaret and Tam would find themselves dragged into the ensuing hunt for the culprits. But that was in the future.

If drugs were sold, they were not carried on any van operated by the McGraws. That is not to say that the police did not take an interest in what Margaret carried: 'Like a lot of other van operators, I found crisps were really too bulky, so I looked at other items to sell. Obviously, cigarettes were a favourite and tobacco for roll-ups or pipe smokers, but then I began selling batteries, mainly as a good turn. An elderly woman neighbour who was crippled with arthritis in her hands and could not walk far complained to me about the price she was having to pay at the local corner shops for batteries for her hearing aid. It was just the sort of situation in which Tam wanted to help out. But it led him into serious trouble. I said to him, "Get some batteries for the old woman's hearing aid, will you?" And he did, probably when the Barlanark Team was knocking off some store somewhere. But it was all in a good cause, and when I next saw the old woman, I gave her batteries and told her, "There you are. That will be ten pence." She was over the moon but unfortunately went straight down to the guy who ran the nearest corner shop and complained. "My ice-cream van can sell those for ten pence, and you're charging a fortune," she said. "You're robbing everybody in Barlanark." The upshot was the guy rang the police and said that for us to be selling them so cheaply, we must have been stealing them from somewhere. The police came and wanted to know where we got the batteries. Tam came up with a story, and they eventually went away, but his "Good Samaritan" act nearly landed us both in jail.'

In fact, not long after starting up her ice-cream-van operation, Margaret found herself on her own with her infant son when Tam was jailed for three months at Glasgow Sheriff Court for breaking into stores in the area. She had, in reality, little time to worry about what her husband was up to. While running the ice-cream van gave Margaret and others in the business plenty of opportunities for laughter, it could at times prove a headache. The simple matter of keeping the vehicle on the road was a necessity. Margaret's van could bring in £500 a week, a considerable sum then, and to have a van off the road even for a day would result in substantial losses. Of course, other vans were available for hire, but the cost could quickly eat up any profits. The lengths to which van operators would go to make sure they kept going are testament to the ingenuity of some. In one case, an operator discovered that an ageing van was developing a worrying knocking sound beneath the bonnet as it trundled its way around the streets of an East End scheme. A mechanic friend soon discovered the cause of the din: 'It's your gearbox. It's splitting. You need a new one.' That meant not just a healthy bill for a replacement, to which had to be added the cost of labour, but, even worse, the van being off the streets until the operation could be performed. A call to the manufacturers, Mercedes, produced the information that it would be at least a week before another gearbox could be delivered to Glasgow.

The situation was serious but was resolved with the spirit of ingenuity that is a trademark of Glasgow East Enders. An almost brand-new Mercedes ice-cream van was hired for one day from a Glasgow company. It was happily driven off to a waiting mechanic, who, in a matter of only a few hours, swapped the gearboxes over. Then, with screws tightened, seals sealed and hoses secured, oil was poured in. The new van, now with highly unreliable innards, was towed to a spot just around the corner from the garage where it had been obtained and then, with the utmost care, driven a matter of 100 yards or so back to its owners, who expressed surprise that it had been returned so quickly. And there it waited for another customer. That unfortunate drove it as far as the gates of the garage compound a few days later, only to be deafened by an ear-splitting din as the gearbox split asunder, leaving oil and fragments scattered across the road. While the inquest into the cause raged, the ancient Mercedes was purring its way along familiar streets, where customers remarked on how well it sounded. 'As good as new,' commented one, and the operator gave a wry smile.

As the years drifted by and William went to school, Margaret's routine left her little time for herself. 'I was working almost every night. At about 4.30 in the afternoon, I'd be off on my rounds, and after the last round at 11, we returned to the garage where the van was kept. It had to be cleaned and restocked, and although that could have been done in the morning, I preferred doing it there and then. So while I was working out what we needed, my driver would load up the ginger beer and drinks and whatever else we could get at the garage. Only once that was done could I get home. By that time, Tam was probably out with the rest of the Barlanark Team, although he preferred waiting for me to get home before he left to join up with the others. Sometimes I only found out where they had been if he was arrested and it was the police who came to the door. At home, I would get William's clothes and whatever else was needed ready for him to go to school later that morning. By the time I'd done that and some household chores, Tam might be coming back, and it was often well after three before I got to bed. In the morning, he would go to the garage and the cash and carry to complete the restocking of the van, then he'd drive it down and park it in Burnett Road ready for me to go out in the afternoon. It was hard work, but I loved it.' There was an added reward. Eventually, she was able to afford to hand over £15,000 for a brand-new ice-cream van.

Tam, a notoriously difficult man to get out of bed in the morning, was usually awakened by another van operator, his near neighbour Tommy 'T.C.' Campbell. T.C. did not drive, so the two men came to an unusual arrangement in which Tam drove his neighbour to the garage to stock up his own van in exchange for T.C. getting him out of bed. It was purely a business arrangement, and the two never socialised. In 1984, T.C. and Joseph Steele, both from the East End of Glasgow, were convicted of murdering the Doyle family and would spend 20 years in prison protesting their innocence before they were finally declared the victims of a miscarriage of justice. But the bitterness that surrounded the Ice Cream Wars would never go away. In a book outlining his experiences, T.C. would point the finger at Tam, his one-time acquaintance, as the culprit.

Yet most of the operators were on friendly terms with one another, and friendships that would endure over difficult years grew up, not least that of the McGraws with Eddie McCreadie, who ran a van in Castlemilk, another of the giant Glasgow schemes. Likeable Eddie, a man with an inexhaustible supply of witty stories, impressed Tam so much that he became a valued member of the Barlanark Team. He and Margaret remain firm friends.

Starting in 1974, Margaret would operate her vans for nearly 14 years, making scores of new friends in that time. Billy McPhee, her youthful neighbour from Burnett Road, would become one of her assistants, her van boy, when he left school in his teens and remain close to Tam and Margaret until his death. 'The thing I liked best about the van was that I knew everybody – the weans and their mothers who had been at school with me,' Margaret says. 'I'd have a laugh with the weans and always knew everything going on in Barlanark. Not a thing happened in the area without word of it being passed through the window of the van. Working on the van provided non-stop laughs.

'One day, a couple of weans came down. They were living two-up in one of the tenements along the route, and I watched them make their way to the window. One of them, the smaller of the pair, said, "Wanna buy gnomes?" I said, "Where did you get gnomes from?" Then the second wean, who was the cousin of the first one to speak, piped up: "They're fae oot ma da's garden." I said, "But you don't have a garden? Is this a concrete garden?" The first one says, "Do you want to buy the gnomes or do you not want to buy them?" I could hardly speak for laughing. I said, "No, I don't want to buy your gnomes." And off they went. I went another three stops and passed a guy whose mother had a garden full of gnomes. He was taking his dog for a walk, and I wondered if the dog was trying to sniff out the gnomes. Anyway, he gave the impression that he was looking for something, so I shouted to him, "You're not looking for gnomes, are you?" He replied, "Margaret, as a matter of fact, I am. Somebody's nicked all the fucking gnomes out of my ma's fucking garden." I said, "I know where they are." When he asked where, I said, "Never mind. We'll go round and get the gnomes, but don't touch the weans. They're just tottie weans.' He said, "My ma's had those fucking gnomes for 30 years." But I said, "You walk around to Barlanark Road, and we'll drive around in the van." We then met up outside the tenement where I'd seen the weans.

'When I got there, I realised I'd seen the weans on the same landing where a guy I knew lived. So I shouted up to him, "The weans have stolen his gnomes, and he wants them back." But when I saw the guy, I realised he was pished [drunk], and then his relatives appeared beside him, and they looked drunk as well. They all looked at each other and said, "Stolen gnomes? Gnomes?" I said, "They're on your fucking veranda." And the guy said, "I'll kill them." I was sure he meant the weans, not the gnomes, so I shouted up to him, "That's just the sort of thing weans do. This man here is getting his mother's gnomes back. There's no point in killing the weans." And the boy whose mother owned the gnomes agreed: "Aye, you're right, Margaret, but how are we going to get all these fucking gnomes down the road?" I said, "Just throw them in the ice-cream van, and I'll run them to your mother's for you." There were seven or eight pretty big gnomes, and we piled them into the van and returned them to their home. Once we got them there, I told the owner, "If I was you, I'd make sure they are concreted into the garden so they can't go walkies again." Later on, one of my customers asked me how I knew that the guy's mother owned the missing gnomes, and I said, "I don't know. I just saw him walking past, and he reminded me of gnomes." Every single night something happened to make you laugh.

'I got on fine with the weans in the area. Some of the other van operators complained that the youngsters were cheeky, but they were perfectly polite to me. I'd sometimes tell those who were grumbling, "You treat that wean the way you want him to treat you, and you can't go wrong." It's true there were a lot of cheeky weans in Barlanark, but I never had any hassle from any of them. One of them might come to the van with a couple of pals who were getting crisps, and I'd just know he didn't have any money. So I'd ask him, "Want to do me a favour?" When he said yes, I'd dig out some rubbish from inside the van, pass it over and tell him, "Take this to the rubbish bin, and I'll give you a packet of crisps." It was better than simply saying, "Your pals have got crisps, so here's a packet for you as well," because had I done that, the others would have said, "Margaret's given him a packet for nothing." Instead, the boy would put the rubbish in the bin and come back for the crisps he'd earned. It meant all three were equal – each had their own packet of crisps.

'Because of the fun we had, the time on the van seemed to pass so quickly. It was as if you went to work one moment and the next it was time to clean up and go home. There was gossip at each stop, such as "This fucker's got the jail" or "He's left his fucking wife" or "The police have been around, what should we do?" That was it, night after night.

'In the early days, the police were OK. But sometimes you came across one who wanted to make a name for himself. The rule was that you weren't allowed to play your chimes after a certain time, usually half-past seven in the evening. Now and again, they went off by "accident" to let customers know you were there. Nobody complained, but you'd get some copper following you around checking to see what time you switched the chimes off. Once I asked one, "You been promoted from the Serious Crime Squad to the Serious Chimes Squad?"

'One night, a police patrol car drove up to the van and stopped. An older man in uniform came across, leaving his younger colleague in the motor. My driver had gone off to deliver a message somewhere, leaving me alone for a few minutes. I thought, "Trust them to turn up now." But they didn't want any trouble. The older one waited until all the customers had been served and then said, "Can I ask you something, Margaret?" I said, "If you think you'll talk me into persuading Tam to join the police force, you're mistaken." But he said, "One of our guys is leaving. This is his last night, and we're having a wee party for him when his shift finishes." I said, "So what's the problem?" And he said, "We need to get a carry-out so we can have a few bevvies with him." I asked him why he couldn't get it himself, and he said, "I cannae. It's against the law. They aren't allowed to serve me when I'm in uniform." It was obvious that he wanted me to get the carry-out for him, but that meant driving the ice-cream van to an off-licence. That created a problem. I couldn't move the van, because I didn't have a licence to drive, and there was no sign of my driver. At the same time, I knew this guy, and he was OK. I wanted to help if I could. Then I hit on the answer. I said to the copper, "You take off and send your wee boy over to me. He can drive me." The policeman said, "Right, it's a deal." He went over to the car and told the younger constable to get into the van. He was just a wee boy, no more than 19 or 20, and I said to him, "Jump in and cover me while I get the carry-out." He was embarrassed and asked me what he should do. "Just drive me to the next stop," I said. "I'll do the rest. Stay in the driver's seat and don't let any fucker see you." He wanted to know what would happen if a customer looked in the window and recognised his uniform, so I told him, "Never mind about that. Just you stay there and don't come in the back or you'll get me a bad name. And take your hat off."

'The police didn't come to me for information, because they knew they wouldn't get any. At the same time, I was kind of pals with them all, but it was only a case of chatting with them when they called at the van to get something. One policeman I came to know pretty well was very well liked in the area. One day, he brought a younger colleague to the van. I said to the newcomer, "Would you like a KitKat?" and he took one plus a bottle of Irn-Bru. His colleague took the same and winked. He did that because they weren't supposed to take stuff. This effectively meant that they would never do me, because I could get them both into trouble for breaking regulations. The older one made sure his pal had taken the point. "He'll come and have a KitKat with his tea, Mags, and you won't have problems with chimes or anything else." And it was true. I never had any problems. Once, they came to the van and tipped me off about the Serious Chimes Squad: "Watch your chimes, Margaret, because they're on the prowl tonight. Just blow your whistle after half-past seven.' It was a friendly warning, and I even had a laugh with the Chimes Squad when they showed up.'

7

A LETTER TO THE QUEEN

MARGARET WAS NEVER SURPRISED BY HER HUSBAND'S NOCTURNAL disappearances. He would frequently leave the flat as darkness was falling, sometimes returning in the middle of the night as she was cooking, ironing or maybe preparing the breakfast table for William after a long stint working on the ice-cream van. She was not alarmed by hearing a sudden tap on the rear window and on opening it finding Tam on a ladder preparing to clamber back into their home. There were even occasions when, before climbing up, he would remove his outer garments and rejoin his wife dressed in just underpants and vest. He explained this peculiarity to friends and other members of the Barlanark Team as being a security precaution, pointing out that dust or flakes from the scenes of their crimes could easily transfer on to their garments, so these should be removed and thoroughly shaken before entering their own houses. That way no traces would be left for clever police forensic specialists searching homes and clothing.

And there were searches. The police became regular visitors to the Burnett Road address, opening drawers, looking into wardrobes and searching behind doors in a vain hunt for signs of stolen property. After a time, the police knew that Margaret's assurances that they wouldn't find anything were true but ploughed ahead with their probing regardless, telling her, 'Sorry, Margaret, but the bosses tell us we have to do this.' Their excuse for these constant intrusions was always that they had 'received information' and doubtless were able to convince a sheriff, when seeking his signature on a search warrant, that the informant was known and reliable. When Margaret asked, as she did on each occasion she answered a knock on her door by the police, who had said that she was hiding a cache of knocked-off property, the standard response was that the information had come via a telephone caller whose identity was known only to 'the bosses'.

Once, not having had her home raided for some time, Margaret made a spoof telephone call to the Strathclyde Police, disguising her voice and telling the operator that she was a neighbour of the McGraws in Burnett Road, Barlanark, and had seen 'stuff' being furtively carried into their house by two men from a Ford Granada and a black Ford Capri. By adding this detail to the mischief, she knew that alarm bells were sure to sound once the information was passed to CID. Drew drove a Granada and Snads a Capri, and even the most dim-witted detective would think that the Barlanark Team had been at work and this time had left itself open by being spotted stashing the night's swag.

Margaret made the call intending it as a joke, but she was astonished by the reaction. Within minutes, police had charged into Barlanark, sirens wailing and blue lights flashing, sealing off Burnett Road and menacingly telling onlookers, 'Get to fuck and go home.' On hearing boots charging along the close and up the stairway, Margaret opened her door to be handed a hastily scribbled search warrant. She had to endure demands for the whereabouts of Drew, Snads and Tam, but it was soon clear to the police that they had been taken for a ride. However, they did not suspect that Margaret was the caller, because they knew that not only would she never play informant, but that the targets in this case had been her own family and friends. The look of genuine astonishment on her face at being given the answer to her question of, 'What the fuck's brought the Seventh Cavalry?' was evidence in itself of her innocence.

She had not known it, but the previous night a gang had staged an audacious and terrifying armed hold-up on a major Glasgow cash and carry. A nightwatchman had been brutally attacked and beaten, then tied up and left in his own blood while the robbers made off with a huge stash. Violence apart, there were similarities between the raid and those made by Tam's Barlanark Team, and an anonymous call tipping off the police that two men known to be part of his gang had been spotted unloading goods at his home arrived just as a major manhunt for the culprits got under way. However, satisfied that the McGraws were not involved, the police did not linger long in Burnett Road before charging off elsewhere. They consoled themselves with the thought that it had been time to take a look in Margaret's home anyway. She thought the episode was hilarious.

Some people might have wondered if she had psychic powers, that some inner sense had told her that it was such an opportune time to make a prank call. In fact, it was pure coincidence. But there was no doubt that she had a gift given to few – that of being able to see and interpret signs and portents of things to come. Even as a child, she understood that things about her that caused alarm in others were not to be feared. On one occasion, she had asked her mother not to replace a flickering lamp in her bedroom because she enjoyed watching and interpreting the images created by it on her ceiling. Many children, and perhaps some adults, would have been disturbed by these visions made up of darkness and light, convincing themselves that their ghostly appearances were the work of spooks, not a faulty wick. Margaret was not afraid but fascinated, reasoning that if some unseen apparition was responsible, then it must be friendly, because it did her no harm.

She grew up with a sympathy for the spirit world, not knowing that in future decades it would provide her with terrible knowledge. Her adolescence, her marriage, the starting of a family and her venture into business had left her little time to ponder on matters outside her immediate circle of experience. But the time was coming when members of the Barlanark Team would try making use of her sixth sense.

During the middle and late 1970s, both Tam and Margaret found their separate enterprises becoming increasingly profitable. More and more customers were signalling her ice-cream van to stop, while Tam's team were in full flow.

For all his tough exterior, Tam always had a streak of vanity. He liked to think that his wife thought of him as being handsome and manly. Using extraordinary exertions to lift a heavy cash-filled safe that he and two gang members had extracted from a business in Mosspark, Glasgow, into their getaway car one night, Tam felt, to his horror, one of his teeth pop out. The three men spent half an hour crawling in pitch darkness before it was found. Tam claimed that the tooth could not be left because if it was discovered by police, it might lead back to him, particularly if he sported a tell-tale gap. But there was a suspicion that the real reason was that he did not want Margaret to see him toothless. 'She always looked good for me. I wanted to do the same for her,' he admitted 30 years later. 'Even if it meant risking prison.'

A later episode exposed Margaret and the family to close scrutiny by the Special Branch; even the movements of her ice-cream van were carefully and discreetly monitored. Encouraged by the success of the Barlanark Team, especially in raiding sub-post offices, other crews from the Glasgow area formed themselves into gangs and embarked on their own thieving sprees. For one group, the motive was not personal gain, but the advancement of the political and civil unrest in Northern Ireland. Postal orders stolen from Scotland turned up in the hands of paramilitaries in Ulster. It was worrying for the authorities, and Tam's family was watched in case he had anything to do with it. Checks were even made on Margaret's customers in case an Irish contact was being handed postal orders with his cigarettes and vanilla wafer. However, Special Branch detectives soon satisfied themselves that her business was strictly legitimate and the Barlanark Team was not involved. Tam was routinely interrogated, but it was plain from the tone of the police questions that they simply wanted to spread the word that no mercy would be shown to the culprits if they were caught.

Tam's dealings with the police were not always so amiable. Margaret recalls one especially unpleasant incident in which a blatant attempt was made to fit up Tam for a crime he had not committed. Indeed, the memory of it was so strong that on later occasions when police were pressurising him she would write to the Queen asking her to intervene with the Scottish Office and chief constable to ensure her husband was treated fairly.

She had known it was inevitable that Tam's chosen profession would land him in serious trouble from time to time. In 1976, a year after his imprisonment in Glasgow, the activities of the Barlanark Team resulted in his being fined in Perth after a series of raids went wrong. These were crimes in which he accepted he had been involved. But Margaret remains angry about the attempt by a prominent senior detective, now long retired but whose name she still treats with loathing, to warp his authority: 'This guy came to our home and said the police wanted to examine my black Mini car, which Tam had been using and which the police had seized, claiming he had driven it on a raid. The individual in charge, a detective inspector, ordered one of his subordinates, a constable – fortunately, a very decent and honest guy – to go and check the Mini. The constable replied, "That's already been done, and it's clean." Following that initial examination, the detective inspector decided to check out the vehicle alone. After doing so, he ordered the constable to look over the Mini again, and when the man protested that there was nothing to find, said, "Make sure you check the hubcaps." The subordinate was forced to do so and inside found keys for a cellar in which a huge stash of stolen cigarettes were later discovered. In the glove compartment, they even found a map of Scotland marked with crosses where there had been robberies. It was blatantly obvious that the inspector had planted the keys and map there while going over the Mini on his own. It was a fit-up of the worst kind, so amateurish to be laughable, only it wasn't funny.

'Tam was arrested, and because the Mini belonged to me, I was taken in for questioning. I rang our lawyer, a man in whom we had complete faith and trust, and explained what had happened. He was unable to come and sit in on the interview but said he would send a colleague. I was not impressed by the newcomer, who sat taking notes and seemed out of his depth and unsure what to do to get me out of there. The inspector was making mincemeat of him. He seemed so confident and was getting no challenge from the man my lawyer had sent along. Eventually, I said to the copper who was threatening to put me in the cells if I persisted in arguing that Tam and I were innocent, "Look, if you are going to charge me with anything, fucking do it or let me go home to make the dinner. It's as simple as that. If you're going to sit there and threaten me, you are wasting your time, because the only person that frightens me is the fucking dentist. Are we going to sit here and argue or are you going to do something, because your threats about doing this and that aren't going to work with me."

'When the lawyer at last spoke up, he said, "Have you any charges?" The cop just shouted at him, "You fucking shut up or I'll put you out of here." The man said nothing to that, and I thought, "I don't believe it. What's my lawyer sent me here?" Anyway, we got out, and when I got home, I rang my lawyer and said, "What a fucking halfwit you sent. That inspector's been giving him fucking dog's abuse. He even said he'd chuck him out and the guy said nothing." My lawyer said, "Margaret, trust me." I said, "Trust you? Fuck it. I could be getting the jail while you're out having an afternoon booze-up." But he only laughed and said, "Just trust me."

'So, anyway, the case came to court. I wasn't charged, but Tam was, with theft. According to the inspector, Tam had admitted everything, but his version of what we were supposed to have said was very different to how Tam and I remembered things. It all boiled down to who the jury believed was telling the truth – the policeman or us. The Mini was mine, and according to the inspector I was supposed to have said this and that, incriminating Tam. I knew I hadn't. My lawyer also represented Tam, and he called in the young man he'd sent to sit with me while I was being interrogated by the inspector. This man repeated what was said in the interview room – that I said from the outset we had done nothing wrong and that there was nothing in the Mini from any raid. He told the jury that he had carefully noted down everything that had been said by everybody there. My lawyer then asked his younger colleague, "So you write everything down every time you go to a police station? Every single word?" And the reply was, "Yes." Of course, our lawyer already knew the answer when he asked his next question: "What is your job?" The man answered that he was training to be a solicitor and was taking his final examinations in four weeks.

'As I heard this, I thought, "Fucking doughball. He hasn't even passed his exams. He's not even a lawyer." Then our lawyer said, "Previous to that, what was your occupation?" The man replied, "I was a police officer for 15 years." There was a bit of a gasp in the court, and our lawyer said, "So that explains why you write everything down." Then he said, "This all comes down to who is telling the truth and who is lying. You are used to writing everything down because you were a police officer, and by doing that you couldn't be accused of making things up and lying?" The man naturally agreed. Our lawyer then said, "Before you were asked to go to the police station, did you know the McGraws? Had you ever met Mrs McGraw?" He honestly replied no to both questions. Our lawyer said, "Is your account of what the inspector said during the interview at the police station truthful?" His colleague replied, "Definitely the truth."

'When it came to summing up the evidence, our lawyer said to the jury, "This person was a police officer for 15 years and is about to become a lawyer. Why should he become a liar and risk his career for Mrs McGraw, somebody he's only just met? I sent him out to the police station to meet her for the first time, and he's never met her since." So, it all boiled down to whether the jury believed the trainee solicitor or the inspector. They trusted the ex-policeman, and Tam was cleared. It even turned out that the trainee had spent some of his training working under the sheriff.'

But Margaret was enough of a realist to know that things would not always go her way. And much as she warned her husband to be careful, there were times when he ignored her advice and as a consequence found himself in deep trouble. One such example occurred in the mid-1980s. With their usual care and attention to detail, the gang had spent time surveying a general dealer's store in the Falkirk area. It was a thriving concern, serving a busy housing scheme, and a reconnoitre showed a raid would produce healthy pickings. Watchers were posted at main roads around the area and issued with hired walkie-talkie sets to report on police activity. Telephone lines were cut to avoid an over-inquisitive local ringing the police to report strange noises or the suspicious appearance of men in dark clothes. The store alarm was disabled and the box covering the electronics removed from the wall. Meanwhile, locks were cut through and replaced with brand-new padlocks. This was a routine precaution. It meant that patrolling police checking the security of the premises would not be suspicious.

In this case, it was also a precaution well taken. No sooner had the locks been changed than the lookouts reported that a police car was on its way. The vehicle stopped outside the store. It was a dark, cold night, and the officers in the vehicle carried out a cursory check, testing the strength of the padlocks but failing to note the disappearance of the alarm box before driving back into the darkness.

Once the policemen had left, the gang got to work. Cigarettes, tobacco and spirits were the main targets, but shelves filled with sweets, chocolates and soft drinks were also quickly cleared.

During the robbery, two young women appeared. The activity in the shop as they were passing had led them to believe that the store was unexpectedly open late, and they had decided to take advantage and buy some groceries. The kindly gentlemen who informed them that the men were fitting new shelving units even helped them with their purchases and guided them on their way, giving a friendly warning to 'get home soon out of the dark'. By the time the gang dispersed, they were confident that they were in the clear, but the sound of their operation had attracted local residents, who had made for the police station when they had been unable to use their telephones. The outcome was that Tam and some of the others were arrested not far from the scene. Later, police would say that they had found a soft-drink bottle nearby with Tam's fingerprints on it. It was a rare lapse by the team leader, which threatened to be a costly one.

By the time of their trial at Stirling Sheriff Court, considerable interest had built up in the gang. Most had been allowed bail, but after the first day, the sheriff ordered each of the defendants to be held in custody for the remainder of the case. This meant a strange circus each morning, consisting of a plethora of police and prison-service vehicles carrying the accused from Saughton Prison in Edinburgh. Traffic in the centre of Stirling was held up to allow the convoy free movement, and some locals were heard to wonder if the miscreants behind the barred windows of the prison vans were in fact dangerous terrorists. The case lasted a week. A close friend of Margaret remembers what happened: 'As the trial approached, the procurator fiscal announced he would be impressing witnesses. It meant he could force anyone to give evidence who didn't want to do so. The two people he most wanted in the witness box were Drew and one of Margaret's relatives, John Healy.

'So Drew, who was accused of being involved in the raid, went in first, and in answer to the opening question told the jury, "I am not going to answer on the grounds that I might incriminate myself." There was a recess, at the end of which the fiscal came back into court and handed Drew a letter guaranteeing his immunity. But it meant that he could not refuse to testify. So he went back into the box and just said, "It wasn't me, and I don't know who did it." Then it was John's turn, and the fiscal had a letter guaranteeing immunity ready for him. John hadn't ever been arrested. And he wasn't there when the police seized the gang close to the scene of the crime. Some people suggested that John might have been coached by friends of the accused as to what he should say in court. There was a rumour that he had agreed to take the heat off the others by saying that he had committed the robbery. It was an outrageous suggestion – as if anyone would do such a thing.

'The sheriff asked John, "Do you understand that you have to answer the questions?" and he replied, "Yes." He was then asked, "Did you rob the post office?" When John admitted that he had, he was instructed to tell the jury what had happened. He said, "Well, we took the stuff out in the van, drove down the road and that's when the police stopped us. They took the stuff out of the car and jailed us." At that, he stopped, and all Tam's friends put their heads in their hands. John realised that he'd dropped a clanger and tried to put it right, but it was too late. He said, "Oh, no, I meant I got away." But he knew that he had made a fatal mistake. Everybody was now convinced that he had been tutored and that whoever had coached him must have told him, "Look, say you did it and that you got away." Sadly, John got confused and placed himself and the others at the scene of the crime when he wasn't even arrested. Everybody in the courtroom was trying to hide that they were laughing.

'One of the defence witnesses indignantly told the jury when he was asked if he was being honest in his evidence, "I am a Catholic, and I cannot tell a lie. I have never been in trouble with the police before." The truth was that he was a Protestant who had been released from prison a few days before the robbery after having served an 18-month stretch for burglary.

'The girls who had been passing the scene as the robbery was taking place were also called as prosecution witnesses. They were asked, "You were confronted by masked men. Weren't you scared?" They both replied, "Oh no. They let us go in and get our messages." Drew even took the two of them out for lunch during the trial. "Not proven," announced the jury foreman.'

8

SHOELACES CLUE

THE ROBBERY NEAR FALKIRK WAS ONE OF SCORES COMMITTED BY THE Barlanark Team over the years. Many people in the East End of Glasgow thought that it was Tam and his team who robbed the post office, as some members of the gang also happened to run ice-cream vans and these vans sold many of the types of goods that had been stolen, not least cigarettes and sweets. It surely wasn't mere coincidence that stock similar to that which had disappeared from a store in Stirling one night was being offered for sale from ice-cream vans around Easterhouse or Castlemilk the next. But no one accused Tam of being involved.

However, he was caught on a number of other occasions. And unlike in Stirling, where the slip by John Healy caused such confusion that the jury let Tam and the others go free, he did find himself doing time. After what many saw as leniency by the sheriff in Perth in 1976, he was given twelve months by another sheriff in Linlithgow a year later and six months at the Glasgow Sheriff Court in 1983.

Before his death, Tam gave a clue as to how the team managed to have such a high percentage of success. He said, 'I realised not long after we married that Margaret had second sight. She definitely had a gift or knack of seeming to know what was coming, although I always made out I was never much interested. A few of the Barlanark Team said we should make use of this by taking her out with us when we were doing a reconnoitre and finding out what sort of vibes she received, good or bad. I told them there was no way I would put my wife at risk, and, in any case, Margaret would have been furious if she'd thought she was being involved in what we were doing. However, the more I thought about it, the more tempting it was. One morning, I persuaded her to come out with me for a run in the car. We went out towards Denny and Stirling, and I asked if she would take a look at one or two businesses that I'd heard might be coming onto the market. I said I'd been thinking that it might be worth our while opening a store or sub-post office somewhere outside Glasgow, because the police there were never off our backs. She was certainly surprised, because I'd never mentioned this before, but she agreed to come, pointing out that she would have to be back by the middle of the afternoon for the van round.

'I took her round a few places that the team had been looking at as possible targets. Margaret had a good look at them and mostly said they were OK, but there were some where she told me, "Tam, I don't know what it is, but I have a bad feeling about that one. I don't think we should have anything to do with it. My advice would be to stay away." That was enough for me to tell the others I wasn't happy and that we should maybe call things off. Margaret genuinely didn't have a clue that we were using her to gauge whether or not it was safe to turn over some place or other. Had she known, she would have hit the roof. She really thought I was thinking of buying the premises, and I had to evade her questions about where we'd get the money from. I told her we could get a loan on the strength of the income from the ice-cream van and that her experience running it would be useful.

'Was she right in what she told us? We mostly laid off, but a few other crews were doing the same sort of work as us, and one of them hit a store that Margaret had told me she was uncomfortable about. It was sheer bad luck, but while they were inside, the police turned up, because one of the cops thought he'd dropped his torch there earlier on. They heard a noise inside, and when the guys came out, the place was surrounded.'

During the research for my book about Tam called *Crimelord*, he took me around a number of the areas where the Barlanark Team carried out their raids. He told many stories about heists, safes being stolen with the contents, sometimes amounting to thousands of pounds, still inside, narrow escapes and even one incident in which he was almost fatally electrocuted. I asked what he did with his share of the booty. 'Gave some to Margaret and had a good time with the rest,' he said. 'I was never short of friends.'

Margaret has admitted that 'I spent what he gave me, because he told me I had earned it.' Those close to her believe that Tam was right in that respect. Margaret did earn what her husband gave to her.

'How did I feel the first time he got caught? Well, it was no use going to my ma and telling her, "Ma, Tam's been arrested and he's in the jail," because she'd warned me from the very first time she knew I was going out with him that prison and Tam went together like mince and tatties. And I knew that if he was caught, it was odds on Drew and Snads would be too, because the three of them were inseparable.

'Was I upset when he was in prison? After he'd been arrested a few times, there wasn't much I could do except get on with life. I'd just say to myself, "Well, it's six months. That's it. No use moping." Prison was a part of the job, a risk they all had to take. Can't do the time, don't do the crime. At the end of the day, they all get caught at some stage. When Tam was in prison, either on remand awaiting trial or doing a sentence, I'd visit him every day. In the end, it simply became a routine, adding prison visits to looking after William and doing my rounds on the van.'

Like during the 1970s, the early '80s were a constant sparring match against the police. Over the years, Margaret's experience of dealing with police surveillance on her and her family would hold her in good stead when the degree of monitoring became intrusive.

During the heydays of the Barlanark Team, police operational methods were hardly as sophisticated as they are now. For instance, any self-respecting thief would always make sure he had in his possession a short-wave radio in order that he could tune into police wavelengths and find out where the 'enemy' were and what they were up to. Margaret remembers that Tam and the team were no different, constantly listening in to find who the police were chasing, who they were tailing and who they were eyeballing – frequently other team members. On occasions, she'd go out for a drive with Tam or Drew, manoeuvre behind a police vehicle and listen to a frenzied policeman telling his controller, 'Fuck sake, they're tailing us.'

Mostly the banter was friendly enough. A policeman who knew the ropes realised that a harmless word here or there could make his life considerably easier, especially in the relatively hostile environment of the East End: 'I have a warrant for you over an unpaid fine, but I've left it in the office. I'll be back out here next week with it in my pocket, and if the fine isn't paid, I'll have to take you in.' Such a seemingly insignificant snippet of information could save a man from jail and earn the bobby respect.

The hostility towards the police in the East End was caused by flagrant attempts to fit up men and women for crimes they had not committed. Police might suspect a man of being a persistent, indeed major, lawbreaker, but that did not give them the right to condemn him for something he had not done. The McGraws had experience of this with the planting of the map in the Mini, but an even more glaring example occurred in the early 1980s.

Before then, the police made an appallingly amateurish attempt to seduce Tam into unwittingly giving away information. Margaret recalls what happened: 'Tam was arrested and taken to Baillieston Police Station in the East End, where he was searched. His pockets were emptied and his watch, jewellery, belt and shoelaces taken from him. He was then put into a cell, where he was joined by another man. They were chatting away: "What you in for, big yin? Where are you from? Where did they get you?" It was the usual blah, blah, blah and seemingly friendly, but the other man appeared to be trying to find things out from Tam. Then Tam noticed that something was wrong. He asked the time, and the other guy automatically looked at his watch and told him. Tam was furious and said, "Do you think I'm fucking daft? Next time you want to put somebody in to get information, at least make sure he takes his watch off and his shoelaces out. You've still got your watch on. Mine is outside the cell door with my shoelaces. You're a fucking cop." When he eventually got home, Tam could hardly speak for laughing about it, and later on he got to know the cop, who saw the funny side himself.'

Margaret also stuck up for what she considered to be her rights and those of other women operating and working on the ice-cream vans. She discovered that the main supplier of ginger beer and other soft drinks for the vans had arranged a men-only night at Shawfield, the renowned greyhound-racing stadium in the East End of Glasgow.

There would be free drink, a meal and free bets. It was a night for the drivers, owners and workers. One for the boys. But there were also many women workers, including Margaret. When she was told of the freebie, she warned representatives of the firm that female operators would boycott the company's products. At first, the company's management failed to take her warnings seriously, but when word filtered to the top that if Margaret said there would be a boycott, there would certainly be one, a clear change in attitude came about. The result was that while the men had their night out, an equally lavish evening was provided for the women. The soft-drinks suppliers kept their business but had learned their lesson and vowed never again to mess with Margaret McGraw.

9

HORROR MOVIE

IN BETWEEN DOING HER ROUNDS AND WONDERING IF TAM WOULD survive a night's thieving, Margaret loved life in Barlanark. Each day might have brought new problems, but there were also laughs, and there are incidents that she still remembers as though they were yesterday – the horror movie, for instance.

'Colour televisions were starting to be the thing,' she says. 'Most people had been happy with their massive black-and-white sets, even though they often didn't give a very good picture. But once colour had appeared, black and white was not the same. Everybody wanted a colour set, but most families couldn't afford them at first, and that created demand. Colour televisions were being knocked off all over the place, and because of the reputation that the Barlanark Team had built up, Tam, Snads and Drew naturally came in for a lot of police attention. One of the problems of Tam being so well known was that when the police did one of their very regular searches of our home and discovered something new, no matter what, they automatically assumed that it had been stolen. So, while most other people in Barlanark had colour sets, we did not. If there was a particularly good programme that we desperately wanted to see in colour, we'd have to knock on the door of a neighbour and watch it in their home.

'The team had done a couple of big stores that stocked electrical equipment and got a load of colour tellies, which they hid in a house up a close in the area. It was the home of someone elderly who was grateful for a few quid to look after stuff, and there was no way this individual would ever be suspected of hiding stolen goods, so

Tam knew they were in safe hands. We had a friend staying with us, a cracking wee guy who had been a member of the Barlanark Team on and off over the years, although he wasn't the brightest. As a result, some people made use of him, which used to annoy me, and I'd tell them when they were going to take him out on a job, "You're not doing that. He's fucking staying with me. That's not going to happen." The trouble was, he could be his own worst enemy, because he'd do anything anybody asked. I tried to keep an eye on him, but doing that landed me in trouble now and again, I can assure you. One night, I loaned him Snads' beautiful white suit to go to the dancing, and he came home looking as though he'd been rolling around on the dance floor and in the street outside. You can imagine Snads wasn't at all happy, and I had to talk my way out of that one.

'Anyway, one of the television channels began showing a horror film every weekend, probably one of the Hammer series. They were in colour – the blood vivid red and the costumes every shade under the sun – but we had to watch them in black and white. One night before one of them was due on, I was thinking that it would be brilliant to watch it in colour when our wee pal piped up: "Can't we get one of the TVs down?" I said, "No, we can't have anything stolen in the house. It would be just our luck if the police came while we were watching it." But he persisted: "It would only be for one night, then we could put it back up." I said, "I don't know about that," but he had set me thinking, and when Tam came in, I asked him, "Can't we bring one of the colour televisions down so we can watch the horror film?" Tam was adamant: "Oh no, no. No chance." I said, "Just bring it down, and as soon as the film's finished, the wee man can take it back again." Tam would watch the telly 24/7, and he eventually gave in and said, "Aye, all right." So, the telly was collected.

'We watched the movie, but by the time it was over, it was too late to return the set, because it would have meant disturbing the friend who was looking after the stash. It was decided to take it back first thing the next morning instead. We were sure nobody would shop us – our neighbours weren't the sort. All the same, even though it was late we knew we couldn't leave the set in the sitting room. Because we'd had to disturb some of the furniture to make room for it, I wanted to replace everything as it had been, so we put the set in the bedroom cupboard, where we kept our suitcases – we hadn't been back long from working in London at that time. I'd actually intended to get rid of the cases the next morning, so dumped them on the bed and the floor to make room for the television set. Everything else was put back in its place, including our wee black-and-white TV.

'We were sitting down having a cup of tea and getting ready for bed when there was a knock on our front door. I instinctively said to our wee pal, "That's the fucking polis," and sure enough when I opened the door two policemen I knew were standing there. They said they were looking for a colour television, so I asked them, "What is the script with you? It's two o'clock in the morning." One said, "Well, we've had a phone call." And I said, "About a colour fucking telly? You've got to be kidding." I was sure they believed me, because they turned our house over twice a fucking week and didn't find a thing for the simple reason that I didn't allow anything stolen in the place because I knew how regularly they came. I said to them, "I've got a fucking pal up from London. What do I tell her? That it's the fucking milkman? During the night? She's hardly had time to unpack." One of them said, "Margaret, where is your pal?" I said, "Where the fuck do you think? She's in the toilet, but she was sitting in the living room when you woke the neighbourhood up." He said, "Go and shut the living-room door. Tell her it's one of the neighbours." Our wee pal looked at me as though I was daft, because as I shut the door, I shouted, "Och, it's just a neighbour for some milk. I'll be back in a couple of minutes."

'The policeman looked in the bedroom. He saw the cupboard was shut and that there were cases on the bed and floor, and it was obvious that he thought I was telling the truth about having a guest. He didn't even bother looking in the cupboard or taking a peek at who was in the living room. Instead, he said, "Margaret, I'm really sorry." I said, "I'm going to tell you something. Somebody must have a fucking big phone bill. Are they having a laugh? There's no chance of you finding anything stolen in here." He said, "We know. But if it was a woman across the road who phoned and we didn't come, she'd be telling her pals, 'Oh, I phoned and they didn't show.' That's why we're here. I know there's nothing stolen in your house." The coppers left, and I swear I've never seen a telly leaving a house so quickly, even though it meant waking up our elderly neighbour.'

Barlanark might have been home to men who were thieves, robbers, shoplifters and even murderers, yet Margaret remembers that it was a time when many families felt sufficiently safe to not bother locking their doors at night or even during the day when they were out. Occupants of closes looked after each other and each other's property. They could be trusted to keep secrets.

Most of the properties in the scheme had concrete floors, particularly those at ground level, and during a search police soon realised that there was no point in lifting carpets or moving furniture to see whether stolen property was hidden underneath. However, the police knew that some homes did, in fact, have areas of wooden flooring, under which were deep spaces that could be used to secrete considerable volumes of items and materials, people even, merely by lifting up four floorboards. Margaret found that she had such a space in her bathroom. It was exceedingly useful for hiding away cigarettes and drink, for example. She believed she was being extremely discreet as to when she accessed the secret room, always making sure that the front door was locked, and she certainly never did so when there were visitors in the house. Unfortunately, she didn't reckon on the normal but insatiable curiosity of William. One day, a friend who lived in the next close paid a call on Margaret and, after the customary pleasantries, said, 'Do you keep stuff under the toilet floor?'

Startled, Margaret said, 'How do you know that?'

'Because William's told my wean, and who knows who else he might tell that his ma's got loads of drink under the bathroom floor.' The hiding hole was promptly opened, the contents removed and the floorboards nailed firmly and permanently back in place.

There were, of course, other secrets in the house. Margaret was a resourceful woman who knew the value of looking after her friends, especially when they were in trouble and needed help. In the living room, there was a fireplace in which sat a fire that could be pulled out should workmen require access to the workings. On either side of the fire breast were alcoves that were not to her taste. Margaret told Tam that she wanted to cover them up. A workman was hired to carry out this very simple operation, and having been instructed as to what was required, got on with the task. He might have been a little surprised to be told not to fix the fire back in its place and even more astonished had he been able to see, after he left, that a few adjustments were made to his completed work so that enough space was left for a man to squeeze in behind the fire if it was pulled forward and into one of the alcoves.

A friend on the run suspected of being harboured by the McGraws needed only to duck in, wait patiently and quietly, and re-emerge when the police had left – Jonah McKenzie was one friend who made use of the facility. Sometimes when a visitor was in the hiding place during a police visit, Margaret would turn up the volume of the television or radio to cover any accidental noise – a sneeze or cough perhaps – and wait for the hunters to depart. Officers, no matter how skilled in searching or how wise to the devious ways of the folk of Barlanark, never thought to remove the fire from the fireplace.

For as long as she could remember, Drew Drummond had been a close friend, the best pal of her brother Snads. Often Drew would seek her advice. They were always close friends, shopping together and talking over problems. The gender difference was not a factor in the relationship. They were never boyfriend and girlfriend, and Tam happily accepted that when he became Snads' confidant and Margaret's boyfriend, Drew would be an intimate of the little group. If some people noticed the closeness of the friendship, they kept their views to themselves.

However, one incident gave rise to the police gossip shop having a field day. A bookmaker's premises in the East End had been raided late one night, and the break-in seemed to have been perpetrated by the Barlanark Team. By chance, Tam and Drew had been out and about at the same time as the robbery, although there was never any evidence to connect them to the crime, which would always remain unsolved.

Drew had a day job, and rather than return home he agreed to secure an additional hour of sleep by staying with his friends until the time came for him to go to work. The problem was that there was only one bed, so Drew climbed in to sleep on one side of Tam, with Margaret on the other. Hardly had they pulled up the covers when there was a bang on the door. 'That's the coppers,' Margaret said, and Tam leaped up to answer it, without thinking that he had left his wife in bed with another man. The police immediately charged into the bedroom. 'I saw the way they looked and thought, "Fuck it. I'm not explaining the situation to them. They'll come to their own conclusions,"' says Margaret. Clearly, the three-in-a-bed discovery distracted and embarrassed the callers, who were barely able to conceal their sniggers as they departed.

There were many other occasions when police came to Margaret's house, including a couple of times when the officers were armed. One of these visits followed a strangely coincidental raid on a thriving general dealer's store in Barlanark. Coincidental because a few hours earlier the storekeeper had been involved in an argument with the mother of a man with connections to the Barlanark Team.

There is no need to identify this delightful lady other than to say that she survived on her old-age pension, which meant that her every penny counted. She went to the shop to make a few small purchases and handed over a £20 note to the counter assistant, only to be given change for half that amount. Naturally, the lady was upset but was told that she would have to wait until the end of the night when the till was checked to see if there was a tenner over. Only then would she get her money back. It was clear that the assistant thought she was lying.

The customer was still distressed when she got home and told her family the reason for her discontent. They were, not unnaturally, more than a little angered. That night, the shop was raided and emptied – totally gutted. Even the calendars and flypapers were removed. Nothing was left.

The theft bore all the hallmarks of the Barlanark Team. Telephone wires to nearby houses had been cut so that the police could not be alerted that a raid was in progress, but during the operation, a local resident happened to come out of his front door. One of the thieves, the likeable Colin Campbell, was holding a crowbar that had been used to jemmy open the doors of the target building. But in the dim light, the local resident was convinced that he had spotted a gun. Colin's warning shout of 'Get back in the house' made the witness all the more convinced that an armed gang was involved. Colin adding 'And mind your own fucking business' merely added insult.

During the period when the Barlanark Team could be said to be in their prime, guns were largely restricted to London gangs. They were, of course, in circulation in Glasgow but not in the profusion they would be later, so the sight of what appeared to be a gun caused considerable consternation. That concern extended to the police when they began making door-to-door inquiries in the Pendeen area of Barlanark the next day and were told that one of the robbers had been carrying a weapon. The media played up the gun angle, and it was hardly surprising that armed officers were among the investigating detectives. Sure that the Barlanark Team were the culprits, the police confined their searches to the area where the members were known to live.

Those who had been responsible for cleaning out the store were more than certain that their swag would never be found. It had been carried a short distance to the family home of one of the team members, who was fortunate to have one of the houses with space underneath their floor. In the past, police had carried out searches of the house without discovering the hidden area beneath the floorboards and at the time the store was raided confined their hunting to the area above ground, not bothering to examine any flooring. Their search that day drew the inevitable blank. But armed police remained outside the house, as well as that of Margaret and the other wives of the Barlanark men while the searches went on inside. Making no effort to hide their weapons was a clumsy move by the police and did nothing to improve relationships with locals.

For some days afterwards, police threw a virtual cordon around Barlanark, searching cars and vans entering and leaving the area. They found nothing. Had they bothered to confine their inquiries to the scheme itself, however, their curiosity would doubtless have been aroused by the seemingly never-ending trains of baby pushchairs and prams entering a particular close and leaving when they were evidently considerably bulkier and heavier.

There were other times when the police came closer than they realised to property the source of which could be said to be questionable. Following a successful raid by the team one night, the McGraw home was packed to the ceiling with cigarettes and drink. It was a temporary measure: the loot was to be removed to a safer hiding place the next morning, but for now, with no time to put it from sight, it lay piled everywhere.

That night, a car alarm went off in the street. One of Margaret's neighbours, a businessman, had a car with an alarm that took it upon itself to go off night after night. He was rarely, if ever, affected, as he slept in a room at the rear of his house where the din could not be heard, leaving others to suffer the racket. Sometimes, investigating the alarm was all the excuse the police needed to search nearby homes. There was no way Margaret could afford to have the police in her house, no matter what the grounds.

It was the early hours, and after hastily dragging on a housecoat over her nightwear, she headed out to find her neighbour, intending to say, 'Your fucking alarm's going off.' She could not add, 'And if you don't stop it, I'll have the cops turning my place over.' Margaret had just stepped out of her door when she met policemen coming into her close. It was a heart-stopping moment. They were only feet away from a discovery that would have enhanced their chances of promotion. She had to make sure they came no further. 'Do you know where the owner of the car lives?' she was asked.

'They sleep at the back, so they don't hear it. I chap them up all the time.'

'That's really good of you, hen. You're a good neighbour. We'll just leave it to you.' The two policemen then headed back to their beat car and drove away. It was a close thing, and the episode strengthened Magaret's resolve not to allow stolen material into her home.

There would be other close calls, such as that of the 'Invisible Goodies'. 'One night, I was out in the ice-cream van when a cop car pulled up and a policeman told me he had a warrant to search our house,' Margaret remembers. 'He said he was looking for stolen cigarettes, and I assumed the phantom phone caller had been at work once again. I was worried, not because they'd find any stolen cigarettes, but because the spare bedroom was piled from floor to ceiling with stolen sweets. Tam found a huge stash at a garage and guessed that they'd been stolen. Whoever had knocked them off had evidently got windy and had abandoned the haul. Tam was Tam, and there was no way he was going to abandon them, but by taking them he reckoned he was stealing stolen sweets. There was enough to fill a van, so he brought them home. We had nowhere to put anything so just piled them ceiling high in the spare bedroom. "What am I going to do with these?" I asked Tam. He said, "Sell them off the van." I replied, "If anybody asks where I got them, what do I say?" He said, "Just say you got them off me and that I found them."

'So, when the police came to the van with the warrant and said that they wanted to search our house, it's not hard to guess how I felt. There was no point in trying to stop them, so I just took them to the house, opened the door and invited them in. One of them searched everywhere, opening and checking every wardrobe and cupboard, including in the spare bedroom, looking for cigarettes. He couldn't have missed the sweets but never once mentioned them. When he appeared to be finished, I said, "Is there anywhere else you want to see?" And he replied, "Well, there isn't really anywhere else you could hide a pile of fags." As he was leaving, he said, "Sorry, Margaret." I replied, "I know – the phantom phone caller. It's OK, any time. But don't keep me off work in the future. This has cost me money." He then apologised again. I was amazed that he had never once mentioned the sweets. How could he have walked by them without asking where they were from? The police came with warrants many times and searched our house, but they found absolutely nothing.'

In that instance, the joke was on the police, but a time would come when it was Margaret, Tam and their friends' turn to be on the receiving end. During one of his frequent spells behind bars – many of which were served on remand, at the end of which the case against him was not proven – Tam met an older man who had been held for some minor infraction. The two found themselves being freed at the same time, and they asked the customary questions of one another, such as where they lived and whether they were returning to their families. In the case of his new friend, whom we shall call Robbie, Tam was told that he had nowhere to stay. So Tam invited him to spend a few days with him, Margaret and William. Margaret remembers thinking that he was a strange man but likeable: 'He was on edge, and I thought, "What weirdos Tam brings into the house." I was always worried about William, but Robbie turned out to be harmless – just a drunk who would disappear for a year and then, out of the blue, knock at our door.

'He was always clarty, living much of the time in the streets. When he turned up, I'd say, "Fuck, Robbie, it's you. Strip and I'll get

Tam's housecoat for you." Then his stuff would go into the washing machine, and he'd sit while his clothes were being washed and dried. I'd ask him what he'd been up to, and he'd tell me, "I haven't been up to anything. I was working down the covered market in the Glasgow Barras." I'd say, "Are you lying?" And he'd protest, "No, I'm not lying." So I'd ask him, "How the fuck are you in that state?" And he'd say, "Oh, well, I've not been at the Barras." He'd then try to get out of answering by talking about something else.

'He came from a wealthy family who had disowned him. Years earlier, he'd done a robbery, and he and his mates were caught. When one of them got out of prison, he threatened Robbie's wife about some money, and she killed herself. After that, he just didn't care. Everybody knew him, because he went around helping everyone else except himself. And it always seemed to end with me or one of my friends telling him, "Oh, all right then. Just stay."

'If he didn't stay with us, he'd go to my brother John's house and stay there. We had a bar in the house, and there was always drink in it. The bottles were always full. Robbie would lodge for a week, then one morning he'd just get up and disappear, and you wouldn't see him for a year.

'One time, he'd been staying with us and John for a while before heading off. A few weeks passed, and I had some pals over for a drink. When I asked what one wanted, she said, "Whisky, please." After taking a sip, she held up her glass and said, "Margaret, that's not whisky." I said, "Of course it is," but she was adamant it was not. I took a sip and knew what had happened. Robbie had drunk all the whisky and had filled up the bottles with cold tea. He'd gone through the vodka and gin, too, replacing them with tap water. I told John, and he checked his bar to find that the same thing had happened. Conned again.'

10

THE PETRIFIED PLUMBER

RUNNING THE ICE-CREAM VAN MEANT HARD WORK AND LONG hours, but the financial rewards, fun and gossip made it worthwhile. It left little time for home life, but what there was of it Margaret valued and treasured. She never minded the interruption of a knock on her door from a neighbour seeking help or just a natter. The endless visits from the police, disturbing her few hours at home, were an irritation, but she had known the life into which she was marrying, and over the years came to accept these searches as others in Barlanark would regard a visit from a social worker or probation officer. Not everyone, though, was able to deal with the police in the same casual way. One visit in particular would have bizarre consequences.

In early summer, Margaret decided that the kitchen sink at Burnett Road had seen its best days and needed to be replaced. She contacted a local plumber, and after a preliminary visit to look over what was needed, the tradesman agreed to carry out the work. He arranged to remove the old sink and take it away, fit another that was to Margaret's liking, and complete the job in a day, with a minimum of disruption to the family. And true to his word, he duly arrived on the morning of 23 June 1980. By the time he left to return home, he would have plenty to talk about.

The old unit was soon disconnected and placed in the hallway while the workman began preparing the pipes for the replacement. The talk that day was of a dramatic prison break the previous morning. It was natural that Margaret was interested. The escape had been from Barlinnie, and Tam was being held there, accused of the customary break-in of some store or post office. He was in the remand wing but would not be there long, the charges failing as the result of a lack of evidence. Margaret intended to visit Tam later that day before heading out on her ice-cream round. Snads had arranged to take her to the jail and bring her home again, and she was waiting for her brother as the plumber worked away.

The breakout was so ingenious that it is worth examining in some detail. One of the escapees was a family friend, but Margaret had never heard of Archibald 'Big Archie' Steen, who had been sentenced to life imprisonment in 1975 for murder, attempted murder and bank robbery. His murder victim was John Stillie, aged 27, who had been shot dead by two gunmen during what had been described at the time as a gangland vendetta. Archie had also been convicted of robbing the Clydesdale Bank in Albert Drive, Glasgow, stealing £12,290 and threatening staff and customers with a shotgun and revolver. At his trial, it was said that when he was eventually arrested in Edinburgh, he had fled into a Princes Street store and struggled with chasing police. The judge who sentenced Archie had described him as 'a menace to the community'.

Steen's was a name Margaret, and others, would not forget. In prison, he had become close to John Steele and his elder brother by two years, James. Both Steeles were serving 12 years: John for assault and robbery and James − known to his family as 'Jim' − for attempted murder. They were well known to the McGraws, and Jim in particular was a friend of Margaret and Tam.

It was not surprising that the three prisoners associated together. Theirs was a natural friendship because they were all from Easterhouse in the east of Glasgow and had known one another before they fell foul of the law. They had initially been sent to Peterhead Prison in Aberdeenshire to serve their sentences. The jail was a grim place that had a terrible reputation for violence − violence between inmates and violence perpetrated by the guards on their charges. In winter, men were left in freezing, unheated cells with only a single threadbare blanket for warmth. The food was appalling, and because it was almost 200 miles from Glasgow, the home city of many of its inmates, families found it a nightmare to pay visits, particularly during the winter. Rather than put their loved ones through the ordeal of these journeys, most men opted to forgo visits at Peterhead, instead saving up their allocation and applying for a temporary transfer to a prison nearer their homes, where they could use their allotted number.

Archie and the Steeles had made use of this regulation, and in June found themselves at Barlinnie, on the doorstep of Easterhouse. By the morning of 22 June, with their visits used up, all three knew that they would be returning to Peterhead in three days. Time, therefore, was short. But their stint at Barlinnie and the chance to meet old acquaintances had not been wasted. An escape plan had been drawn up.

At about eight o'clock that morning, an off-duty officer looked out of his prison-service house and watched in amazement as three men slid down a rope taking them from the roof of one of the prison blocks and over the encircling wall around Barlinnie. He telephoned a warning to his colleagues, who initially thought that they were victims of a practical joke, and by the time staff had reached the spot, the three men had disappeared. The only trace that something untoward had taken place was a rope, about 40 feet long, dangling from the roof of one of the prison buildings, a new shower unit. It had been tied to a clothes pole in the communal area used by the wives of guards for hanging out their washing. Clearly someone on the outside – almost certainly two men at least – must have known of the plan and been in place to tie the rope at their end, hold it taut as the escapees slid down and then help them make their getaway, presumably in a car.

When he was telephoned within hours of the drama, a furious Malcolm Rifkind, then a Scottish Office minister with responsibility for prisons, ordered an immediate investigation into how the men could have got away in broad daylight when closed-circuit television cameras were trained on the wall over which they had abseiled. His staff announced that the escapees were all 'violent and dangerous'.

Strathclyde Police placed Detective Superintendent Norman 'Norrie' Walker in charge of the hunt to find the men, and he called a press conference at which he announced, 'We would warn the public that these men are vicious and dangerous. Nobody should attempt to tackle them if they are spotted. Telephone the police immediately and leave it to us.' Walker would later play a significant role in the lives of the McGraw and Steele families.

The police had special cause to be worried about Archie now being at large. He had threatened Chief Superintendent David Frew of the Serious Crime Squad, one of the officers involved in his arrest, and the policeman's family. Such threats were surprisingly uncommon, but when they were made, officers were quick to rally round their colleagues. In this case, it had been made five years previously and might well have been a remark uttered in the heat of the moment, but the police still took it seriously. Any prison escape received maximum attention, but there was also a potential threat to a policeman and his family, which guaranteed that the case would be treated with the utmost priority.

Walker and his team were soon inspecting the jail, trying to ascertain the various stages of the break. They found that as other inmates were doing their morning's vile slopping-out operation prior to taking a shower, the plotters had slipped away unnoticed, headed to the third floor of the unit, climbed to the roof through an inspection hatch and waved to waiting accomplices.

Jim Steele, still a likeable and well-respected figure in the East End, remembers the morning well: 'The treatment at Peterhead was so bad that any man held there would want to escape. We were about to go back when I had an idea as to how we could get away. The others were enthusiastic, and we had many friends on the outside willing to help. We got word of it to Tam, who said he would arrange any assistance we needed. The plan was that once we were on the roof, we would throw down a light line with a weight tied on the end to our friends waiting by the washing lines. They had bought a long stretch of mountaineering rope from a shop in the west end of Glasgow a few days earlier. The two ropes were tied together, and we pulled the heavier up and tied it, with our helpers securing the other end.

'I was last to slide down, and by the time my turn came, the rope had sagged. When I grabbed it, I suddenly dropped about six feet, and I thought my end had come. I looked down, and the prison yard seemed to be at least 100 feet below. As I slid, I expected the guards to come haring around the corner of the outer wall at any second. Another pal from the East End was waiting in a motor, and as soon as I hit the ground, I ran to his car. Archie and John were already in, and off we went. The police never did discover who our helpers really were.'

News of what had happened spread like wildfire, and soon dramatic stories of the escapees' plans were swamping Glasgow. It was said that they planned a massive bank raid to finance their new lives abroad, that mistresses were waiting for them on exotic islands, that an hour after the break a private aircraft had been seen leaving a disused airstrip to the south of the city and even that major London crime gangs were harbouring them. Police might have thought that these rumours were fanciful, but they were taking no chances. Descriptions of Archie and the Steeles were circulated to every force in Britain, while authorities at ports and airports were asked to be on the lookout. Police were paying especial interest in the East End and the known haunts of the escapees. Detectives banged on the doors of friends and associates, while the homes of the men's families were put under permanent watch. Even telephone calls were monitored.

Margaret and Tam liked Jim Steele. While he was held at Barlinnie, he had given his visiting passes to Tam, because he had not wished to place the burden on his own family, and he had known that they would reach their destinations. Tam simply handed them on to Margaret. Making sure that they reached those for whom they were intended was no problem. Almost all of those meant to receive them lived in Barlanark, and Margaret simply passed them out as she went around in her ice-cream van.

While the rumours circulated and the plumber worked away, the day wore on, and Snads arrived. He was interested to see the plumber's progress, but he had some difficulty getting in, because the old sink was leaning against the front door and needed to be moved to allow him to enter. 'John was no sooner inside than the most almighty din started,' says Margaret. 'There was shouting and banging and something being smashed, and then the front door was kicked in. They must have been charging against it, because when it gave it crashed down onto the sink, and the coppers went over with it. I ran out of the kitchen, yelling, "What the fuck's going on?" and a voice shouted, "Police." At that, the officers picked themselves up off the floor and extricated themselves from the sink and what was left of the door. I then saw that they were holding guns, which were pointing at John, the plumber and me. The police had come to my home many times before, but never armed. One of them shouted, "Right, everybody, stay where you are." It was exactly like something from a television programme, but I didn't react the way actors do. Instead, I shouted, "Fuck this. What do you think you're doing? Get out of this fucking house. Now. Out."

'But the police were running all over the place and in and out of all the rooms, even the toilet. They pointed a gun at John, and I shouted at them, "Get that fucking gun off him. Get that fucking gun away from my brother." You ought to have seen the policemen, with both hands on their guns, pointing them at John as if they were terrified. What was really scary was that they could have shot him. They were in the house about 20 minutes, checking that we were who we claimed to be. And that included the plumber. While all this was going on, they continued to stomp about, shout questions, point their guns, go in and out of rooms, and search cupboards and wardrobes.

'The head guy then pulled me into the bedroom. "Who is that in the kitchen?" he wanted to know. I said, "It's the plumber and John Adams." He said, "What's John Adams doing here?" I replied, "He's got more right to be in here than you fucking have. He's my brother. He came here to take me to Barlinnie to see Tam, my husband." The cop clearly thought he'd better do some explaining: "It's like this: John looks very like Jim Steele. They really are similar. And Jim Steele has escaped from Barlinnie with Archie Steen. John has been seen coming here, and Archie is very dangerous." I thought, "So that's it. It's really Steen they're after."

'When they left, I went into the kitchen to see if the plumber was OK. He was a big guy, but he'd been so terrified that he'd swallowed a whole bottle of whisky and had peed himself. There he was, sitting on the floor, non compos mentis, holding the whisky and muttering, "I've never had such a fright in my whole life." And he looked that way.'

All three escapees were recaptured the following month, and it was their own kind who shopped them. Such was the intense level of police activity, particularly in the East End, that the search for the missing men was hampering the efforts of criminal gangs to make a decent living. Crooks could barely move without a police car pulling up alongside them and officers opening the rear doors and inviting them to 'come down to the station for a wee chat'. The police seemed to be everywhere, because senior officers knew that this tactic might pay dividends. It had certainly done so in the past. They realised the value of patience and were confident someone would eventually decide that enough was enough and that it was time to clear the decks. Before long, telephones began ringing in police stations, and detectives started picking up snippets from informants.

The outcome was that after two weeks on the run, Jim Steele was the first to find himself back behind bars. He had been enjoying himself in a busy bar one Saturday night. Drinks were flowing, women were giggling and men were arguing when someone told Jim that a visitor wanted to talk to him outside. He immediately realised that the game was up. The man was a detective, and the pub was surrounded by armed police. Jim was not the sort of individual to want innocent friends to get hurt. He went out and gave himself up without a struggle.

The next day, exactly two weeks after the escape, police arrived at a house in Starpoint Street, Cranhill, the district separated from Barlanark by just the width of Edinburgh Road. They smashed down the door and emerged with John Steele. While there, a taxi arrived and out stepped Archie Steen. Paying off the cabbie, he turned to find himself staring into the barrels of many guns, all pointed at him. The following month, all three appeared before the High Court in Glasgow to deny a charge of escaping from prison. They defended themselves after their trial counsel withdrew, telling the judge that he could not continue because none of his clients wanted to accept his advice. In turn, each defendant told of appalling conditions at Peterhead, describing in graphic detail, which had spectators gasping in disgust at times, of being handcuffed, stripped naked, savagely beaten up in cells specially soundproofed to drown out their screams and of having urine put in their mugs of tea. The prosecutors said the escape was the brainchild of Archie and during it the three had sawed through an iron bar before getting onto the roof, where a weighted rope was thrown over the wall to waiting accomplices. Their stories of inhumane treatment found little sympathy with the jury, and they were convicted. Archie was sentenced to four years and the Steeles three.

But the saga was not yet over. In October that year, T.C. Campbell from Easterhouse, who had regularly roused Tam from his bed in exchange for a lift to the garage where their ice-cream vans were housed, was charged with organising the escape. He would use his own liking for a lie-in as an alibi, telling the jury, 'On the Sunday morning when they escaped, I was in bed with my girlfriend. The first I knew about a breakout was when I read of it the next day. I'd visited Jim in Barlinnie a couple of days earlier, but we never talked about escape.'

In the dock with him stood Thomas Lafferty from Garthamlock. All three escapees were called to give evidence, and each in turn told the jury that the police had arrested the wrong men – T.C. and Lafferty had not been involved. They named two other men as having been behind the escape. Jim Steele even briefly brought laughter into the staid surroundings of the High Court at Glasgow when he described sitting in a safe house after the escape and being warned that the police had been tipped off about where he was hiding. 'The others got out and ran off, but I couldn't go with them,' he said. 'I was trying to alter my appearance and had curlers in my hair. There wasn't time to take them out. All I could do was sit and wait and hope that the information was wrong. I would have looked conspicuous running down the street with my head covered in women's hair curlers.'

His brother John admitted that Thomas Lafferty had been at their hiding place but had stumbled into it by accident: 'We gave him a drink and then kept topping it up. We kept him drunk for two days in case he blabbed to the police, and by the time he sobered up, we were long gone.'

At the start of the second day of the trial, the Crown withdrew the charge against Lafferty. It was pointless continuing. There was no evidence against him. He walked free but waited in the court, hoping to be joined by T.C. And he was when the jury announced, 'Not guilty.' Outside the court building, T.C. told reporters, 'I am glad this is over, because it has cost me a lot. I have been unable to pay the rent on my council house while I was in prison for three months waiting for the trial, and I have been evicted and am now homeless. The embarrassment and worry caused my girlfriend to leave me, so I'm now on my own. All I want to do is pick up the threads of my life once again.'

T.C. and Margaret went back to their ice-cream rounds, and Tam was soon released to rejoin his wife and his friends in the Barlanark

Team. The plumber completed his installation of the kitchen sink, but he would never forget the day armed police forced a halt to his work. It had all been caused by mistaken identity, Snads being a Jim Steele lookalike. The episode ended reasonably well, but another incident of mistaken identity would not have such a harmless conclusion. The story was related to Margaret by a friend who was sufficiently circumspect as to withhold from her the names of those involved. We will simply call the principal 'Jock', a common enough name and not that of anyone involved.

Jock had arranged to visit a friend in Barlinnie, but as he was on the verge of heading to the prison, two associates called to see him. He explained that he had a prior appointment, apologised and asked both to wait in a well-known East End pub. Returning from Barlinnie, Jock was dismayed to discover that one of his friends had been badly beaten up. He realised who the offender was and confronted him. 'You've done enough, now just fucking leave it at that,' Jock told him.

The suggestion did not go down too well. The culprit carried an ugly, gaping facial scar. Pointing to it, he said, 'You fucking want one of these?'

'Don't be stupid,' replied Jock.

This response was met with a belligerent look and a clear threat: 'Well, cunt, mind your own fucking business.'

Jock was not the sort of man to allow such a threat to pass. In addition, his friend had been given a hiding. Leaving the pub, he called on a contact and that night could be spotted heading back to the bar carrying a shotgun. The next day, news of a ghastly shooting and a photograph of the victim were plastered across the front pages of Glasgow newspapers. Jock read one of the articles and gasped as he put the paper down: 'That's the wrong guy. He hasn't got a scar. That wasn't the one I meant to shoot.'

'Why didn't you just stab him?' someone asked.

Jock was appalled at the suggestion: 'Stab him? You should have seen the size of the guy. He would have leathered me. I'm afraid I've shot the wrong man.'

11

STARSHIP ENTERPRISE

O NE DAY IN 1980, JIM McMINIMEE AND HIS WIFE DEBORAH SET off on a shopping expedition that was to change their lives and those of Margaret and Tam McGraw. Leaving their beautiful detached home in Mount Vernon, they headed for Glasgow city centre, intending to browse around the shops and stores in Argyle Street. Then curiosity led them into the Barras market at the edge of the East End, as it has done to so many millions of other Glaswegians over the decades. The marketplace is a remarkable mix of stores and stalls offering every imaginable item, old and new, legitimate and otherwise. The couple had planned their outing well and knew where they were heading and what they wanted. Their final call was a video shop in the nearby Saltmarket, and having arrived there Deborah spent a few minutes making her selections while her husband sat patiently outside in the family car waiting to collect her for the journey home.

Neither of them had any reason to believe that all was other than normal and well. They were regulars at the shop and both were known to the staff. But then as she stood near the door, Deborah was amazed to find herself looking into the eyes of a total stranger who seemed to have run in from the street and was trying to hand her an item. It was a bizarre meeting, to say the least. Her reaction to put forward her hand was almost instinctive, but then she seemed to hesitate and draw back. The man was breathless, but a slight smile appeared when Deborah seemed alarmed, as if he was anxious to put her at ease in the shortest possible time. For a split second, she wondered if he had mistaken her for a store employee and was attempting to deliver a package.

The meeting was over in a flash. The newcomer took to his heels and vanished. Deborah looked at what had been pressed into her hand. It was a ring and, judging by the diamond set within it, an expensive one at that. She rushed outside to see where he had gone, but there was no trace of the man – her benefactor had vanished. Jim recalls what followed: 'Deborah came over to the car and said, "A guy's thrown me this diamond ring and said to me, 'Watch this for me, will you? The polis are after me.'" I said, "Who is he?" And she said, "I don't know." I then asked again what had happened, and she said, "He just ran in the door, threw it into my hand and said the police were after him." I said, "Well, where is he now?" She said, "He just ran away. I've never seen him before. What should we do?" I said, "We'll hold on to it, then." We must have sat outside the shop for an hour and a half, but nobody came back for the ring, so we just went home. Deborah asked what I thought we should do, and I said, "We'll go back to the shop tomorrow and ask the guy in there if he knows who the stranger was."

'The next night, we were sitting at home when there was a knock at the door. I opened it to find two men standing there. When I asked, "What is it?" one of them said, "Eh, we're here to see your missus." I said, "Aye, and what about?" One of them said, "She did us a wee favour." I then realised who the man talking must be. "You're the guy with the ring," I said. He said that he was, and I told them both to come in. When they were inside and seated, Deborah immediately brought the diamond ring she had been given and handed it over. The same man who had given it to her took it and without even looking at what was in his hand smiled at Deborah and said, "Thanks very much for that." We then all introduced ourselves. That was Tam, and from that day on we became great friends.

'Tam told us that he and his colleague had not hung around the Saltmarket because the police were about and had decided to wait until the next morning, by which time things would have calmed down. They knew the owner of the shop and had called in to ask him who we were and where we lived. I don't know if it was someone at the shop who gave Tam our address, but by the time he set off for Mount Vernon, he knew precisely where we stayed.

'He sat fingering the ring and suddenly asked, "What were you going to do with it?" I said, "Go back later on today and find out who you were. There was no way we would have kept it. It wasn't ours."

'His name meant nothing to me then, but when I asked him how he'd found out who we were and where we lived, he said, "I know everything about anything that goes on around here. I'm from the East End, and I know lots of people." We chatted for quite a time, and he said that he and his wife Margaret lived in Barlanark and that she ran an ice-cream van. I told him that I rented and sold videos, which interested him.

'When he left, we told him he was welcome to call back any time, and about a week later Tam and a friend turned up. Deborah never forgot that visit. We had a big bay window at the front of the house with a couch under it. Deborah was lying on it while I was opposite on another couch. We were chatting away while watching television, and it was about half-past eleven in the morning when Tam and his pal walked past the window, clearly heading to our door. At that time, we had a Doberman and a Labrador, and on seeing the men, the Doberman jumped up on the couch with its paws on the window and leaned over Deborah. When it saw Tam, it barked and peed all over her.'

That second meeting was the start of a relationship between the families that would survive two deaths and reach a dramatic climax. Just as the men shared a friendship, so did Deborah and Margaret, the women often meeting, confiding in one another and taking a deep interest in one another's families. Jim realised from the outset that Tam was a career criminal, but the two men did not enquire into one another's backgrounds. Had they done so, Jim would have admitted that as a teenager he had been convicted of burgling a Co-op in Castlemilk and had served a short spell at Her Majesty's pleasure.

The couples often socialised with each other, but there were times, as in any relationship, when the friendship became strained. Tam admired the McMinimee home and once told Jim, 'I'd like to live here. If you ever sell up, let me know so we can have first option on buying.' When Jim and Deborah did decide that the time had come for a change of surroundings and opted for a move to the countryside to the south-west of Glasgow, they had forgotten Tam's request. When a buyer appeared almost as soon as it became known that the house was for sale, they went ahead with a deal. Tam was furious when he found out that he had been overlooked. 'He hardly spoke to me for six months,' said Jim.

Jim's own business interests would soon integrate with those of the McGraws. The video market was expanding quickly, and the public demand for films was seemingly insatiable. Tam and his Barlanark Team realised that there was an opportunity for them to enter the supply chain, and soon their list of targets would include stores holding videos. 'He passed them on to me, and I rented them, but I never asked where they came from. In a way, I legitimised Tam.'

Jim would come to know members of the Barlanark Team and as a consequence become involved in several of their scrapes with the law. Following one escapade in the late 1980s, he found himself in Hamilton Police Station to the south of Glasgow, called upon to take part in an identity parade. Tam and a few friends were with him. At times, Tam could have a wicked sense of humour, and he decided to have some fun with the police. He told everyone that when they were asked for their names, they had to give that of somebody famous to see what the police reaction would be. The first to be called was Jim Steele, whose brother Joe had been convicted of involvement in the Ice Cream War murders in 1984. Jim announced that he was Patrick Hamill, the then chief constable of Strathclyde, and gave an address in Pitt Street that happened to coincide with that of the force headquarters. The name was carefully written down without comment. The next man in line admitted to being a well-known politician, getting precisely the same response even when the address of a popular Glasgow bar was added.

'Jean-Luc Picard,' said Tam, who had been following with keen interest the adventures of the spaceship skipper played by Patrick Stewart in *Star Trek: The Next Generation* series.

'Address, Mr Picard?' he was asked.

'The Starship *Enterprise*.'

'Get the fuck out.' And after debate and a hasty consideration of the list of names and addresses collected so far, those who had gone before received a similar directive. It was then Jim's turn: 'When we arrived at the police station, the officer in charge put us all outside the line-up room and said, "When I shout, just come in and stand where you want." He shouted for us, and everybody went in, but I remained outside. I could hear him saying, "James McMinimee, take your place and stand where you want to." Then after a few seconds, "James, are you happy with the line-up?" I said, "Aye," but nobody had noticed that I was still not in the room with the rest of the guys. Then I heard a voice calling, "James? James?" A policeman's head poked around the door and said, "James, what the fuck are you doing out here?" I said, "Well, you told me I could stand where I wanted." After the line-up, none of us heard anything further.'

Such an end result was not always achieved. Some years earlier, Tam had been arrested after a police investigation into a series of break-ins in central Scotland and was held on remand in Barlinnie. Each day as she made her way to visit her husband, Margaret recalled the words of her mother that her marriage would descend into a non-stop round of prison visits. She had soon managed to get into the dreary and enthusiasm-sapping routine that is known only to those women who have undergone years of sitting in drab prison visiting rooms.

Each time the women of the team discovered that their menfolk had been lifted, they would rush home to prepare suits for their partners' court appearances. But why the hurry? The answer was that the suits needed some slight alterations made quickly. Seams would be carefully opened and tobacco and matches slipped inside before they were sewn back up. Prison guards did search clothing that had been handed in before it was passed to the inmates, but there was not the time to make inch-by-inch examinations of every raised seam. Thus the prisoners knew that they could rely on extra smokes, in Tam's case a desperately needed perk. Margaret and the other women debated whether it might be possible to smuggle in tobacco sewn into ties, but experiments suggested that they were too thin and were the attempt detected it might lead to suggestions that more careful checks should be made of other items of clothing.

The need to help her man led to a non-stop battle of wits between Margaret and the warders. After a while, however, she discovered a chink in the Barlinnie armour: 'It was Tam's birthday, and I wanted to take him a cake, even though he was in prison. I gave a photograph of him to a friend who was a baker, and he baked the cake and copied the picture onto it. Nowadays, it's very easy to have a photograph imaged onto a cake, but not then, so I was very pleased with the result. However, I needed to make sure we could give it to Tam, so I asked Jim to come along to help. I knew he had the gift of the gab and was certain he could talk us in. When we arrived, Jim said to the screws, "It's her man's birthday, and we've made him a cake. OK if I bring it in?" One of the screws said, "Oh all right, as long as we get a slice." That was Jim in. He said, "All right, no problem. What else do you fancy? Next time I'll look after you." One of the officers said, "Any cream cakes?" And Jim replied, "Aye, nae bother."

'After that, it was plain sailing. When I went for visits, Jim would come with me, and he'd bring great big wooden bakers' trays packed with all sorts of goodies: cakes, strawberry tarts, chocolate eclairs and meringues. The screws would see us coming and open a side door to let us in. We'd leave the trays for the staff, and then it would be straight to an interview room to see Tam. The visits were meant to be closed – made in the presence of an officer – but they'd say, "Give us a shout when you're finished." You weren't supposed to hand anything over to the prisoners, but after a couple of visits, Tam said, "If you stick some tins of tobacco in your pockets, nobody will notice, because they'll be too busy eyeing up the trays of cakes." So that's what happened.

'While he was on remand, I was able to see Tam every day, except for a Sunday, but after he was sentenced to six months, I should only have been able to get occasional visits. When I turned up, a record was taken of my name so that they could check how many visits I'd had. But the cakes came in useful again. Tam would ring up and say, "The record of your visit last night is off the card so you can come up again." That meant I'd have to get on the phone to Jim and ask him to get more trays of fucking cakes and pies. We paid for the extra visits with sweetmeats. In the end, I was visiting Tam so often I got fed up looking at him.

'One day, Jim wasn't able to take me, and a taxi I'd booked didn't turn up, so I just went up in the ice-cream van. One of the screws spotted me as I was checking in and said, "You might have brought me in a wafer." I said, "No problem. Just take my name off the record card, and I'll get you a wafer." And that was that. Extra visits cost me an ice cream.

'I was up seeing Tam almost daily, and my brother John, who was being held on remand, was allowed defence visits, which were supposed to be restricted to meetings with witnesses. So, I'd go along on occasional evenings as a witness but had to keep changing my name. One night I'd be Mrs Snow, another Mrs Frost. It ended up with me going in at two in the afternoon for Tam and the same officer who checked me in then would still be on duty when I went in at the evening visiting session. He'd ask, "Well, who are you tonight?" I was there so often I became quite pally with them all.'

Jim discovered an alternative to cakes. After driving his video van into the jail car park one day, he began talking to an officer who looked at the array of films on offer and commented that some of them were not yet out on general release. Jim told the man, 'Oh, a friend gave me a copy. It's totally legitimate.' The officer then asked if it was possible to get a copy. 'Nae problem. What films do you want? Give me your address and I'll drop them off.' The upshot was that Jim was also able to secure extra visits to accompany Margaret to Barlinnie to see Tam. Jim remembers, 'They must have loved me there, because if they weren't getting cream cakes or cigarettes, somebody was calling on them with videos.'

His video business was a thriving concern, and his vans were delivering films all over Glasgow. But, like the Barlanark Team, he had to live with the constant suspicion that his films might well be from illegal sources. Some officers were convinced that Tam's team were his main suppliers, and the fact that Tam was in prison did not prevent them from turning up at Jim's home one day following a major robbery of a store selling movies. The police arrived, banged on his door and commanded him to open up. On doing so, he was told, 'Eh, Clydebank Police here. We understand you're in receipt of a lot of stolen videos. Could we look?'

Jim responded by saying, 'Not a problem. I'll put the dogs away.'

At that time, he owned two Rottweilers, whose menacing appearance belied the fact that they were harmless. Jim asked Deborah to take the dogs into the master bedroom. The police were clearly relieved and told him, 'We appreciate that.'

'Anything to help the police,' he said. It so happened this was the room in which he had been surrounded by videos when the police arrived, and he had good reason not to want the officers to see inside. Deborah took the dogs into the bedroom and firmly closed the door.

Video tapes carried a special marking or code that only showed up under infrared light. The object was to give each tape a unique identity, enabling the police to ascertain whether or not it was in legitimate circulation. Devices into which tapes could be placed to reveal the existence of these marks were widely available. These devices could also delete or alter the markings, and it was said that traders who dealt in stolen videos used them for that purpose.

The police announced that they would need to examine many thousands of videos at Jim's home, but it would be necessary for them to send for a device. At that, he said that he had such a machine and was happy for them to make use of it, knowing that there were no infrared marks remaining on any of the tapes in his possession.

'One of them shouted that he'd found a tape that had the original markings on it, indicating that it had been stolen,' says Jim. 'I knew that was not the case and that they were trying it on, hoping I might suddenly make a mind-boggling confession of having the stolen consignment. To try and add to the pressure, they said that they would need to send for a van to take every tape away so it could be further checked at the police station. That's when I said to them, "No you're not. Get to fuck." At the same time, I thought, "They're lying, because I know the marks have already been changed."

'The police started pissing me about, and I was getting fed up, so I said, "Away to fuck. I'm letting the dogs out. They'll be getting sick of sitting in the bedroom." One of the policemen clearly thought he was a bit of a hero and showed me marks on his throat where he said he had been bitten by a dog previously. I said, "You'll not be scared when I let the dogs out, then." They thought about this, had a quick chat and left. They'd tried it on, and it hadn't worked.'

His relationship with the police had always been like this. While living in Carrick Drive, his home was besieged one day by a team of police officers who told him that they were looking for stolen videos. A sergeant who would go on to rise to a very senior rank in the police force in Scotland was in charge. 'They searched the house but found absolutely nothing,' recalls Jim. 'Nothing they'd hoped to find, that is. They did come across something that interested the sergeant, though. I'd just bought a couple of brand-new three-wheel motor bikes that were about to become all the rage. The sergeant got his eye on one, said he'd seen and read about them in a magazine, and wondered if there was any chance of my letting him have a go. I told him to go ahead and couldn't believe what happened next. His team sealed off Carrick Drive while he raced the bike up and down the street. Traffic was stopped at both ends. He enjoyed himself so much I wondered at one stage if I'd get the bike back, and when he was finished, he thanked me profusely.'

Another good turn with an item of machinery would not end quite so happily for Jim: 'Tam had borrowed my motor, a little XR3, for a couple of days while his was off the road for some reason. It was parked in the street about 100 yards from his house, and somebody clearly got the idea that the car belonged to him. Tam spotted the car cruising up and down and believed that the occupants were going to attack him and Margaret in their home. Joe Hanlon, who used to work for the McGraws, was with Tam and the two men had a couple of guns to hand in case the would-be assailants tried to get inside or smash the windows.

'They watched the car drive past again and relaxed when nothing happened, thinking that everything was OK. But then they heard a bang. Somebody had put a scaffolding tube through the back of my car window with a petrol bomb in it, obviously believing that it was Tam's motor. Tam raced out of his close with Joe on his heels, but it was too late. The attackers had driven off. I was raging. Tam thought it was funny and watched me sprinting up and down the street shouting, "My fucking motor. My fucking motor."'

Jim had lost his car, but it was beginning to dawn on him that another loss was developing. That of his heart. Jim was becoming increasingly drawn to Margaret. And he wondered whether his feelings were being reciprocated by her.

12

THE CELTIC CROSS

F ROM CHILDHOOD, MARGARET FELT AN AFFINITY WITH THE SPIRIT
world, but it is not always easy to admit to having an interest
in a subject steeped in mystery. Believers convinced that the dead
communicate with the living are frequently misunderstood, ridiculed
even. Many people find it difficult to believe that ordinary men and
women, acting as mediums, are able to receive messages from the
dead and pass these on to family, friends and loved ones. Skilled
mediums will strive to convince an audience by giving to a recipient
intimate details of which no outsider could ever have knowledge:
the hiding place of a favourite piece of jewellery, for instance, or a
secret imparted before death. Many spiritualists, Margaret among
them, acknowledge taking great comfort from these messages.
Similarly, mediums look upon their abilities as being a God-given
gift and are grateful for effectively being the chosen.

Communication from the spirit world can signal what has
passed or hint at what is to come. It is the latter that provokes most
interest. While few are selected as mediums, the capability to look
into the future might seem open to all simply by purchasing a pack
of Tarot or fortune-telling cards. In fact, possessing these cards is
one matter, the ability to interpret their meaning another entirely.

Margaret's initial interest in and understanding of spiritualism
has enabled her, over the years, to put at ease others who are
convinced that they are 'seeing things and going mad'. Many years
ago, she was approached by a trusted friend who told her, 'I think
I'm going daft. I can see things in an ashtray, and I hear voices.'

Margaret told her, 'You aren't mad. You're psychic.' The friend was unconvinced and Margaret had to persist: 'You're not going wonky. All of us can see and hear things, but you must be able to understand and interpret them. Don't sit and stare at ashtrays or tumblers and then say you can see things, because anyone can do that if they stare long enough. Unless you can understand what you see and why you are seeing it, you'll go demented. It's no use telling a spirit to go away, because it won't.' She solved the problem by taking her friend to a spiritualist church in Glasgow, where a medium explained how spiritualism worked and assured her that she was not going out of her mind.

Over the years, mediums had often told Margaret that she was psychic and demonstrated a rare sensitivity to the unseen and unknown. And she had often looked in shop windows and seen the brightly decorated cartons of Tarot cards, but she had never opened or handled one until she attended a fund-raising event for her spiritualist church in about 1980. She saw some packs of Tarot cards among the items for sale and, on the spur of the moment, bought one: 'I used to read a lot about the future and bought a book all about Tarot. It explained how to understand the cards and the meaning of each one. The book said that when I eventually came to buy a pack I'd know exactly which one was best for me out of all the many different varieties available. I'd really decided to buy the pack just for fun, but that day I had an odd feeling that something was telling me I just had to buy it. And so I did.'

Margaret went home with a set of cards named after one of the foremost authorities on Tarot: Ryder Waite. Later, she would buy other sets. She examined and experimented with the cards at home, but the many demands on her left little time to develop a serious interest. That would come later. She admits, 'Maybe I started doing the cards because I was just nosey. But I very quickly learned to take them seriously.' The book had explained how the content of a forecast came not merely from the information contained on a card, but also the position in which it was laid down. When she came to look through the various layouts and positions, she read that one was known as the 'Lawsuit Spread'. It was one she avoided then and still does. Her favourite became and remains the 'Celtic Cross' in which the cards are laid out to form an image of the ancient sign. From then on her interest would never wane, only growing in intensity. She preferred doing readings for herself but would very occasionally look into the future to see what it held for others.

Tam, a constant sceptic, never asked for a reading, although she would, over the years, lay out the cards while she pictured his face to see what lay in store for him. This was as much for her own peace of mind. Tam was constantly in trouble with the police, and Margaret often wanted to know how his latest scrape would end. Usually, the portents were good. 'Right from the start, I was never afraid of the cards,' says Margaret. 'I believed that if I knew what was likely to happen in the future, then I could prepare myself for it. I could do a reading for someone else so long as I knew what they looked like from seeing them in person or from being given a photograph. But these readings were exceptions to the rule.

'Most people have the totally wrong impression of Tarot cards and how they work. It isn't just a question of shuffling a pack, laying them down then turning them over and seeing what's on the other side. The death card, for instance, doesn't necessarily mean someone is about to die. It stands for change. What that change is and when it will happen comes from the position in which it sits in a particular formation of cards and what the others around it show. The death card could actually mean a change of job or a move to a new house. It doesn't necessarily mean something bad. It was this huge combination of interpretations that made me increasingly interested in Tarot.'

Despite his protestations of a total lack of interest, it was Tam who introduced Margaret to a set of Russian gypsy fortune-telling cards that gave her huge pleasure from the first moment she unwrapped them: 'Tam used to bring a different Tarot pack back every time he went away on a trip somewhere. Eventually, I said to him, "Tam, it's fine buying all the different packs, but I only use one set, because you need to get to know your cards and the cards to know me. Nobody changes their pack every week or month." But the next time he was in London, he arrived back with a bag from the airport shop at Heathrow. Inside were the beautiful gypsy cards. I've treasured them ever since.'

She continued visiting the spiritualist church and still does. But she also booked private readings for herself. More than one of these would have terrifying consequences, but because she came to discover that the medium in question had an uncanny ability to foretell the truth, Margaret knew that what she was told would indeed come to pass.

As time passed, the cards would come to have a significance not just to Margaret, but to many of her friends as well, and she would occasionally treat herself to a night in with a friend. 'We'd have a drink and say to ourselves, "We'll do the cards." We'd then do a reading but forget all about it. Then, much later on, something would happen, and I'd remind myself, "Fucking hell. The cards said that." That is what makes you go back to them again and again. That voice saying, "They said that. The cards said that was going to happen, and it's happened." They draw you to them, because you know that what they say is the truth. I very quickly learned one lesson, and it is that the cards never lie. Never.'

Bringing up William, operating the van and visiting Tam in jail in the late 1970s and early '80s left little time for card readings or for simple relaxation. Friends were forever advising Margaret, 'Mags, you need a holiday.' And she knew they were right.

Holidays had never been high on the agenda for most citizens of Barlanark. Simple survival was difficult enough, but as incomes rose and, more particularly, the fortunes of ice-cream vans and the Barlanark Team increased, more and more families were able to afford to take an annual break and even travel abroad.

Margaret was looking through holiday brochures one day while chatting with a workman who was carrying out repairs in her home. Margaret had noticed the man's grey pallor and asked if he was ill. 'Oh, no. It's just these jags,' he told her.

'Jags?' she inquired.

'Inoculations. I'm going on holiday and have had to have injections.'

She would later tell Tam, 'Honest to God, I thought he was going to die on the premises. He looked terrible, and I was glad when he finished his shift. I'd wanted him to go home early, but he said that would only make him feel worse and he was better to carry on working until the effects wore off.' His plight made her decide that any holiday destination would be one where injections were not required. Her tick list also included a requirement for sun – and lots of it.

Margaret and Tam took William to Spain and enjoyed it, although they found that the weather could be uncertain. Tenerife, she was assured, guaranteed heat and blue skies. And so began a love affair with the island off the coast of North Africa that was to last for well over two decades. The family explored every inch of the island but preferred the southern resort of Playa de las Américas. They did not mind the flight of nearly five hours at the start and end of each trip, but Margaret particularly loathed the cockroaches that proliferate the lower floors of seemingly every hotel in Tenerife. On the plus side, though, she adored the guaranteed good weather.

Many of their friends and relatives would travel with them. They would sit in groups at Verdes restaurant, eating steaks and drinking beers while they watched buses come and go at the terminal opposite. The spot would come to have a special significance a decade later.

Ultimately, as with so many love affairs, the affection faded, jaded by an overabundance of visits. But these balmy days were among the happiest of their lives. During our trip to Tenerife to research *Crimelord*, Tam told me, 'I'd love to be able to turn back the clock and relive the days when Mags and I would come here with William and some of our pals. So much was happening around us then, but as soon as we stepped off the plane, it was as though we didn't have a care in the world. I used to wonder what it would be like to live here full-time, but I know that despite the pleasure Tenerife gave her, Mags could never have moved lock, stock and barrel. Her family and friends meant too much to her. She and I had brilliant holidays here, and it's only 20 years later that I realise how much those times meant.'

As the visits continued, the McGraws debated whether it would make sound sense to invest in a holiday home on the island. They would eventually settle for such a second home, but it might have been its very existence that signalled the end of the romance. That was, as the cards would have foretold, in the future. For the present, a nightmare was about to descend. It was 1984, the year in which George Orwell had set his classic novel about state oppression. Glasgow in 1984 would be remembered as a year of state terrorism, operated by a handful of police officers, and it would wrap Tam and Margaret McGraw firmly in its clutches.

13

LUCKY THIRTEEN

THERE IS AN OLD SAYING IN SOME AREAS OF GLASGOW THAT MOST policemen couldn't lie straight, even in their coffins. It is a maxim that has been, for many, born out of bitter experience. The McGraws had already tasted the sour tang of an attempted fit-up when a detective planted incriminating evidence in the hubcap of their car. That had ended sweetly for them, but only because of the integrity of others. However, there were certainly men and women in prisons throughout Scotland because unscrupulous police officers lacking hard evidence had simply provided it.

In 1977, Thomas Ross Young, a Glasgow lorry driver, was convicted of murdering bakery worker Frances Barker. He was taken to Peterhead Prison to start a life sentence, protesting that he was the victim of a fit-up. It would take nearly 30 years before the courts accepted that he was telling the truth. Others were about to share his disgust for what was offered up as justice. Tam and Margaret would be caught up in the middle of one of the most reviled crimes in Glasgow history.

By 1984, Margaret was installed in a much newer model of ice-cream van that gaily chimed its busy way along her little round in Barlanark. She bothered no one, and no one bothered her. That was the case with most other ice-cream-van owners, but not all. Elsewhere, stories were emerging of vans being driven off the road and even shots being fired at drivers and assistants.

In one notable incident in Barlanark, Margaret was doing her round when the sound of children playing and laughing in the street and adults shouting greetings to each other was broken by an ear-splitting bang. The van gave a slight lurch, and the driver braked to a halt. One of the van's tyres had blown. Margaret looked out of her serving hatch, and to her amazement saw youngsters with their hands over their ears and adults running for cover. A few moments later, as the wheel was being replaced, one of her regular customers told her, 'You read so many stories about trouble with the vans that we thought somebody had fired a shot at you, Mags.'

Newspapers dubbed the trouble the Ice Cream Wars. Such squabbles would normally attract little attention, because arguments and disputes, feuds even, had always occurred. Spats blew up, blood might even be shed, but they normally died down. But ice-cream vans could be the source of big money. They could, for instance, come in very useful for selling stolen goods. In the East End of Glasgow, some among the criminal fraternity assumed, without having any firm evidence to support their suspicions, that goods stolen by the Barlanark Team ended up being sold from the vans, although there was never any suggestion that Margaret fenced stolen property in this way. However, the success of the team in its thieving exploits encouraged others in Glasgow to go down a similar path, and the belief grew that booty taken by these new teams ended up in the vans of relatives or friends. The number of disputes over routes along which this plunder could be sold escalated and so did the certainty of a full-scale disaster. But while the outcome of the Ice Cream Wars was predictable, the extent of the outrage that turned it into a national scandal was not.

Not long after midnight on 16 April 1984, someone set fire to the door of a flat in Ruchazie. It was the home of ice-cream-van driver Andrew Doyle, aged 18. The fire killed him and five of his family members, including an eighteen-month-old baby boy. Public horror and revulsion followed. Immense pressure for an arrest came to bear on the team of detectives hunting whoever was responsible. It was unfortunate that the squad was led by Detective Chief Superintendent Charles Craig, aided by Detective Superintendent Norrie Walker, because Craig had a reputation for getting results with methods that were not within the rules. When normal techniques of detection did not work, he used violence and intimidation, and if that didn't work, he simply fitted up his adversaries. As the days went by, Craig became increasingly agitated at the failure to make an arrest. It was time to refine the process of collecting evidence.

Tam McGraw was walking to a meeting in Edinburgh Road, close to his home, when three police cars hemmed him in. Without explanation, he was handcuffed, dragged into the back of one of the vehicles and driven to a police station, where Craig was waiting. Ordering Tam to be shackled to a radiator, Craig pressed his angry, red, sweating face close to his prisoner and said, 'You did it.' Then he ordered that Tam be thrown into a cell. Tam telephoned Margaret to tell her what had happened. She was incredulous: 'I was numb with shock and horror and kept saying, "What's this all about? You had nothing to do with this. You were with me the whole night when it happened." What made it all the more dreadful was that I knew he was innocent and yet the police were trying to find evidence that would convict him.'

Tam was joined in the remand wing of Barlinnie Prison by T.C. Campbell, Jim Steele's brother Joe – a friend of T.C. – William 'Tamby the Bear' Gray and Gary Moore. T.C. later explained that police stormed into his home early one morning and that he was dragged away to Baird Street Police Station, where he was handcuffed to a table and told by a senior member of the investigation team, 'This is where we do the fitting up. I am going to nail you to the wall.'

An infamous police informer, William Love, had claimed that while he was in the Netherfield Bar in Glasgow, he had overheard T.C., Joe, Tamby and Gary plotting the fire. Love was himself facing serious charges at the time detectives helped him to write his incriminating statement, and after telling his tale, he was given bail and the charges reduced.

Naturally, Margaret wanted to know what the allegations against Tam were. Knowing Craig and Walker's reputations, she became even more alarmed when she discovered the nature of the so-called evidence they were trying to pin on him. It was claimed that on the night of the fire a woman neighbour of Campbell had seen Tam driving a black Ford Escort XR3i, registration number A32 VNS, and carrying a can, evidently containing petrol, into T.C.'s home. Margaret knew that to be false. She had had an evening off from operating the van that night, it being a Sunday, and Tam had been with her in the house throughout. More sinister than that was an attempt by Craig and his team to show that Tam had been driving the XR3i near to the scene of the fire at about the time it started.

Margaret was furious and even more so when she discovered that an effort had been made to intimidate a witness into changing his story to make the situation look bad for Tam: 'We had ordered a new black XR3i, and the garage in Rutherglen got in touch to say it was all taxed, registered and ready to collect that day, 13 April 1984. The registration number, A32 VNS, reflected my age at that time, 32. They asked if I wanted to come over and pick it up, but I said to Tam, "The 13th? They've got to be kidding. I'm not collecting a new car or a new anything on the 13th of the month. Tell them they'll need to wait a day before I get it." So, Tam rang up and told the garage, "We're going to come across and check the car but won't drive it away until tomorrow." When we got there and saw it, the brand-new car had a bash in the side. The salesman said he could get us another black XR3i from another garage nearby, but Tam was determined to make sure they didn't just move the damaged car there, plug the dent with filling, spray it over and tell us it was a brand-new motor. As a safeguard, he removed the registration plates. The garage selling us the car managed to get a black XR3i from a branch in England, and we took delivery of it, fitted with the registration plates Tam had held on to, on 19 April. On the night of the fire, we didn't have it yet, but the police thought we'd collected it on the 13th and set out to come up with so-called evidence that would show that we had.

'The woman who told the story about Tam and the petrol gave the police the registration number of the car. But we knew we could prove it had not been on the road until three days after the fire. When the police arrested Tam, they'd come to me to ask about his movements and had said, "Don't worry, Margaret, we know it wasn't Tam."

'Tam and I made statements to our lawyer as to when the car had been collected, and these were given to the police. We naturally thought that would be the end of it but then found out the police had gone to the garage from where we'd been due to collect the car on the 13th and had tried to get the people there to say I'd picked up the motor that day. To his credit, the salesman there refused to go along with them and stuck to telling the truth. As a result, they had to release Tam without any charges, but it was a terrible time.

'I knew for certain he was innocent, but they still used the woman neighbour as one of the witnesses at the trial of the others. She got a new house after the police asked where she would like to live, and one of her close relatives was let off after having commited a minor offence. As soon as the prosecution told the defence lawyers about her statement, she was moved to the new place. I knew that at the end of the day it would work out all right and nothing would happen to Tam, but it wasn't easy trying to get the police to understand why the car had not been collected on the 13th.

'About two months later, the garage that had supplied the motor called to say we would need to return it because my registration number, A32 VNS, was actually assigned to the damaged car. It was a fairly simple matter to have the plates registered to the motor I subsequently bought.

'For some reason, the police got it into their heads that Tam and T.C. knocked about together, that they were pals. But it was only because T.C. did not drive and relied on Tam for a lift that they met up. The police were convinced that T.C. and Joe and the others knew all about the fire and would for certain have confided in Tam. So they arrested Tam, and he later told me that Craig had threatened him by saying he had evidence to prove that Tam was there and advised him to make a statement implicating the others. He refused, and Craig didn't like that. All of us with ice-cream vans had to take them to the police station in Easterhouse, where they were photographed and checked over to see if there was any evidence linking them to the fire. T.C.'s wife Liz, who had a van, was there along with both of our respective families.

'I was as upset as anybody about what happened to the Doyles and as keen to find out who was responsible. But even while Tam was in jail and under suspicion, life had to go on. I still got up in the morning to make sure William left for school. I'd then go up to the garage to load the van, because Tam wasn't around to do that job, and bring it to the house and park it up ready for the day's shift. Then I'd go to Barlinnie to visit Tam, and when I came back, I'd get the van on the road and around the streets, where everybody wanted to know what was going on. When the shift was over, it was back to the garage, then I'd grab a few hours' sleep before starting all over again. The days just seemed to roll into one, but being so busy helped take my mind off what was happening. Fortunately, I didn't need to look for something to do to stay occupied. It was a huge relief when Tam was finally freed without charges, but he ought never to have been arrested in the first place.'

Later that year, after a trial lasting 27 days at the High Court in Glasgow, T.C. and Joe Steele were found guilty of murder and jailed for life. Tamby Gray and Gary Moore were cleared of murder, but Tamby received 14 years for shooting at an ice-cream van. He has since died from throat cancer. It was only the start of a nightmare for T.C. At Peterhead Prison, he was constantly beaten, once to within an inch of his life, and the prison service was forced to pay him damages as a result of the attack. Joe made a series of dramatic prison escapes, on one occasion chaining himself to the gates of Buckingham Palace, to draw public attention to their unceasing campaign to be declared innocent. Both would win, but it took 20 years before they were set free and declared to be the victims of a miscarriage of justice. But then another fight ensued for compensation for the lost years of their lives. They had hoped to come face to face with their tormentors Craig and Walker, but that opportunity was denied them. Four years after watching them be led to the cells to begin their sentences, Walker attached a hosepipe to the exhaust of his car, turned on the engine and killed himself. Three years later, in 1991, an overweight Craig died of a heart attack. Life plays cruel tricks. It would go on to demonstrate that Craig had at least something in common with Tam McGraw.

14

A THOUSAND REGRETS

THE TRAGEDY OF THE DEATH OF THE DOYLES SPREAD OVER GLASGOW, marking the city as a place where evil lingered. For those running ice-cream vans, these were difficult days. The media in general, and sections of the local press who ought to have known better, hinted that the vans were merely there as a front for selling drugs, ignoring the crucially important service they provided to schemes void of shops and a half-decent transport system. Margaret, and more importantly her customers, knew that she found the suggestion of selling drugs from a vehicle that based its business on attracting children and mothers loathsome. These were her friends, many from her schooldays, and she was as protective of their children as of her own son.

At the same time, she could sense the writing was on the wall – that the days of the ice-cream vans with their multitude of offerings, from batteries to biscuits, were numbered. There would always be a demand for them, but the reliance on vans to supply families with the bulk of their needs was diminishing. This was not a development resulting directly from the Ice Cream Wars, although the outrage of the fire surely played a part in the decline of the van trade. Large superstores offering free parking and cheap products were springing up. And petrol stations began to provide shops that in some cases opened all night and offered the same cigarettes and sweets as the vans. Margaret could see what was happening. She had bought other vans that like her own were giving a healthy return but wondered whether it might be time to move on and branch out.

While she still enjoyed the patter with her customers, the long days were tiring – whenever the opportunity arose, she would pack her family's cases and all three would fly off to Tenerife – and she worried. Tam was not a selfish man. Indeed, it was generosity not meanness that was his weakness. He showed an increasing willingness to take part in exploits devised by others that lacked planning and encouraged risk. In 1983, he had been sent back to prison for theft. The horror of being arrested and threatened with a fit-up after the death of the Doyles had happened the following year. Margaret knew that had the police not switched their attentions to other, easier, targets, then it could well have been her husband staring at a 20-year spell behind bars and vainly protesting his innocence. Wasn't it time, she reasoned, with William approaching adolescence, for Tam to abandon petty crime?

'Were there times when I regretted marrying Tam? A thousand times, but there's nothing unusual about that. Every woman probably feels that way at times about her husband. The thing was that even if Tam was away in jail, I still had my pals. And just because the main man was out of the way, the Barlanark Team didn't stop working. And I knew them. They carried on. My friends were still around, and the ice-cream van remained on the road. The difference was that without Tam to help, things just got busier. I looked on myself as any other worker – as someone getting up in the morning, going to the office, doing my job, going home, having dinner, reading a book and going to bed. It all became a habit.

'Then Tam would get out of prison and go off with the other members of the team to eye up turns, decide which ones they fancied and which they didn't, do a few and then have a wee break in which he would stay in bed and sleep for days. He might work one night, come home and sleep for a couple of days then go off again. The difference between us was that I had a routine while he did not.

'All the wives of the Barlanark Team were friends and looked after each other if our men were in jail. One of my best pals had five weans, and if one of them wasn't well, I'd dive up to see if she and the youngster were all right before William came home from school and before I went off in the van. Looking back, I sometimes wonder how we survived. I worked the van five nights a week. On those two nights off, we never really went to pubs. Instead, one of the wives would have us round to her house and we'd have a few drinks and a laugh. I thought I was entitled to the break and a bit of fun. What I had, I had earned. Nobody gave it to me, not even Tam, because anything he had, he gave away.'

A nagging doubt lingered about how long the vans could survive in their current guise. Margaret had always known about The El Paso pub in Barlanark. It had closed in the late 1970s, largely because it was said that the brewery that owned it could not find a manager capable of running it. The place had a bad reputation as a gathering point for troublemakers, and decent folk who went along for a quiet half and half too often found themselves drawn into fights that started out as harmless arguments but ended in vicious slashings. Sometimes these developed into full-scale brawls, with furniture wrecked, glasses smashed and the police called to separate the standing from those barely recognisable beneath the blood masking their heads and faces.

All pubs were subject to fights and varying degrees of violence, but what had spelled the death knell for The El Paso was that it had begun attracting young men and women who brought along drugs. At that time, these were limited to dope and a few pills, but the police had made it plain that drugs would not be tolerated in licensed premises. Bars with a reputation for attracting users would find the granting of their licences challenged. If brutality was the nail in The El Paso coffin, dope was the hammer that drove it in.

As she passed the empty building, a bleak windowless block with its boarded-up front door and fading signs, Margaret often pondered as to whether it could be resurrected. She saw it each day and knew it well. Before the closure, she and friends had gone there to women-only nights, and it was a regular stopping place for her van to supply tobacco and cigarette papers to customers who found it cheaper to buy from her than to use the vending machines inside. True, there were other drinking holes, one of them close by, but most people found the outdated ten o'clock bells, when they would be kicked out onto the streets with their thirst unquenched, a grim block in the way of their having a proper night's enjoyment. The closing time, to them and lots of other Scots, was too early and meant that customers invariably headed into the city centre in search of a club or night spot where they could drink on.

The availability of public transport in Barlanark was never a major inducement to live in the area, so pleasure seekers were forced to hang about after closing time, hoping to spot a passing taxi or to persuade a friend to take a chance and drive into the city centre, risking being stopped by the police. It was all very unsatisfactory, with the result that too many people just got on a bus and headed straight for the bright lights of Sauchiehall Street or the lively area around the Barras, instead of starting their drinking in Barlanark once they had returned from work and finished dinner.

Margaret saw the possibilities. If The El Paso could be opened and remain open until the early hours, then the potential for success was there, certainly as far as attracting custom was concerned. As for the concern about violence, she felt sure Tam and the Barlanark Team could be persuaded to hang about and give the pub a reputation as somewhere that brawling was not tolerated. She contacted the brewery to sound out whether they would be willing to sell and was answered in the affirmative. At the same time, she was warned that the police might well oppose the granting of a licence unless they could be satisfied that the pub would not once more become a haunt for drug takers and dealers. And there was a further bridge to cross: how would Tam react to her idea?

'The Paso had been shut for ages, and the way I saw it was that I knew everybody in Barlanark, got on well with everyone, and knew all the gossip and what was happening, so why couldn't I be talking to folk in my own pub? Those same customers could be going to The El Paso. So why not get it?

'I don't think Tam was keen on my taking the pub at first. It had been empty for a while, and he realised a lot of work would need to be done to persuade the old clientele to return. And, naturally, he wanted to know where the money would come from. The brewery was asking for £80,000. I told him we'd just sell some of our vans. If he had reservations about buying it, he made no serious protest. In the end, I told him what we were going to do, and he went along with that. I kept on thinking over the idea and then just rang the brewery and said they had a deal. It was almost a spur-of-the-moment decision. The upshot was that in 1987 The El Paso became ours.

'Looking back, it was a bad idea. My idea, but a bad idea – a bad brainwave – even if it was a good money-maker. It's only when I got the pub that I realised the people going to it were not the same people who came to my ice-cream van. They might be the same faces, but once they filled themselves with the firewater they became entirely different people. My customers, those who came to the van, didn't get drunk, whereas those who visited The El Paso did. And then we would get all the others: the strangers, the outsiders, people we couldn't trust until we got to know them. But it did make money.'

The El Paso reopened and was granted a licence to remain open until 2 a.m. at weekends. There had been the expected and unexpected objections from the police. The former involved drugs and, in particular, a Glasgow band that had a reputation for attracting dope users among its followers. A condition of being granted her licence was that Margaret had to agree that the band would never be allowed to perform at The El Paso again. Not anticipated was a police objection based on the fact that Margaret intended to employ a man with a criminal record. The crime? Playing ice-cream-van chimes after the allotted time, for which a small fine had been imposed. That objection was dismissed. Friends joked that while the police might try to prevent her from reopening the pub, her neighbours on Hallhill Road would not be making any protests. The El Paso sat next to a cemetery.

Margaret debated on a name. The pub had originally been The El Paso before the name was converted to The Viking, later reverting to The El Paso Bar and Caravel Lounge. Although the pub became widely known as The Caravel, to Margaret and the regulars it was The El Paso, and that is what she settled on.

At weekends, the place was heaving. One of her barmen was John Carr, a long-time friend. Later on, another jack of all trades worked at The El Paso by the name of Joe Hanlon, a likeable young man who was fancied as an amateur boxer. They, together with Tam and the regular presence of members of the Barlanark Team, ensured that the pub was relatively trouble free, although there was occasional bloodshed.

Margaret became the official licensee. That title would later be used to describe Tam, his rivals claiming that he had an arrangement with the police – a licence to get away with crimes in exchange for passing on information. Tam and Margaret found it offensive and insulting, but it stuck. Was it true? Was Tam a grass? Not according to the police and in particular Les Brown, a former senior detective with Strathclyde Police and a man well positioned to know if Tam was an informer. 'Nonsense,' was how he described the suggestion. 'I saw no evidence of McGraw ever helping the police.'

By buying the pub, Margaret simply gave herself extra work to do: 'I continued working in the van for a wee while, because we didn't have enough money to pay for The El Paso and needed to save enough to clear off the debt. When I finished my round on the van and had cleaned and loaded it at the garage, I'd get down to the pub just before midnight, by which time the bar had closed and only the lounge remained open. I would clean the bar floor, and by the time that was done, the last customers would be leaving the lounge. Everyone would come through to the bar, where we'd do the bookwork, and we'd all go home about two in the morning.

'We only lived a couple of minutes away, but that proved to be a problem. Whenever anything went wrong at the pub, I'd get a telephone call. If a pump wasn't working or a delivery hadn't arrived, someone would ring me, and I'd go down to sort it out. My telephone would ring and a voice would say, "Can you ring Tennent's?" and I'd just say, "It's all right. I'll just come up." The alarm might go off, and I'd go to reset the alarm and then get back home. Sometimes I'd be back in ten minutes, but there were many times when I felt as though I was living in The El Paso, and I knew I'd have to do something about that. I thought that if I lived further away, the staff would have to sort out for themselves all the stupid things they called me in to handle. But I wondered how Tam would feel about a move.'

15

THE EL PASO

MARGARET RAN HER PUB FOR TEN YEARS. THAT DECADE WOULD BE a never-ending battle against the various authorities responsible for granting the necessary licences, represented by men in grey coats who seemed hell-bent on finding fault and only cheered up when they did.

Most of the ordinary policemen who worked the beat around The El Paso would have conceded that it gave them little trouble. They knew most of the staff and the customers from way back and were on first-name terms with them. Yet there were a handful of officers whose concept of policing seemed to be the closure of anywhere that men and women congregated with the intention of having fun. They supported and were encouraged by one or two local diehards who seemed to take exception to anyone, especially anyone from Barlanark, proving that they could make a success of themselves.

The constant battle to hang on to her licence would ultimately prove to be too energy sapping and financially draining for Margaret. The end, when it came, was dramatic and unexpected, and would give the McGraws' enemies licence to spread astonishing rumours as to the reason why the pub had closed. But while it was in operation, The El Paso was rarely short of action: some good, some bad; some happy, some sad – just like the men and women who drank there.

Most people in Barlanark approved of The El Paso reopening. And there were many who would benefit as a result. Countless thousands of pounds were raised for charities, in particular for a school standing directly opposite that looked after children with special needs. Scotland's first children's hospice, Rachel House, opened on the banks of Loch Leven at Kinross in Fife in July 1996 at a cost of £4 million and run by the Children's Hospice Association Scotland, was another organisation that was helped as a result of voluntary efforts by customers, some of whom were popularly conceived as being more used to helping themselves than others.

John Carr, now a successful businessman, has fond memories of working there: 'Pool was a big favourite, and some of the customers fancied themselves as real experts. Maybe they'd been watching the Paul Newman film *The Hustler* about a guy who gets into really big money by being a sharpshooter on the pool table. There was a small group, mainly made up of friends of Margaret and Tam, who would play pool for hours after the bar was closed and everyone else had gone home. The games might go on until the next morning and only end because some of the players had to go to work. Big money was at stake. We'd play for £10 or £20 a game, and there were nights when I left The El Paso having won £300, which was a lot of money. There was just one stipulation by Margaret to playing for cash, whether it was during normal hours or after closing, and it was that you had to leave a percentage of whatever you were playing for in the fund for the school opposite. No one ever objected to that. In fact, everything possible was done to raise money for those kids, because we admired the work their teachers did.

'We ran dances at The El Paso, and when the teachers told us they needed some item of equipment for the school, we'd set to work and start raising money to pay for it. There was a giant whisky bottle on the bar in which everyone put change and the pool players slipped a few notes. It was a real time-consuming task emptying it out once a year and counting the money. When we happened to mention this to the school, the teachers asked if the children could do it, as it would be good therapy for them and could be used in one of the lessons to teach them to count, add and distinguish between the various coins.

'We organised a day out for the kids once a year. Margaret would go around all the ice-cream vans and be given crisps and cartons of juice. Then we'd hire a bus and give the children a really great time. We got huge pleasure from seeing the happiness this gave them. When it was announced that a fund had been set up to raise enough cash to build Rachel House, we all agreed to help. And everyone agreed that they had a great time doing so.'

There was never any shortage of volunteers willing to help, even with a variety of money-raising stunts in which their participation had to be seen to be believed, and John and his entire family would always be at the forefront. Much to the amusement of their friends and families, Charles 'Chick' Glackin, his friend Trevor Lawson, who lived on a farm at Dunipace in Stirlingshire and ran a demolition company, and taxi driver George McCormack from Glasgow took part in a bungee-jumping event on Glasgow Green, the scene of a huge rave.

Glasgow has a reputation for bitter sectarian divide, but Margaret watched as fans of rivals Celtic and Rangers happily drank side by side in her pub. Only once did the inter-club rivalry force her into action when a Rangers supporter, having overimbibed, was ordered out. He had broken an unwritten pub rule by dancing around the pool table and giving what appeared to be a boozy rendition of 'The Sash'.

On 15 April 1989, Hillsborough football stadium in Sheffield witnessed the worst football disaster in Britain when 96 fans were crushed to death, the cause later being attributed to the failure of the police to maintain proper crowd control. The tragedy would have far-reaching repercussions, and the ensuing Taylor Inquiry resulted in the introduction of safer all-seater stadiums. The sadness spread to Glasgow, where memories of a similar disaster at Ibrox, the home of Rangers, still remained. Also, it was mainly Liverpool fans who died, and that city has an affinity with the East End. The El Paso raised about £1,100 for the families of the victims, and at a sombre ceremony a cheque for that amount was handed over to the well-known football player Pat Nevin.

That spontaneous generosity was typical of The El Paso drinkers, who never failed to react to pleas by Margaret to raise money, especially for their young neighbours who attended the school. Customers often brought in second-hand clothing and ornaments for jumble sales, but it was unkindly rumoured that some of the donated items had spent most of their lives in the homes of strangers until disappearing in the dead of night through a broken window or jemmied door. The pub also held coffee mornings, which were popular with local women who felt they had too little opportunity to meet with one another.

'The customers were brand new,' says John Carr. 'I knew most of them from way back. A local newspaper published the names of everyone and every organisation, company, pub, club or team that gave money to Rachel House. We raised £3,000, but somehow the words El Paso or Caravel were never mentioned.

'There was rarely any trouble, and if there was any, it wasn't caused by the regular customers for the simple reason that nobody wanted to be barred, because The El Paso was the only pub in the district that had a late licence. If you weren't allowed in, it meant you would have to go all the way into the city centre to get a late drink. Our licence was until 2 a.m., which was when the doors officially closed, but that didn't necessarily mean the drinking stopped then. By and large, the pool players needed to stay sober because of the amount of money at stake, but it wasn't unknown for others to drink right through until morning and then head out to look for a coffee and a roll and a bus to work. It was a very eventful and lively pub, where the unexpected was very often the norm.'

One night, a stranger appeared in the pub. It was cold and frosty, and he was not dressed for the sub-zero temperatures. It was soon plain that something was not quite right with him. The bar was a friendly spot, and some of the regulars began chatting to him, but they were astonished and worried when he said that he didn't know his name, where he was or where he had come from. Margaret offered to make sure that he got home safely, but as no one knew where home was, the only thing they could do was phone the police, so John Carr called Strathclyde's finest.

What happened next took everyone by surprise, not least Margaret: 'At some time in his life, the guy must have had a bad experience with the police, because as soon as a couple of them arrived, he went ballistic. The police were trying to search him, purely in the hope of finding something that would tell them where he lived, but he was having none of it. He was holding a can of Pils lager in each hand, and he set about the cops with the cans. They called for reinforcements, but even then they were unable to calm him. Eventually, the police turned up in force, but he still managed to rattle a few of them with the cans. Some of the regulars were in stitches of laughter, while others had dived for cover. After a while, the police were able to find out that the man had come from Riddrie in Glasgow, having walked all the way. When we heard that, we wondered if he had broken out of Barlinnie, which is in Riddrie. Finally, when everything calmed down, the police agreed to let him go, but he said he would only do that if one of our regulars went with him. The stranger had taken a liking to him, because my customer had talked to him when he arrived and had been kind to him. So he got home, but we never solved the mystery of how or why he had turned up in the first place.'

John Carr says there was a particular factor that helped keep trouble to a minimum: 'People respected Margaret and Tam, largely because most who went to The El Paso had grown up with them. The weekends were particularly busy. There was piped music, a karaoke until about 11.30 p.m. and then a disco, although the older men didn't like the music much. But the younger ones did, and the place would still be crowded at closing time.'

At Christmas, Margaret laid on a special party and dinner for up to 160 local pensioners. Those who had no transport or were unable to walk any distance would be collected by regulars and returned to their homes afterwards. Much of the cost of the event was covered by money raised throughout the year in the bar and lounge. Customers would tell John or the other staff to 'Put the change in the old folks' fund' when they were buying their drinks. John played Father Christmas at the events, dressing up in the traditional red outfit and white beard to hand out gifts. One year, his enthusiasm for the role landed him in hot water. After performing his task, he was invited by one or two of the recipients to join them in a Christmas drink. He agreed to do so, and as the night wore on forgot he had been meant to return to his own family, where his arrival and the distribution of presents was to be videoed. At eight the following morning, he was still in The El Paso as anxious family members wondered whether Santa had suffered a mishap on his sleigh.

But the Christmas party was not always plain sailing, and the old adage that 'the older they get, the worse they get' could have a ring of truth to it. 'One year, one of our regulars announced there was no way he'd be coming to the party or dinner,' Margaret remembers. 'He was in his 80s, and one of my staff members had barred the old guy for being cheeky to him and to some of the customers. The man could be a nuisance at times and was quite a character. Despite his age, when he got into an argument with one of the younger regulars one day, he picked up a chair and tried to bash the guy over the head with it. He'd be barred one day and back in 24 hours later. It was true that he was occasionally cheeky, as the member of staff had complained, but he was a part of our pub, and a lot of us were disappointed when we heard he wouldn't be coming.

'On the day of the party, I went to see him at his home and said, "Are you coming for Christmas dinner today?" He replied, "No, I've got visitors." I asked his daughter, who was there, "Who are the visitors?" and she said, "Just my brother, and he can come any time." So I asked again, "Are you coming?" He was adamant: "No, I'm not." I said, "Look, I've told the guy who barred you not to do it again. I apologise that you were barred. You know you'll always be welcome," but he still insisted that he wouldn't come. Even his family tried to persuade him, telling him, "Go on. Get your coat on and go." But he was stubborn: "No, I won't." So I asked him what time he was having his dinner at home, and when he replied, I said to his family, "Well, just lay a plate for me." At that, the old man said, "What for?" and I replied, "Well, if you're not joining us at my place for dinner, I'm coming to your house." That did the trick. He relented but still was stubborn: "I'll come on one condition: that William brings me." I made a telephone call, and ten minutes later William arrived and took the man to the party.'

It was at The El Paso that Tam would meet for the first time some of the men who would later come to play such a huge part in his and Margaret's lives. One of these introductions was born out of near tragedy, and when Margaret remembers it, her hackles still rise: 'Trevor Lawson used to call in occasionally, but we didn't really know him too well. He was never any trouble, likeable even, but for some reason he got himself involved in an argument with a stranger that escalated into a fight. We didn't know that this guy, who had wandered in through the rear of the pub, was carrying a knife. It was late one Boxing Day, and towards the end of the evening, Trevor decided to go home and went outside. The guy with the knife was waiting and the fight started up again. Tam went in to stop it, not knowing that the nutter was trying to stab Trevor. The knife ripped into Tam's arm instead. William had seen his dad trying to break it up and went in to help and was stabbed as well.'

Tam stopped the fight, but there was a cost, as John Carr recalls: 'Tam came in when it was over, threw the keys on the counter and said, "John, you'll have to lock up." I asked him why, and he just said, "Because I've been stabbed." He didn't appear to have been badly hurt, but when he raised his arm, I could see that his clothes were dripping blood.'

Tam, William and Trevor were taken to hospital, where doctors discovered that Trevor had lost so much blood that his life was in danger. Thanks to their skills, he survived, but it was touch and go at one stage, and a priest was called to read him the last rites.

Margaret was at home, as it was her night off. There was a knock at the door, and when she answered it, Snads came into the house: 'He said, "Look, hen, there's been a wee accident. William's been stabbed." It was as though a bolt of lightning had hit me. "How could he be stabbed? He's at that fucking pub? William didn't go to the pub. Tam was at the pub. What was William doing there? One fucking night. I'm off for one fucking night, and Tam can't look after the pub for one fucking night." Snads said, "William's absolutely fine. I'll take you to the hospital. Tam's been stabbed as well." When he told me that, I said to Snads, "If he survives, he's lucky, because I would have stabbed him for letting that happen to William."

'Snads and I went off to the hospital, where I went to check up on William, who had four stitches in a stab wound in his side. I never even went to see Tam. If I'd been there, nothing would have happened to William. They could have stabbed me, but they wouldn't have stabbed him. I was so furious. At the hospital, I asked some of the others who had been at the pub, "What did Tam do? Did he throw William in front of him?" I later heard that a few nights after this the guy who did the stabbing opened his door and somebody stuck a hatchet in his head.'

Father and son were kept in overnight, but Tam's arm had been slashed so severely that it would leave him scarred for the remainder of his life. Trevor made a full recovery, and the incident cemented his friendship with the McGraws.

One evening, another stranger wandered in with a handful of regulars. He was introduced to Margaret and Tam as Gordon Ross. He would become one of Margaret's closest friends and confidants, seeking advice and help from her in the years ahead. Unlike other women, she was not bowled over by looks that many a movie star would have craved, rather his sense of fun and spirit of adventure. Gordon would play a major role in the future of the family, and, in turn, Margaret would come to learn a secret about him that even he did not know.

Manny McDonnell, the Irishman from Belfast, who had connections to a leading terrorist organisation and who would move to Glasgow after being offered work by Tam, would also become a member of the family circle. Then there was Paul Ferris from Blackhill, younger than Tam but seemingly hell-bent on taking on the mantle as the number-one gangster in Glasgow. That was a title to which many had aspired following the demise of Jimmy Boyle, whose cruelty during his youngster days as a racketeer and moneylender had been cut short when he was jailed for life for the murder of a petty crook named 'Babs' Rooney. Ferris would try but never succeed in overtaking 'Big' Arthur Thompson, known as 'The Godfather', and Tam as top dog, although neither would ever claim such a title.

Ferris had worked as a debt collector for The Godfather and seemed anxious to have a foot in both the McGraw and Godfather camps, something that was never attainable. He courted publicity, and at one stage acted as a form of unofficial and unwanted public relations adviser to Tam. However, if there was ever a genuine friendship between the two, it did not last and instead turned to bitterness and hatred.

Margaret makes no bones about her feelings for Paul Ferris: 'Ferris? I never, ever liked him. You get a feeling, an impression, about somebody, and mine of him was that he just wasn't right. I just knew he was a wrong 'un. He once gave an interview in our pub. I knew nothing about it until I saw it on television and said to Tam, "That's our fucking pub. What the fuck is he doing in our pub?" I couldn't quite put my finger on what I distrusted and disliked about Ferris, but I never had any doubts that he wasn't right. I didn't like him then, and I don't like him now. He would sometimes come to my door asking for Tam, and I'd say, "He's not in," even if he was lying upstairs in bed. I just didn't want him in my house. It is a fact of life that when you're honest with people, when you tell them you don't like them and they know you don't like them, instead of respecting you for being honest, they give you a load of abuse. But my attitude, which I made plain to Tam, was, "I don't give a fuck. He's not coming in here. Like it or lump it."

'I said to Tam, "Tell him I wouldn't go to his house if I knew I wasn't wanted, so he need not come here. If he does, he's not getting in." He came to my home one day with a mate, and when I opened the door, he said, "Oh, Mags . . ." Before he could say another word, I told him, "He's not in. You can try coming back another time when he is." Then I just shut the door on them. Tam was in, and I told him, "That fucking Ferris was at the door." Tam started to say, "Oh, tell him . . ." but I stopped him and said, "Tell him fuck all. He's not getting in here. If you want to meet him, do it outside." The trouble was that Tam picked up all the shite. People latched onto him because he was a soft touch. He was generous and helped people, and then they'd turn around and stab him in the back.'

There were men who drank at The El Paso who would come to know the consequences of violence. Robert Mills, a soldier on leave in Glasgow, was stabbed to death after an attack outside the pub in August 1991. Robert, aged 19, was on leave from the 16th Army Air Corps after serving in the first Gulf War. He was based in Lincolnshire but had returned north to spend time with his family in Uddingston, to the south of Glasgow. He went with friends to The El Paso, intent on having a good drink. Sadly, a good drink became too much drink, as is so often the case, and the mood turned from one of joviality to hostility. Staff at the bar were forced to eject him when he began fighting with his own friends. He re-entered but was told to leave once again, and when he refused, he was kicked out. His struggles continued outside, and the scuffle became ugly and deadly. A short-bladed knife appeared, and the soldier was stabbed. Despite the attentions of doctors and nurses at Glasgow Royal Infirmary, he died. Later, two men were charged with his murder. It was alleged that they and others had kicked and punched the teenager on the head and body before stabbing him. However, the charges were dropped.

Thankfully, that terrible incident was an exception during Margaret's tenure. However, the regulars had known tragedy previously, from an era before she took over the pub, resulting from an incident that showed just how sudden and unexpected the arrival of death could be. Two elderly customers, both of whom had enjoyed a good drink, set off at closing time to take a short cut to their homes. It was later surmised that one of them fell and was unable to get to his feet. It seemed that the other tried to assist but could not manage to do so and lay down to keep his friend company, hoping a passer-by would find them and bring help. Regrettably, it came too late, and they were discovered the next day frozen to death.

'The El Paso was a dump, but it was our dump,' says John Carr. 'It took a lot of courage for Margaret to reopen it, but we had some wonderful times while it was in her hands.'

What Margaret saw as constant harassment and badgering by the authorities, a never-ending search for even minor transgressions in the terms of her licence, was a continual thorn in her side, however. One example of this occurred when she decided to provide an evening's entertainment with a difference, the star of which was to be a hypnotist. 'I applied for a licence, but it was surprisingly rejected, even though the police raised no objections,' she recalls. 'It looked as though the whole thing would have to be called off at the last minute. I didn't really know what to do, and right up until the big night was asking the licensing authority to let us continue, but they were adamant in their refusal. A couple of hours before the hypnotist was due to appear, the police showed up and said that they were as baffled as anyone by the knock-back. I asked what we could do, and they said, "Go ahead. There's no reason to stop this." And they stayed discreetly away. The police rarely checked up on us anyway, because there was very little trouble – certainly no more than at any other pub in Glasgow. Am I sentimental when I think about the Paso? No, I think I must have been mental to buy it.'

Tam believed he was having mental problems one night, telling Margaret that he was convinced he had seen ghosts: 'He came in one night as we were getting ready to close and said, "There's ghosts outside, Mags. I've seen them. They're all over the place." I said, "If you drag me out, there had better be ghosts." Sure enough, there were figures wandering around outside the pub wearing long, flowing white robes. I went back inside, and he said, "Did you see the ghosts?" I said, "Ghosts? These ghosts are walking off along Hallhill Road. When did you see fucking ghosts getting into big motors and driving off?" Tam said, "So they're not ghosts, Margaret?" and I replied, "No, Tam, they're not ghosts. They're Asians. They've been to some festival in their national dress, and they're going home."'

16

FINGER OF FATE

Margaret knew Jonah McKenzie from their youth. Although a few years younger than her and Tam, he had been on the fringes of their group and was an occasional visitor to the home they set up in Burnett Road after returning from London. Like most of his generation in Barlanark, Jonah was fascinated by cars – fast cars and flash cars. But to own a car meant having money, and he constantly complained of being short. Tam and the others in the Barlanark Team helped out by now and then inviting him along on their robberies, and Jonah leaped at the chance to make a few pounds. But even these infrequent pay days could not solve his problem of never seeming to have enough cash in his pocket.

At about the time Tam was coping with the nightmare of being persecuted during the Ice Cream Wars, Jonah was also finding himself staring at the inside of a police cell. He was arrested after a car he had been driving in the East End was stopped and a routine search turned up a haul of stolen videos. Where, the police demanded, had they come from and what was he doing with them? These were questions he knew would have to be answered at some stage. In the meantime, he was released on bail while detectives carried out their inquiries into the source of the stolen films and, more importantly, continued their hunt for whoever it was that had arranged for and financed their theft.

Jonah was 29 and old enough to know the probable consequences of informing on friends. Any self-respecting gangster finding himself in a tight corner knew the rule was to bear the burden of guilt and suffer what was coming. By looking after his friends, he would be rewarded with respect, while his needs and those of his family would be met whilst he served out his punishment. Perhaps the police simply terrified Jonah, or maybe he just lacked backbone. Whatever the reason, Tam was appalled when he called on Jonah after his release. 'I'm going to say I got them from you,' said the younger man.

Tam hauled his accuser off to see Margaret, who had always liked Jonah but who now listened aghast as he relayed to her the tale he intended to give the police. She was horrified and not unnaturally concerned. Her husband had found himself unwittingly drawn into one of the worst murders in Scottish history, and the last thing Margaret or Tam needed was more trouble. 'The cops want to know who sold them to me, and I'm going to say it was you. I'm not going to prison,' said Jonah.

'You can't say we sold you the videos, because then they'll come down on us,' Margaret angrily told him. 'Just say you found them. They'll make a few threats against you, but, take my word, nothing else will come of it. Jonah, you can't go around dropping your friends in trouble. You know what can happen to you.'

The matter went no further. It was trivial anyway, and police had other fish to fry. But it left a nasty taste with the McGraws and taught them and the others in the Barlanark Team that Jonah could no longer be trusted. He became a semi-outcast, despised and mistrusted. As a consequence, he turned bitter and could constantly be heard muttering threats against Tam.

In the early hours of 20 October 1984, Tam was returning home from a visit to friends when three men armed with knives and a machete leaped on him. Newspapers reported that 'a man linked to Glasgow's Ice Cream Wars' was 'comfortable' in Glasgow Royal Infirmary, where he was recovering from a fractured skull, two stab wounds and a severed finger. According to police, the attack was not linked to the murder of the Doyles. They were right. Margaret knew what lay behind the ambush. Tam had made it plain to Jonah that his threat to implicate him and Margaret in the video seizures was unacceptable and that he was no longer welcome in the circle of which he had once been a member, albeit on the fringe. 'Another thing, Jonah,' Tam had told him. 'If you are thinking of joining up with another crew, remember you can't work with two teams on opposite sides. You have to make up your mind which side you are on.'

Jonah promptly threw in his lot with Arthur Thompson's son Arty, known rather cruelly as 'Fatboy' due to his liking for Mars bars. Arty was a young man who loved the good life, driving showy cars and trying to impress cronies by playing around with handguns. His father was generous to all his family, but Arty's appetite for money was insatiable. When The Godfather came up short, Arty decided to make money by becoming a heroin dealer. It was a potentially lucrative business, but the risks were huge. Judges chastised those who dealt in dope, but they positively hammered anyone found to be involved in the distribution of smack. Arty needed outlets for his supplies. Jonah knew Barlanark. The pair teamed up.

The Thompsons and the bulk of the Barlanark Team had never hit it off. They maintained a discreet distance, one side never deliberately encroaching on the territory of the other. In this way, an uneasy truce was maintained. Tam and The Godfather would never be friends, but neither would they ever go to war. By deciding to move camps, Jonah exiled himself from the Barlanark Team for ever. Conversely, Paul Ferris would desert the Thompsons, believing that he was entitled to a more generous share of the substantial amounts of money he and his fellow enforcer Tam Bagan collected in the way of loans and drug debts, and end up siding with Tam, admittedly for a short time only. In each case, once out there was no way back.

The attack on Tam by Jonah and his new cronies was a deliberate attempt to murder him. 'We knew right away who did it,' remembers Margaret. 'The three men came up behind him in the dark, and he had no chance. His injuries were mainly to his hands, because he had put them up to protect his head as the machete and knives were brought down upon him. The men then ran away, leaving him bleeding and with a finger attached to his hand by skin only. I was home, but he didn't want to frighten me and instead went to his sister Nancy, who lived close by, for help. She telephoned Snads, who went to her house with a pal. They took one look at Tam and called an ambulance. When it hadn't turned up after a couple of minutes, they drove him to hospital themselves. They were so desperate to get him there quickly that they drove over wasteland and up a very steep junction to get onto the main road faster. It saved valuable seconds and showed how seriously worried they were about him.

'Tam was kept in overnight and examined the following day by a surgeon. The worst injury was to his hand, and the surgeon carried out an emergency operation to sew his finger back on. The tricky part was joining the tendons together, and although the hospital did a wonderful job, his finger was permanently bent from then on. A day later, he was allowed home. The pain must have been intense, but I don't think he was aware of it. What he was aware of was being intensely angry, and anger and a desire for revenge are great antidotes to pain. You tend not to think about your injury or how much it is hurting if your mind is filled with hatred and an intense desire to seek retribution against those who have made you suffer.'

A few years later, Tam would re-enter hospital for another operation to straighten the damaged finger. Before then, Jonah McKenzie would feel the full force of his victim's wrath. He had already been blinded in one eye when a drunk pushed a glass into his face during an argument in a pub in Shettleston. Now he was a marked man but ignored or forgot the warnings of his cronies to take care. One afternoon, while visiting the home of a relative in Burnett Road, he was spotted by Tam McGraw, who, without hesitation, took savage retribution. Jonah found himself in the same hospital where his attacker had, only a few weeks earlier, been treated. He was asked who was responsible for the wounds to his face, head and body, but remained silent, realising that to apportion blame would be to utter his own death sentence.

Despite the murderous tit-for-tat attacks, Tam would, within weeks, try to save Jonah and Arty Thompson from the folly of their highly indiscreet drug operation, which was becoming the talk of the streets. Arty was a major police target, and he was constantly watched and the movements of his associates monitored. In December 1984, his lawyer, Joe Beltrami, wrote to the then chief constable of Strathclyde Police, Sir Patrick Hamill, complaining that his client had been stopped 28 times in just a few weeks and been forced to undergo constant humiliating strip searches inside police vans, in the street, at police stations and in his family home in Provanmill Road. Now, Tam discovered, undercover police were all over Barlanark looking for whoever was supplying the heroin circulating within the scheme.

Like most others, Tam knew who was responsible and told a friend to warn Jonah and Arty. They ignored him and in February 1985 were arrested and charged with possessing and supplying heroin. Before their trial, Arty's dad asked to meet Tam and offered him £20,000 to give favourable testimony if he was forced to give evidence. He wanted Tam to say it wasn't Arty and Jonah who were selling heroin, but ice-cream van owners such as Margaret. Tam was furious, telling the other man to 'stick it up your backside'.

During a trial lasting two weeks at the High Court in Glasgow, Arty's advocate was Donald Findlay, a man who would later find himself representing Tam in a case with a similar theme. Thompson claimed that he was the victim of a fit-up – that police planted the drugs in order to make it seem as though he and Jonah were big-time suppliers. That did not wash with the jury, who found both men guilty. The man with a taste for Mars was told to spend 11 years behind bars. Jonah was given seven years.

Like most of the mothers who lived in and around Barlanark, Margaret detested and feared the consequences of drugs and was angered by suggestions that they were slyly sold from her vans. The death of the Doyles and the jailing of Arty and Jonah had done nothing for the image of the van owners, innocent though most of them might be. She would always remember the smear the cases cast. She was determined that drugs would never be allowed in The El Paso, and now that the pub belonged to her remembered the claims of the Thompsons that Arty was the victim of a fit-up. Margaret had already seen for herself at first hand how police had tried planting evidence to jail her husband. Now she realised just how vulnerable she and Tam could be. Any member of the Barlanark Team could be fitted up, and the police would doubtless use it against her in the licensing courts should Tam be jailed. It needed only the slightest nudge or the smallest package to suddenly turn up in the boot of a car to convince a jury of a man's guilt.

One incident in particular brought home to her just how fine the line between being caught and staying free was. She had bought another spanking new black Mini in the 1980s and had decided to take it out for a spin along Edinburgh Road, a dual carriageway trunk route running past Barlanark. A friend by the name of David had arrived in his own new car. His problem was that he had never bothered to obtain a driving licence. The two cars set off. Tam drove the black Mini, and Margaret was David's passenger. Suddenly a police car, its lights flashing, forced Tam to a halt. David and Margaret had to continue on until they could find a break in the central reservation that would allow them to turn back, look for another break in the roadway and join up with Tam.

Margaret clearly remembers the ensuing conversation: 'I said to one of the policemen, "What is it with you? What's the problem?" I was told, "Ah, well, the motor might be stolen." I said, "It's not stolen. It's mine. You know it's not stolen, because he wouldn't be driving it if it was stolen. Is this a dig for fuck all, because I'm going to start screaming 'rape' and all the people living along this road are going to come out and start asking questions. They'll want to know what's going on if they see me hysterical." At that, the cop said, "Don't do that," and I replied, "Well, what's the pull for, then? Are you just being nosey?" He said, "This brand new? Where did you get the money for that?" I said to him, "How much do you give your wife for the housekeeping?" To which he replied, "I don't think that's any of your business." I said, "Well, I don't think it's any of your business where I got the money to pay for my car." At that, the cop said, "Shall we just call it a truce, then?"

'I didn't want to push it, because David was there with a new motor and no driving licence, so I told the policeman, "Next time you pull us for nothing, I'm back on to the Queen – getting on to Lizzie." They were so taken aback that they forgot to ask David for his documentation. I don't think they realised that ordinary people could actually write about them to the Queen.'

The promise to write to Buckingham Palace was actually no idle threat. Margaret had already done so following the hubcap incident years earlier. She had complained to the chief constable of Strathclyde Police about the attempt to set her husband up and had said that she was alarmed that the blatant chicanery might reoccur but had received no reply. It might have been that the police hoped she would forget about the letter if they ignored it, but if that was the case, it was a serious misjudgement, because Margaret wrote a letter to the Queen, telling Her Majesty what had happened and asking her to intervene and make sure that there was no repetition. 'Fucking reply to me, so he will,' she told Tam. 'He probably put my letter in the bin, so I'm telling the Queen what's going on here.'

'As far as I was concerned, it was a competition with the police, in which you won some and lost some. I honestly never had anything against any of them, provided they played by the rules. But some didn't. They cheated and planted evidence. Fitting up was entirely wrong. The chief constable might not have wanted to answer me, but I knew he would have to answer the secretary of state for Scotland. And that would be to whom someone working for the Queen would send my letter. The secretary of state would want the chief constable to tell him what was going on. The police would then have to give him an explanation and would be aware that if they did a fit-up on Tam again, the Queen would be told. I got an acknowledgement from Buckingham Palace that my concerns had been passed on, and whenever I was worried that the police were at it, I'd just fire a letter off to the Queen and ask her to investigate.'

It was concerns such as these that contributed to a series of decisions by the McGraws in the second half of the 1980s. At the same time as running The El Paso, Margaret was still operating her vans. At the beginning, Tam had occasionally worked on them with her, but his activities with the Barlanark Team, broken by spells in prison, placed the burden of earning the family bread firmly on her shoulders. The vans were lucrative. At one stage, the McGraws were offered £20,000 for just one vehicle and its route, a small fortune back then. But they knocked it back. Now with a pub to pay for and her increasing workload, Margaret thought that the time had come to give up her rounds. So the vans were sold, and she concentrated on running the pub instead.

Just as she closed one aspect of her business operations, so Tam was beginning to think that the time was approaching when the Barlanark Team should quietly fade from the scene. His explanation that he should be there to help bring up the growing William was one that he would persist with when we spoke during the writing of *Crimelord*. But there were other reasons. Although the hard-core membership of the band of thieves would always remain close, there had been disagreements with others on the periphery, some of whom had taken up with rival crews. But the principal cause for the cessation of activity is most likely to have been the simple advent of change, of the introduction of new methods of security and communication, and huge improvements to the speed with which police were able to respond to incidents such as reported robberies or break-ins.

Margaret had long seen the writing on the wall, her card readings providing her with ample warnings. She would often lay out her pack and be filled with a sensation of unease and try to persuade Tam to stay at home. She would not ask where he was going, but simply tell him what the cards had portrayed. A close friend of Margaret explains: 'Over the years, Mags had become more and more fed up with the thought of Tam being arrested, of seeing him walk out and not know whether he would be home or if her next sight of him would be in a police station or at Barlinnie. She kept reminding him about the warnings her mother had given her when she had said that she was going to marry him. And Margaret would tell him, "Tam, if you go out tonight, you'll end up in Barlinnie." He would argue back, saying, "But all the stuff is out: the walkie-talkies, the cars. All the boys will be waiting for me. I can't not go. I can't let them down."

'Remember, there were no mobile phones in those early days. Had there been, Tam could have just rung up the others and called off whatever it was they had planned or tell them that he thought they should leave it until the next night. He would not, of course, have told them that he was changing the plan because Margaret had said his cards predicted trouble. "Fucking listening to that Margaret, Tam? Come on. Get a grip," they would have said. Once mobiles were introduced, there was no excuse for Tam taking chances when she had advised him against something or other. And, of course, just as mobiles helped the team communicate, they meant that the days when cutting telephone lines left target areas out of contact with the police were gone. Tam knew it was time to move on.'

So did Margaret, but while he looked for some other enterprise to occupy his time and provide an earner, her interest was in finding a new home. Many of her neighbours in Burnett Road were no longer there, and she felt the close was now home to strangers. They might be people whom Margaret quite liked and respected, but they were not friends in the same sense as those people who were already there when she and Tam had moved into the close with William. She knew that she wanted to move and had spent more than a year house hunting throughout the East End, where she wanted to continue to live in order to be near her family and friends. Tam had also kept his eyes open for a suitable home. He and his wife both liked Carrick Drive in Mount Vernon from the days of their visits to the home of Jim and Deborah McMinimee, and Tam had even been upset when Jim moved without telling the McGraws that he was selling up.

Margaret kept an eye on the street of mostly detached bungalows, many of them with upper rooms, wondering when one might become available. When one did, she quickly snapped it up, paying £80,000. It was barely a couple of minutes by car from The El Paso, but it seemed to Margaret that she and her workplace were now on separate planets, instead of being in the same room: 'Our new home wasn't much further from the pub than Burnett Road had been, but, odd though this might sound, it felt as though it was miles away. When I finished at The El Paso, I climbed into the car and had the impression that I was really driving home, whereas in Barlanark it was as though the pub was next door. It was a wonderful change.'

The McGraws bought the Mount Vernon property in May 1991, although it would be some time before they actually moved in. It was to be a year that they would not forget.

17

THE FORTUNATE COOKIE

At about the time Robert Mills was being hacked to death outside The El Paso, Arty Thompson was preparing to return to his family home in Provanmill Road. He was now within a year or so of being released on licence, having served approximately two-thirds of the 11-year sentence he had begun in 1985. It was routine practice for inmates approaching release to spend short breaks with their families to accustom themselves to normality beyond the prison walls. One weekend, Arty caught the Friday-morning bus from Noranside open prison near Forfar and was dropped off at Buchanan Street Bus Station, not far from his home. Before leaving, Arty, along with all the other inmates going home for the weekend, had been warned to be back at the bus station on the Sunday afternoon for the journey back. Anyone who did not show up would, once he was caught, be thrown back into a closed prison and lose the freedom the open system provided.

Arty had made enemies in prison. He failed to appreciate that not everyone actually liked his father and that there were those who, lacking the ability or courage to face up to The Godfather, would instead try to hurt the old man by targeting his son.

Some of the men who had shared a cell with Arty reckoned that he had drawn up a hit list of men whom he insisted should be killed for having offended his family in some way. Among them was Willie Ferris from Blackhill, the father of Paul. Another was his co-accused. He blamed what he thought of as Jonah's incompetence and refusal to listen to advice not to deal heroin in Barlanark for depriving him of his freedom. At the same time, Arty continually reminded his father, who throughout his son's long incarceration was a faithful visitor to whichever prison he happened to be in, of the discrepancy in the sentences, often a sign that one party had curried favour with the authorities by providing information to the police. Arty justified adding the name of Tam McGraw to the roll of death on the grounds that he had refused to allow himself to be called as a witness at his trial. Not that Tam McGraw was worried about Arty.

At the same time as Arty was tasting the fare in a Glasgow curry house on the Saturday evening, Tam, Margaret and a few close friends had been making the most of a rare break from work. It was by chance that Margaret and Tam were out that night. One of Tam's relatives, John Healy, had called Margaret to ask if she could help out a friend who was opening a pub in Thornliebank by loaning him equipment for the first night. She was happy to do so and accepted an invitation to the opening night, which would be restricted to friends and business associates. But her day turned out to be busier than expected, with one chore in particular causing her a considerable amount of trouble. A joiner who was carrying out work at their newly bought Mount Vernon house had complained to Margaret that he was being held up because of a shortage of annular nails, used in flooring. If he were to go off in search of more, it would only add to his delay, so she volunteered to go and buy some for him.

However, after several hours of trawling around hardware stores and builders' merchants, she wished she had not. True, she had finally tracked down the specialist nails to a store in Livingston, halfway between Glasgow and Edinburgh, but after delivering them to her carpenter, she felt exhausted and was simply not in the mood to socialise. She contacted John Healy and asked if it would be a problem for her and Tam to visit the pub the following night instead, after they had been out for a meal. She was told that they would be welcome any night. Margaret would have good reason to be glad that weariness had kept her at home on the opening night – a Friday – and not the following evening.

Margaret and Tam's revised programme promised a busy night. First, they headed to the newly opened Thornliebank pub, had a few drinks and then moved on to another bar in nearby Arden, owned by John Healy. There they enjoyed listening to the music of a popular group called the Marie Saint Claire Band. Tam and Margaret both

knew the group well. The musicians occasionally performed at The
El Paso, where they were well liked and successful.

Margaret and Tam were enjoying themselves, and with good
reason. The El Paso was doing well, thanks to Margaret's enterprise
and hard work, and just a few days earlier she had received a letter
informing her that her purchase of the house in Carrick Drive
had been officially registered. Title number GLA20799 was now
formally her property, and she had followed the advice of her lawyer
in carefully reading through the legal jargon that was attached to the
sale, noting that she had to maintain a 'neat parapet wall' topped
with an iron railing along the front of her home but could not sink
a mine in search of coal, fossils or ironstone. She was thrilled by her
buy. Slogging away long hours in her ice-cream van in the cold and
wet, then gambling everything on making the closed-down El Paso a
success, had taken her from a council flat to a luxury detached home
at which she could shut her iron gates to the rest of the world and
enjoy the trappings of success.

When the time came to move on, the party, now swelled with
friends who had joined them during the evening, moved to a Chinese
restaurant in the city, a favourite spot with those in the licensing trade,
because it opened late, allowing them to patronise it after their own
closing time. Margaret sat back, sipped her drink and ordered her
meal. A couple of hours later, she and her guests were drinking coffee
and opening the brightly wrapped fortune cookies that are a feature
of Chinese restaurants. Inside the crisp cookie was a line or two of
oriental wisdom in the style of the legendary Chinese philosopher
Confucius. One by one, the diners ripped off the wrappings and read
out their messages. Margaret's read 'He who knows he has enough
is rich'. Amongst the laughter and banter, a voice said, 'Come on,
Tam. What's yours say?' Pulling apart the wrapping and crushing
the biscuit inside, Tam looked in vain for the tiny slip of paper with
its words of wisdom. But the cookie was empty, and someone joked,
'That's not a fortune cookie. It's an unfortunate cookie.'

'What does this mean?' demanded Tam, searching among the
fragments of biscuit.

'It means they forgot to fucking put one in when they baked
it,' his wife told him. Tam was not to be outdone. A waitress was
summoned. The McGraws were good customers and generous with

their tips, and the restaurant manager padded over to find the cause of the fuss. Apologies were abject, another plateful of cookies was supplied and this time there was a message that might have come directly to Tam from the great philosopher himself: 'Confucius say: a merry heart make good medicine'. Minutes later, the group was heading off in the directions of their various homes.

Earlier, in the north-west of the city, three men had sat in a car watching Arty's progress. They had been tipped off as to his whereabouts that night. It would later be rumoured that the informant was someone very close to the Thompson family. Two of the men in the white Nissan, stolen earlier in the day from a senior police officer after he had parked it at a railway station and taken a train to work, were Joe Hanlon and Bobby Glover. Later, the police would claim that their friend Paul Ferris was in the car with them, an allegation that was never proved. At a word from one of the trio, the car doors opened. By the time Arty reached home and rang the doorbell, he was dying. Three shots had been fired into his body at close range from a .22 rifle, one hitting him in the cheek, a second puncturing his lung and a third, fired while he lay helpless, entering his backside and hitting a kidney, his liver and his heart. His family rushed him to Glasgow Royal Infirmary, blood pouring from his wounds, but he was declared dead shortly after midnight. Word of the murder spread like wildfire.

When Margaret and Tam reached home in the early hours, their dogsitter informed them that there had been a call from a friend who had insisted that they should ring him no matter what time they returned at. 'What for? What was the call about?' asked Margaret.

'There's been a murder at the pub.'

'Who?' she wanted to know, but the dogsitter didn't know.

Fearing for the safety of her staff, Margaret immediately made the call. A voice at the other end of the phone sounded calm: 'You've heard the news?'

'About the murder?'

'No, murders.'

'Murders? We gather there's been one at the Paso.'

'Yes, a soldier who had been causing a bit of bother. None of your people were hurt. But there's been another murder.'

'Who?'

'Stand by for trouble on this one.'

'Why? What's so special about it?'

'It was Arthur Thompson's son.'

The hunt for the murderers of both men soon began in earnest. It was well known that while his father had adopted a 'so what, let it be' attitude, Arty had been angered by Tam's refusal to help out in 1985 and had badmouthed him, even making threats to attack The El Paso. Word of that had leaked out and reached the ears of the police, who now remembered the rebuff and reasoned that it gave Tam a motive to 'get the first one in'. He too realised that they would be quick to call on him. When they did, that day, it was Margaret who told the two detectives where to go: to the Chinese restaurant, where staff easily remembered 'Missa MaGaw' and the absent cookie message, providing Tam with an alibi for his whereabouts that night. She had little doubt that but for that piece of luck, her husband would have been hauled off and subjected to accusations that he had been involved in the murder.

'We had been laughing and joking with the waitress about Tam's disappearing message,' says Margaret. 'If we had been unable to back up our version of our movements that night, Tam would have been tagged for the murder. The police were continually seeking any excuse to arrest and question him about what he was up to.'

Arthur Thompson was certain that Tam had not been the killer, because he knew the identities of the three men in the car. He might have lacked the resources of the police, but he had a network of informants far superior to that of the murder squad. The police would later admit that every time they followed up a lead or called on a potential witness, they found Arthur or one of his 'people' had already been. The detectives knew that there would be no trial for the men who had slain Thompson's son.

Just to make sure that he was on the right track, Arthur ordered Jonah McKenzie to be interrogated using a method that had been tried and tested by Roman legions 2,000 years earlier. He reasoned that while his enforcers were at the task they could check whether their victim had, as his now dead son had suggested, grassed Arty to the police. So, Jonah, by now virtually sightless after being twice stabbed in the eyes and known as 'Blind Jonah', was summoned to a meeting one night, taken to a deserted building in the area of

Dalmarnock Road and crucified. It was a technique that others who had fallen foul of Arthur had experienced, notably an individual who had reneged on a loan and a well-known car thief of the day suspected of stealing the Nissan supplied to Arty's killers.

Jonah's bloody protests that he knew nothing about the killing of his friend and claims that while they were in prison together he had actually done his best to protect Arty, sounded so genuine that he was believed. And despite his barbaric treatment, he continued working in the Thompson camp when he recovered, reasoning that The Godfather's torture had been a tickle compared to the beating dished out by Tam.

Heartbroken Arthur summoned a long-time lieutenant called William Manson and passed on three names: Paul Ferris, Bobby Glover and Joe Hanlon. He also called a business friend and asked a favour. He then sat back to grieve and wait.

Margaret knew the men now suspected by Arthur of the murder. She disliked and mistrusted Paul Ferris but liked Bobby Glover, who often drank in The El Paso, and she was genuinely fond of Joe Hanlon, who had worked in her pub: 'People go on about Joe, calling him a nutter and so on and so forth, but, at the end of the day, if you didn't do Joe any harm, he wouldn't harm you,' recalls Margaret. 'That was until he got into contact with Ferris and from there into trouble. Give Joe credit. He came to me and said, "Margaret, take me off your books." I said, "What for?" and Joe replied, "Because I'm going to work with Ferris." I said, "Joe, you've got a nice wee flat and a wee motor. What the fuck do you want to do that for? You are going to end up doing life, because he'll use you." He said, "I'll make a few quid." And I said, "OK, Joe, fine. Thanks for telling me." Joe wanted to make sure that if he got arrested, it wouldn't come back and cause problems for the pub and me. He knew that if he was in trouble with the police, they would tell the licensing people that somebody working at The El Paso had been arrested, and it would give the police a chance to cause bother for us and maybe even an excuse to turn the place over. It was really a decent thing to do, but, then, Joe was a good wee guy at heart.'

The night before Arty Thompson's funeral, Manson's nephew, William Lobban, rang Bobby Glover and asked for a meeting. Glover's car had been impounded by the police, and he called Joe to ask him if he could drive them to the rendezvous. Bobby promised his wife Eileen he would not be long. She next saw him in the morgue. The following morning, Joe and Bobby's bodies were discovered slumped in a car parked outside a pub in Shettleston that the cortège carrying Arty's body would pass. Bobby lay across the floor in the rear of the Ford Orion, while Joe was squashed into the front-passenger footwell. Post-mortems would reveal that each had been shot twice, once in the head with one handgun, then in the chest with another. No one can be absolutely certain what happened, because William Manson was mysteriously poisoned in 1997, although the official line is that he overdosed on coproxamol. But theories abound, most of them fantastic.

The most ludicrous one, as it flies in the face of the post-mortem findings, is that they failed to notice their assassin was carrying a sawn-off shotgun as he climbed into the rear seat of the car, and they were shot in the back when they tried to flee. According to this figment of a not especially bright imagination, the bodies were then secretly carried, on the orders of Tam McGraw, past customers to a back room at the crowded El Paso, where they were laid out for Arthur to inspect, and later dumped. In reality, evidence suggests that Bobby and Joe were shot in the head by Manson after agreeing to a request by Lobban to collect his uncle and drive to Hogganfield Loch, half a mile from Arthur's home. A call was then made to The Godfather, who pumped a bullet into the trunk of each with another gun. The bodies were taken to an empty building, which was owned by the businessman Arthur had called, near the city centre then abandoned in Shettleston.

Paul Ferris survived because he was in prison, held on suspicion of killing Arty and of kneecapping Willie Gillen, although he was later exonerated. Bobby had also been arrested over the Gillen attack but, sadly for him, was released the day before his murder. Word was that Jonah was meant to be in the car with Ferris and Glover the day Gillen was shot but had made an excuse so escaped being kneecapped himself and spending what was left of his life carrying a limp.

'Eileen Glover rang me that morning to ask if Bobby was with Tam and me,' remembers Margaret. 'I told her he wasn't, and I had hardly put the phone down when Joe's wife Sharon called asking the same question about her husband. I said that I hadn't seen Joe either. When we finished speaking, I rang Tam, who had been meeting friends, and told him the two women were looking for their husbands, but he had no idea of their whereabouts. At about lunchtime, we went to the Paso to open up, and as we were unlocking the front door, a police car pulled up and an officer wound down his window. He said, "Bobby Glover and Joe Hanlon are dead." Tam asked him what had happened, and he said, "I don't know. Nobody does yet. A guy was passing The Cottage Bar in Shettleston and thought he noticed two men in a car. A few minutes later, he passed the car again and realised that the men were still there but hadn't moved. He called the publican who rang the police. The bodies were in Joe's car." As soon as he drove away, Tam went off to call on Eileen to break the news.'

She recalls, 'He sat down, asked me to make him a cup of tea and then just looked at me and said, "Bobby's dead."' Tam drove her to The Cottage Bar and tried to break through the police cordon so that she could see Bobby, but she was instead taken to the nearby Shettleston Police Station and held there for seven hours before being allowed to return to her infant son. 'Bobby's body wasn't released for five weeks,' she says. 'I went to visit him every day in the mortuary. The guy there was sick of seeing me.'

It was at the Glasgow mortuary, a small but imposing stone building next to the High Court, that the post-mortems were carried out. In a basement room, the bodies of Bobby and Joe lay in cold silence in metal cabinets. While they were still there, awaiting burial, Sharon decided to accompany Margaret and a friend to the nearby Jocelyn Spiritualist Church. 'When we arrived, Eileen Glover was already there,' recalls Margaret. 'At the end of the service, Eileen suggested to us, "Shall we go and see Bobby and Joe before we go home? The mortuary attendant is a really nice guy who has said we can visit them any time." I had parked right outside the mortuary. It was late at night, and as we went to see Bobby and Joe, I remembered that I'd left something in the car. I had this American-style alarm on the motor, which was piercing if you touched the vehicle and it went off. A shrill voice would shout out, "You are too close to this vehicle. Stand back. Stand back." When I ran back, I forgot to disable the alarm, and it went off. As I was trying to turn it off, I thought of Joe and Bobby lying on the other side of the wall and said to myself,

"They'll be telling one another that here we are lying in the morgue and still we can't get peace."

'When we eventually went inside, the attendant recognised Eileen. I also knew him, as he was a friend of mine. I was quaking, expecting to be taken into a room filled with drawers. I thought the man would then pull two out and there would be Bobby and Joe. That's what I'd always seen on television. The truth was that I just wasn't up for seeing dead bodies. I was so relieved when the attendant pointed to a small monitor on which we could see their faces. I took him to one side and said, "I thought you opened a drawer and lifted a sheet." He told me that the mortuary had only just introduced the monitor system to spare relatives what could sometimes be distressing sights.'

Joe had been given the nickname 'Bananas', and while it summarised the personality of a young man who believed in making his way through life with a smile on his face, even if at times it meant acting unpredictably, the tag actually resulted from his appearance at a prison charity day dressed as a banana. One of Margaret's favourite stories about him concerned his attempt to gain entry to a leading nightclub in Glasgow. Joe had arrived wearing what appeared to be a pair of training shoes, thus breaching the club's dress code. Not known as a troublemaker, he argued with the doormen, but he was flatly refused entry. 'Ring the manager and tell him I'm here,' insisted Joe.

Picking up the telephone, the bouncer told the manager, 'There's a guy called Joe here who wants a word.'

'What about?'

'We can't let him in because he's wearing trainers.'

'Well, point to the dress code.'

'We have, and he still insists. Says you know him.'

'What's his name again?'

'Joe.'

'Joe? Joe who?'

'He wants to know your full name,' Joe was told.

'Tell him it's Joe Bananas.'

'Who?'

'Joe Bananas. Just tell him that.'

The odd moniker was relayed along the telephone line, prompting peals of laughter at the other end: 'Let him in and bring him up to the office.' Joe was greeted warmly by the manager, and the doorman was asked why Joe had been refused entry, at which he pointed to Joe's footwear. 'They're trainers,' the bouncer insisted.

'No they're not,' maintained Joe. 'I saw Mike Tyson, the heavyweight boxing champion of the world, wearing a pair of these at some function, and when I heard a friend of Tam McGraw's was going over to America, asked him if he would get me a pair. He brought them back and said the store told him people wore them to dinners and business meetings. They're not trainers.'

Holding back his laughter, the manager relented. But Joe wanted to have the last word. 'Would you get into the ring and fight Mike Tyson?' he asked the burly doorman.

'No, I don't think I'd fancy my chances.'

'I would.'

'Joe, no disrespect, but you're just a wee guy. He'd do you.'

'No he wouldn't. I know I'm a lot smaller than Tyson, but I'd operate a handicap system to level things up. When the bell sounded and he came out of his corner towards me, I'd just pull a sawn-off shotgun out of my shorts and shoot the fucker. Joe Hanlon, new heavyweight champion.'

But William Manson would come to destroy Joe's dreams of fame.

18

ZOLTAN

For ten years, a figure padded about the homes of Margaret and Tam with the assurance of one who knows he is king of all that surrounds him. Among his peers, Tam might have had a reputation as a man not to be made fun of – one to be feared, even. Friends knew, of course, that once through the doors of Burnett Road, or later Carrick Drive, he was ruled, and happy to be so, by his wife. But Margaret and Tam both knew who the real master was: Zoltan, their huge pet Rottweiler.

Margaret has experienced her share of dramas during a lifetime in which she has known many heart-stopping moments. Some she found scary, others sad. For example, she was devastated by the death of her mother Jessie in June 1986. Then she spent desperate, anxious weeks fearing the worst and worrying over her beloved brother John after he underwent a heart bypass in Glasgow. But Margaret freely admits that one of her worst moments came in 1995 when she discovered Zoltan was dead.

Many animal lovers maintain that their dog is their best friend. Others might argue for a pet cat or horse. Perhaps it is the case that only someone who has owned a pet can understand the degree of affection an animal can generate in a human, but to Margaret and Tam, Zoltan was irreplaceable: 'How did I feel when Zoltan died? I don't know. I felt numb, certainly. But how can you explain how you feel when a member of your family dies? And Zoltan was a part of the family. You feel as though you've lost a bit of your own body. Tam felt the loss just as badly. He would sometimes say, "Let's get another." But I will never have another dog for the simple reason that I know it will die at some stage, and I don't want to have to relive the misery that all of us felt when Zoltan died.'

Zoltan joined the McGraws as a pup in 1985 while they lived in Barlanark. He was an instant favourite with William, then aged 13. By some strange canine intuition, Zoltan soon came to realise that he could twist the three humans around his paw. The dog laid down the marker by which he expected the others to abide. Margaret says, 'Zoltan went everywhere with us, even to work sometimes. At home, he was always there, checking up on what we were doing. He even slept with us. The moment I climbed out of bed, he would leap in beside Tam, put his head on the pillow where mine had lain and somehow manage to pull the bedding over his head with his paws. He'd then fall asleep and refuse to budge.

'He could be a very particular dog. If I went out for the evening or to work when Tam was in the jail, Zoltan would refuse to be left on his own, and I had to hire a dogsitter. And he was especially finicky when it came to his food. Much as he might have enjoyed chocolates, his favourite meal was liver, which I would cook for him. Tripe was high on his list of favourites, too. He never ate anything bought ready cooked – no tinned dinners for him. I made all his meals. Looking back, I reckon I did more cooking for the dog than I did for anybody else, including William or Tam. One of our friends, George Reid, used to come to the house and tell us that Zoltan's meals smelled so good he could eat them himself. And to prove it, George would take a nibble out of Zoltan's dish and tell the dog, "That was delicious. You don't know how lucky you are."

'Zoltan was never too happy about having his food pinched and decided something had to be done about it. He worked out a solution that he thought would prevent George eating his dinners. He would pull back the corners of carpets, wander over to his dish, take his meal out and put it on the floor then pull the carpet back over to hide it. When I did the housework and the vacuum cleaner reached near the corners of the carpet where he had his hidden food store, Zoltan would leap up, dive over to where I was cleaning and look up at me as if to say, "Don't you dare go and do this area. That's my dinner under there. Go and clean somewhere else."

'We used to find small lumps near the edges of the carpets, and straight away we'd know what was underneath: Zoltan's dinners.

Dogs are wise, and he was no exception. When he rumbled to the fact that we knew about his little secret stores, he worked out another method of hiding food that he wanted to keep for later. He would hunt about for a newspaper. It might be one Tam had bought that morning and had been reading but had laid down for a few minutes. Zoltan would then drag it off and using his paws and teeth tear it into strips, which he would put over the top of whatever it was he did not want anyone else to find. It might be a meal or even a bone.

'It was impossible not to burst out laughing, watching him carefully cover up something with the remnants of the paper. The little heap he'd made might even be in the middle of the floor, and when he was finished, he would lie there as if he was asking, "Well, guess what's under that lot?" I'd go over to Zoltan and say to him, "What are you doing?" Then he'd look as though he was thinking, "She's not too pleased. Maybe I'd better move this." So he would take all the fragments of paper back to wherever he'd stolen the newspaper from and then eat his food or hide his bone somewhere else.

'Dogs have instincts that we do not. Zoltan always knew when someone was unwell. It was as though he had some sixth sense that sounded a warning bell in his brain telling him that someone he loved was ill and needed his protection. If I was feeling under the weather and had taken to my bed, he would not leave my side unless it was to do his toilet. Then he would come back to lie at the side of the bed, or, if he thought nobody had noticed, on top of it. He was always there, showing total loyalty, willing you to get better.

'Like most humans, he also had a moody side to him. For example, if you went off and left him, even for a short time, he took it as a personal insult. When John had his bypass operation at Glasgow Royal Infirmary in 1984, he and his partner Violet went off to Gran Canaria to recuperate. The break was clearly beneficial to John, and Violet thought it would be a good idea if they stayed on for an extra week. However, they had only taken enough of his medication to last for the period of their original stay.

'When we spoke on the telephone, Violet told me, "He's fine," but I could sense she was worried about something and asked what the problem was. She said that the medication they had changed to didn't seem so effective. John needed more of the tablets originally prescribed by the hospital. I told them to stay put, arranged to get a further supply and flew over with them. I was only away for a couple of days, but as soon as I walked back into the house, I could detect something was not right with Zoltan. He looked at me then walked away as if to say, "So you're back, are you? Where have you been and what do you mean by leaving me behind? You didn't even ask if I minded you going. You went away and left me. How dare you."

'He was clearly in the huff. I looked at him and said, "Come on, son. Mammy's here," but he wasn't interested. For the next two days, he didn't even look at me and seemed to be saying to himself, "That'll teach her a lesson." He acted that way any time I had to leave. As he got older, he got worse. Even if I just went out for a short time, he would be in the huff and sulking when I returned.

'Zoltan was ten when he died. He'd moved with us to Mount Vernon six years earlier and loved his new home. I always knew when he wasn't well. Dog lovers will know what I mean when I say a sort of film appeared to cover his coat, as if he was surrounded by a white outline. He always recovered, but one day I said to Tam, "He's not well." Tam said, "Don't be daft. He's OK." And he was right. In no time, Zoltan was bouncing about, back to his old self. But the next day, he didn't look well, so we took him to the vet, who gave us some tablets to put in his food. They seemed to help, because that morning he was fine, although every time I looked at him I sensed something wasn't right. I was upstairs – to do some sewing, I think – and I don't know why but a strange feeling came over me that there was something very wrong with the dog. When I came down to check, he was lying by the clock, and I knew he would never get up. Ten minutes later, Zoltan died.

'It was a terrible experience. We buried him under some trees at the front of the house. He had been a brilliant friend and a wonderful companion. After Zoltan left us, Tam would say, "Get another one," but I'd reply, "I don't want another one. Zoltan was the best, and there'll not be another like him. No, we won't get another dog." And we never did.'

19

THE DROWNED MAN

THE MURDERS OF ARTY THOMPSON, BOBBY GLOVER AND JOE HANLON, the culmination of a series of shootings in the East End – most down to disputes between rival drug factions or moneylenders, who meted out harsh justice to wayward debtors – had ramifications throughout Glasgow. Overall, the picture was of a city bathed in lawlessness, and there was pressure on the police to act. Senior officers took the view that an effective starting point would be the pubs and bars that were recognised as being the haunts for known troublemakers.

These black sheep of the licensing trade now found themselves frequently visited by uniformed bobbies, who pointedly scrutinised customers for recognised faces. Landlords and managers of bars with a reputation for violence were warned that unless they could bring about a sudden outbreak of peace they would find themselves having to fight to hold onto their licences. Executives of major breweries were visited and advised that it would be in their interests to close down certain premises, the alternative being the threat of what would amount to police harassment of these targeted establishments on the grounds of maintaining good order. Those same brewers were told in no uncertain terms that they should cease supplying particular bars in which they had a financial interest or simply withdraw their mortgage or loan guarantees, effectively putting the owners out of business.

Most of the targets were in the East End, and Margaret discovered The El Paso was on the police hit list. But she owned it outright. She had no obligation to any brewery and, as the boss of a free house, was able to buy from whomever she wished. Knowing they could not close her down, the police began looking for excuses to challenge her licence. With better information, they might have had more success.

Three years after Arty had been huckled away to start his eleven-year sentence for heroin trafficking, muttering threats against Tam for refusing to give evidence, the roof of The El Paso was set ablaze during the early hours. Luckily, there wasn't too much damage. Arty's younger brother Billy was suspected as being the culprit, so Margaret despatched Tam to the Thompson home, ordering him to demand restitution. Crafty Arthur offered to arrange for the repairs to be made using second-hand materials from his wood yard, a suggestion instantly rebuffed, and he was ultimately forced to hand over cash. It was a considerable time before the full details reached the ears of the police. The seriousness of another attack would also be noted by the boys in blue, but not its full consequences, because The El Paso would surely have been closed down had they been.

The bar was crowded when someone opened the door and rolled in a round object. It looked like a potato, and a handful of customers began kicking it around. Eventually, someone took a closer look and reckoned it was a hand grenade. Not wishing to interrupt the drinking, there were calls for a brush to be brought so it could be swept back outside. Then Joe Hanlon emerged from behind the bar to pick it up and throw it outside, where another local gathered it up and lobbed it into the adjoining cemetery. The next day, it was discovered that it was a Second World War grenade. Only a broken firing pin had stopped it from exploding. The bomb squad was called to make the device safe.

Nobody was hurt, and Margaret could hardly be blamed for the actions of a maniac. However, when details of the grenade incident reached local newspapers 18 months later, the fallout was devastating. The El Paso insurers announced to Margaret that they were withdrawing their cover. It was an overwhelming blow and one she had to keep a lid on for three years while she battled to find another company willing to insure the business. Ultimately, she did, but no one knew that throughout that time the premises were not insured. Had that bit of information leaked out to the police, the news would certainly have been shared with the licensing authorities,

Margaret and Tam shortly after their wedding in Glasgow in 1971. They hoped to marry on St Valentine's Day, but Tam booked 13 February instead.

The original members of the Barlanark Team. Tam (centre) with John 'Snads' Adams (left) and Drew Drummond.

One time friend Jonah McKenzie, who Margaret hid from the police behind her fireplace in Barlanark, was blamed for a vicious attack on Tam that put him in hospital.

Margaret and Drew Drummond proudly pose with a racy Ford Capri outside her home in Barlanark.

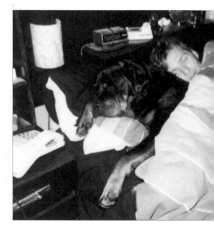

Zoltan, the family pet dog, asleep in bed with Tam.

A cheerful Joe 'Bananas' Hanlon (right) with Tam and close friend James Mullen. Joe acquired his nickname posing as a banana for a charity event.

Paul Ferris (left) and Bobby Glover clearly enjoying themselves during a night out at The Cottage Bar in Shettleston, the pub outside which Bobby's body was dumped after his murder in 1991.

Margaret and Tam in a relaxed mood during a holiday in 1997.

Jim McMinimee (carrying newspaper) followed by
a grim looking Tam during a trip to Paris in 2000.

Gordon Ross and girlfriend Kellie Ann. Margaret knew
from a card reading that he would die but was helpless
to prevent his stabbing in Shettleston.

Billy McPhee looking grim during Gordon Ross's funeral. Billy had been told a contract had been placed on his life, but Margaret had been warned that he would die.

Tam in his trademark blue-denim jacket during a business trip to Tenerife. Few knew it contained a heavy bulletproof lining.

Margaret with her son William during a night out in 2003.

Margaret does a reading with her favourite Russian gypsy fortune-telling cards, a pack bought for her by Tam as a surprise gift. During a reading, she learned that her husband was doomed to die.

Celebrating the Life of
Tam

Thomas McGraw

19 February 1952 - 30 July 2007

The last photograph of Tam, taken at a wedding shortly before his death.

Don't grieve for me, for now I am free,
I'm following the path
God has laid you see,
I took His hand when I heard him call,
I had to go, but I'll watch you all.

If my parting has left a void,
Then fill it with remembered joy,
A friendship shared, a laugh, a kiss,
Oh yes, these things I too will miss.

Be not burdened with times of sorrow,
I wish you the sunshine of tomorrow,
My life has been full, I savoured much,
Good friends, good times,
a loved one's touch.

Lift up your hearts and peace to thee,
God wanted me now; He set me free.

The message to mourners at
Tam's funeral in August 2007.

Tam's death certificate. Despite pleas to
cut down, he continued chain smoking.

Margaret looking relaxed in the luxurious home
that she and Tam created during the years she
ran The El Paso bar in the east end of Glasgow.

Margaret and Jim McMinimee after announcing they
were in love and planned to marry.

Looking thin and gaunt, Tam leaves the High Court
in Edinburgh in 1998 after being cleared of major
drugs charges as Margaret had predicted.
(Photograph courtesy of Ciaran Donnelly)

resulting in her being forced to shut up shop. That would have been shattering, because business was thriving, and Margaret had even considered expanding into another field.

Police were growing ever more enthusiastic in their efforts to crack down on drivers who drank, so much so that some publicans reported a severe slackening off in business. Not so in the case of The El Paso. After closing time one night, Margaret watched as her customers looked for a lift home or vainly waited for the appearance of a taxi and reasoned that the solution was simple. Why not start a taxi company of her own? She discussed the idea with Tam, and the result was the formation of Glasgow Radio Cars, later to become Mac's Cabs, based in an office adjoining the pub. Soon it was operating around the clock, 365 days a year, and it would form the basis of a business that would serve the family well, providing a solid long-term investment.

The taxi business belonged to Margaret, and Tam had no part in it. Margaret sold it in 2001 and paid £97,000 to the Inland Revenue, the government's share in taxation, evidence that she was the sole owner. Tam was never investigated in connection with the company and was never required to make any payment to the Inland Revenue in relation to it.

The success of the cab experiment was a beacon for Margaret in a seemingly never-ending battle to hold onto her licence. Having failed to close her down during the campaign against targeted bars following the 1991 murders, the police began raising frivolous objections to her licence and eventually succeeded in having it suspended. It meant that she could carry on trading, but only so long as she had the means and the will to continue the fight to stay in business. Through a succession of appeals and by switching the licence between companies, she was able to continue for three years. By 1996, she had had enough.

Continual summonses before the licensing authorities interspersed with a succession of adjournments were threatening to cut a huge hole in the money she had made, so Margaret called it a day and closed for good. Three weeks later, Trevor Lawson, the man whose life Tam had once saved, was in the area carrying out demolition work. By now a friend of the McGraws, he pointed out the folly of leaving the building derelict. 'Somebody might climb on the roof to break in, and if they fall, you'll be responsible,' he told Margaret. 'Just get rid of it.'

'How?' she asked.

'I'm just about to finish another contract and have all the equipment I need,' said Trevor. 'I can knock the place down and clear the site in a couple of hours. But I literally need to do it now, because tomorrow I'll be elsewhere.'

'Go ahead,' Margaret replied.

When she next passed by, all that remained of The El Paso were a few lumps of rubble, a posy of flowers left by a disappointed regular and memories by the score. Joe Hanlon was among those she remembered: 'I took a liking to Joe from the very first time I met him when William brought him home one day. Then he began coming to The El Paso, and finally I gave him a job. He just seemed to fit in with everybody, because he was such a jolly wee guy. Joe was a kind of jack of all trades. Sometimes he worked as a barman, on other occasions as a steward, and if we'd organised a women's night, he'd get the older ones up to dance and have a carry-on with them, making them laugh and enjoy themselves. He was full of the fun, was Joe. But what happened to him was unbelievable. If he had continued to work for me, he would still be alive.

'There was one especially funny incident involving Joe and Billy McPhee. The pair of them were arguing in the bar one night. Suddenly, Billy bolted out the door, followed by Joe, who was carrying a shotgun. I gave Tam pelters for letting Joe have the gun until he gave me a little smile, opened his hand and showed me the shotgun cartridges. Joe didn't know it, but he was running around with an empty gun. The next night, Joe and Billy were back in the pub, laughing and joking together as though nothing had happened, and back to being the best of friends.'

Margaret also remembered Jonah McKenzie, who had once been a trusted friend: 'Jonah tried to have a foot in opposing camps and was warned that didn't work. After the fall out with Tam, he simply became a nutter. We all used to go to a little club in Barlanark, where the police and everyone else went for a quiet drink. There was never any hassle. Nobody caused the police any trouble, certainly, and they left everyone else alone until Jonah went out of control and smashed up a couple of the police motors – a panda car and one of the CID motors. That not only fucked it up for everybody, but brought down a lot of bad feeling on Jonah.

'Until he wrecked the cars, the police had an unwritten rule about the club: "Don't do anything here, and we'll not be in trouble. And if we're not in trouble, you won't be in trouble, either. If you want to do something wrong, go and do it somewhere else." But they had to explain what they were doing at the club when the cars were damaged, and from then on there were no favours. Gone were the days when Drew and the others could drive about without a licence.'

Margaret also recalled an occasion in which she witnessed relief and happiness being brought back into someone's life. From time to time, publicans would call on one another, mainly to catch up with the latest business gossip. During a visit to a neighbouring bar run by a landlady called Gina, Margaret noticed her friend ejecting a female customer. This woman was a regular at the same spiritualist church that Margaret attended. 'Gina, what's the script with you?' Margaret asked. 'That woman goes to my spiritualist church and is a really nice person.'

The reply shocked Margaret: 'She's my sister and must not have drink. Any time she comes in here, I put her out, and I'd be grateful if you would do the same.'

'Why?' Margaret asked.

'She'll start talking about her son and get very upset and depressed. He was found drowned in the River Clyde. He must have committed suicide. We've all tried to help her, but she'll just not accept assistance or advice.'

The woman's sorrow was made worse by the fact that the dead young man was her only child. Since his death, his mother had tortured herself, wondering whether she could have prevented his apparent suicide. Had he jumped into the river because of something she had done?

In the months that followed, Margaret watched the woman at every spiritualist meeting until one night the medium gently pointed his hand at the grieving mother and asked politely, 'Can I come to you? I have someone here for you.' He described a young man who the woman knew to be her boy. 'He was very close to you,' the medium continued. 'He says he is here to tell you that what happened to him was just an accident, purely and simply an accident. He just fell into the water. There was nothing he or anyone else could do. He wants you to know that and asks for you to take his love.'

Margaret was overjoyed and could see the happiness the mother felt, her face flooded with tears of joy. She ran to her car and drove straight to Gina's bar with the good news. 'Your nephew came through,' said Margaret. 'Now at last your sister knows the truth.'

As she contemplated the site where her pub had once stood, Margaret also remembered the new friends she and Tam had made at The El Paso – Gordon Ross, Manny McDonnell, Trevor Lawson and so many others: 'The El Paso, the Caravel, call it what you will, although to most people it remained the Paso, was a big part of all of our lives. I spent ten years running it but in the end was glad to be rid of it.'

20

LEARNING TO READ

I N 1967, WHEN GORBALS-BORN JIMMY BOYLE WAS JAILED FOR LIFE for the murder of Babs Rooney, men and women unable to meet debt payments could find themselves staring into a mirror at slashed cheeks or looking at hands through which knives had pinned them to bar counters. Businessmen who refused to meet protection levies might find gangs rampaging through their shops or bars, leaving their customers too terrified to return. Moneylending backed up by violence was the standard mode of life for ordinary hoodlums. Two and a half decades on, however, times were changing. The murders of Thompson, Hanlon and Glover made certain of that. Even Jimmy Boyle became not just respectable, but a celebrity, an admired sculptor and novelist, his company much sought after by party hostesses and art collectors alike.

Arthur Thompson, enraged by the loss of his son and his inability to settle with Paul Ferris – largely because Ferris was in jail, although prison bars had never in the past proved an obstacle to The Godfather – did the unthinkable. He collaborated with the police investigating Arty's death and actually went into the witness box at the Glasgow High Court to give evidence against Ferris, who had been accused of the shooting. Much to Arthur's fury, Ferris got off and was released. Arthur would never recover and died from a heart attack in 1993. His death would prompt a major shift in the nature of crime and of criminals in Glasgow.

In the 1980s, a new earner was introduced in Scotland. Quantities of cocaine were smuggled into the country from the Netherlands by a crew who became known as the 'Happy Dust Gang' but whose activities were smashed by the jailing for four years of one of the ringleaders, Glasgow baker Andrew 'Big Andy' Tait, in 1982. The problem for the pedlars was that cocaine was relatively expensive and its sale therefore limited. Few in the working classes could afford it. Cannabis was the opposite. It was comparatively cheap, had a ready market, and Spanish-based representatives of the Moroccan producers were easy to find and begging to sell. Moneylending was an openly nasty form of crime that targeted the working classes and the poor. Moneylenders were unpopular, reviled as little more than low-life scum. Drug trafficking, on the other hand, was a more clandestine crime, and while the introduction of heroin in particular would ultimately lead to a torrent of shootings and murders, violence rarely touched the early hash smugglers or the subversive world in which they operated.

Gordon Ross was one of the early traffickers. Hearing on the grapevine that others were making a cosy if not princely return on their hash rackets, he threw in his lot with a pal, and in the late 1980s the pair drove an ageing car to southern Spain, found a dealer, haggled, handed over cash, filled the seats and roof of the motor, and drove back to Glasgow. The venture was tiring and sweaty but sufficiently profitable to encourage another successful operation. However, their luck ran out on a third trip. Their booty was discovered by Customs officers at Dover, and they were jailed for three years.

In between trips, Gordon often drank in The El Paso, but he knew that drugs were not allowed on the premises. Their discovery would cost Margaret her licence, and nobody would want to find out what the consequences would be for bringing them into the pub.

'Gordon got to know Tam, and then he was introduced to me,' says Margaret. 'He used to drink in another pub called The County, but it closed at midnight, so, like many others, Gordon would wander along to The El Paso and drink until two in the morning when the shutters came down. Although he was Tam's associate, Gordon and I became very friendly. While it was obvious that with his looks he'd never be short of a girlfriend, I think he might have found it difficult to talk to other women about his problems, so he'd bring these to me. I got them all, but I didn't mind, because he was very easy to get along with in those early days.'

Back in Glasgow after serving eighteen months of his three-year sentence, Gordon was undaunted. He called at The El Paso to visit Tam and told the elder man that he believed the enterprise would have succeeded but for the devastating effect a heavy load of hash had on a car making a long journey. Gordon was convinced the answer lay in having two vehicles: one to bring the hash from Spain to a halfway point, probably somewhere in France, and a second to bring it to Scotland from there. Prison had not diminished his enthusiasm for making quick money, but he was short of funds. Tam was happy to help him out. 'Pay me back when you can,' he told Gordon, slipping him a handful of notes.

Gordon's idea of a halfway point was not lost on Tam, who gave it considerable thought. He talked about it with a number of associates, including businessmen and long-time friends from the Barlanark Team, as well as a handful of trusted regulars from the pub. The idea of shuttle runs from Spain to a larger vehicle became increasingly attractive. Tam studied the potential operation from every angle. It would need money, hence the meetings with businessmen, but more than anything else it would require nerve. In the end, a team of around 30 became involved. Initially, cars drove consignments of cannabis from Malaga to a waiting Transit van, but when the amount being smuggled was increased, the contraband was transferred to a specially adapted coach that had carried a party of youngsters on an all-expenses-paid footballing holiday from Glasgow to Disneyland Paris.

This proved so successful and profitable that it was repeated several times. However, the smugglers then came up against an unexpected problem when youngsters began moaning that visits to Disneyland were becoming monotonous. It even became difficult to find sufficient numbers of children to fill the free holiday places. The answer was to find another destination, and southern Spain was chosen. In addition to offering a huge variety of holiday resorts, it had the added advantage that the gang's supplier was based in Malaga. Thus they could eliminate the long and often risky drive from the supplier to the coach. At the same time, the smugglers decided to increase their profits by enlarging the space available to carry drugs. As a result, by the mid-1990s, a newer, larger coach packed with kids on free holidays was regularly journeying from Glasgow to

Spain and returning with up to 710 kilos of hashish worth around £1.6 million hidden in storage space created by raising the seating.

The racket brought in vast amounts of cash. Each trip produced a profit in excess of £1 million. True, there was the constant fear of discovery. Vast amounts of Scottish currency, used to pay for supplies in Spain, was turning up there and in Gibraltar in banks and money exchanges, while in the Glasgow area some of the smugglers were less than discreet in splashing about their new-found wealth. Some even bought expensive new cars from the same supplier used by senior Strathclyde police officers.

What Tam did with his share, no one will ever know. He drove about in modest second-hand vehicles, dressed shabbily and kept a relative pittance in his bank account. Admittedly, the Mount Vernon home he shared with Margaret and William was big and comfortable, but it was bought by her before the beginning of the drugs racket and with earnings from her ice-cream vans and The El Paso.

Shortly after the purchase of the Carrick Road property, the couple decided on major renovations, work that would take almost a year, and it was only when the last workman moved out that they gave up the apartment in Burnett Road that had seen so many happy times. They might have delayed even longer before moving to Mount Vernon to allow their new home to be given a full-scale security check if they had been aware of one worrying incident. One night, a small team of detectives who had been carrying out surveillance duty in the area, although not on Tam, decided, out of curiosity, to take a look at the McGraws' new home. They were astonished by the scale of the alterations. The property was protected by builders' boards and displayed a notice warning that it was guarded by a security company. Neither caused the police to have a second thought. If they were caught snooping, they would simply claim to have spotted a prowler lurking in the grounds while passing and say that they were checking for any signs of an attempted or actual break-in. Any passer-by or neighbour aware of the police presence would have noticed that the search appeared to be concentrated on the interior of the property. The unofficial check unearthed no signs of an intruder or hidden cache of arms or money within.

Amazingly, while the smuggling operation was at its height, some members of the gang relied on Margaret to tell them whether the portents were promising or clouded in risk. One of her closest friends says, 'For a man who said he had no interest in her Tarot cards or any of her readings and who dismissed it as nonsense, Tam would often ask her if she would perform a reading for him. Those who knew what he was up to noticed that these requests usually coincided with one of the bus trips. He never told her why he wanted a reading. It was almost a casual aside to her that he wondered how the future was looking for him. "Gonnae see if there's any problem coming up, Margaret?" he'd say, and when she asked why he wanted to know, he would shrug off the request and say, "Just wondered, that's all."

'Margaret was not involved in the smuggling. In fact, she was deliberately kept out of the entire operation by Tam, who didn't want her getting into trouble if it went wrong and did not give her any of the money. But it's absolutely true to say that the running of the racket, which made a number of men millionaires and was the most successful that has ever come to light in Scotland, was based on predictions made during Tarot-card readings.

'Wee Trevor Lawson was the worst when it came to letting a turn of the card decide whether or not he should do something that could land him in prison for ten years. If he was off down to Carlisle or somewhere in Cumbria to do a pickup or a delivery, he would call on Margaret and say, "I have to do something, and I need you to tell me it's going to be all right." She'd say, "If it's anything to do with drugs, Trevor, forget it." He'd promise her that it wasn't: "Honest, it's not. It's just business, and I need to know if I'm doing the right thing." Then she'd say, "Oh, all right Trevor. Go and get my cards." He'd bring them and she'd tell him, "Just pick three cards, but, I warn you, if one is the tower, that's bad. The tower means destruction and false promises. It stands for disaster, so if it shows among the three, I wouldn't do whatever it is you are planning." Fortunately for Trevor, the tower never came up. Trevor was right in the middle of the whole drug-smuggling thing, but he was never caught red-handed while he followed Margaret's advice after she had consulted her cards.

'Margaret was never happy doing the cards for him, because she suspected that he was up to no good. He'd beg and plead, and she'd give in but warn him, "Look, I don't want to do this, Trevor, because one of these times I'm going to be wrong." But he would just shrug and say, "But you've never been wrong yet." She'd reply, "Look, everything seems OK." If the cards indicated that things might not go too well, Trevor would have a think about what she had told him and say, "Oh, Mags, that's a bit dodgy," and that turn wouldn't be done.

'Trevor was right into the cards. If he was asked to do something at short notice and there wasn't enough time for him to get to Glasgow to see Margaret, he would ring her up and say, "Do me a favour, Mags. Do the cards for me." She would tell him, "Trevor, I don't know what it is you are doing, but if you're so worried about it, just don't do it." Invariably, he'd tell her, "It's important. I have to do it. Just tell me everything is going to be all right." If Margaret asked, "What if I tell you it's not going to be all right?" he'd say, "Well, if that's how it looks then I just won't do it." And he wouldn't.

'Tam liked everybody to think he was different – that no matter what Margaret said about the cards, even if the reading was not good, he would go ahead anyway. He wanted everybody to think that going against her advice when others were about was a sure sign he was the boss. But those closest to him were pretty convinced that privately he always took the advice she offered. Margaret always tried to give the impression that she was just Tam's wife and was only telling him what the cards said when she was asked to do a reading. But some people thought that because Tam was known to ask for a reading and took the advice given, and because Trevor did as well, Margaret was the real boss.'

It was during a holiday in Tenerife with Margaret that Tam came up with the idea of using a coach for the smuggling operation. He later said that he had been enjoying a meal in Verde's and was watching youngsters craning their necks to see through the windows of their coaches as they passed when he wondered why operators did not simply raise the seating levels. He then realised what the space created could be used for. It took considerable willpower not to ask Margaret if they could cut short their break, but once back in Glasgow he immediately summoned the gang leaders and put forward his idea. It was immediately accepted, and a member was despatched to a car auction, where he purchased a second-hand vehicle under an assumed name. The necessary work envisaged by

Tam was carried out, and after a couple of successful runs, the coach was replaced by a newer and larger model.

It was shortly after the first coach was brought into use that Gordon escaped near disaster, and his experience resulted in a radical change of plan by the smugglers. He had agreed to do an additional run from Malaga to Disneyland Paris. Two cars were to be used, but, having reached Spain, he pulled out, at the insistence of his girlfriend, who said he looked tired and she would take his place, just as the loaded motors were about to set off for France. Both cars were caught by French police, and the three men involved were jailed. The girl jumped a bail hostel in southern France and fled back to Glasgow with a fake passport. When a shaken Gordon appeared at The El Paso to break news of the disaster to Tam, Margaret's husband persuaded the others that the coaches would drive direct to southern Spain in future, thus removing the need for car shuttles and therefore reducing the risks.

New faces were appearing. Manny McDonnell from Belfast came over to Glasgow to attend the wedding of a relative. He began calling into The Cottage Bar in Shettleston, where he met Paul Ferris, and Ferris in turn took him to The El Paso, where he was introduced to Tam and Margaret. Eventually, he would become part of the smuggling team.

Margaret, meanwhile, took every opportunity to head to Tenerife in search of the sun and away from the grim clouds that seemed to perpetually drop their rain on Glasgow. She and Tam would often be joined by old friends from the Barlanark Team or, occasionally, some of those participating in the hash smuggling. Indeed, it was sometimes difficult to walk into an island bar in Playa de las Américas and find a table not occupied by a party from Glasgow's East End.

One evening, while enjoying a few drinks in a bar in Torviscas, Margaret and Tam came across the Irish singing idol Daniel O'Donnell, who, like the McGraws, looked upon the island as a home from home. 'Daniel had a pal, Ben, who worked in the bar, and we knew him well because we were often among his customers,' says Margaret. 'One of our party spotted Daniel and told her boyfriend to ask him for his autograph for her mother, who was a real fan. Daniel agreed right away, was very polite and friendly, and everybody liked him. But you don't carry around paper and pens when you're on holiday. We didn't want Daniel to sign a beer mat, so somebody came up with the idea of him signing a Scottish pound note as we were hunting around for a scrap of paper. That's what Daniel did, and afterwards somebody wondered whether that made it the most valuable pound note in Scotland. Daniel was asked if he'd let us photograph him, and he was up for that as well. Tam had had a few beers, but the pair of them posed together. In fact, Daniel took quite a shine to Tam and made a point of coming over to speak to him whenever he saw us.'

The singer owned an apartment in Tenerife, and one day when she was sitting quietly in a restaurant with her husband, Margaret suggested to Tam that they should also become property owners. 'We come over here so often that it would avoid the hassle of booking up, and if we weren't using it, we could let the family or our friends stay,' she told him. They checked out dozens of apartments before deciding to buy a holiday home in Geranios, close to the bars they favoured, such as The Irish Rover, which was run by friends. Margaret says she bought the hideaway for £70,000 in 1996.

'I wanted to be near the sea, because I loved walking down to the beach every day and the drivers over there tend to be pretty naughty, to put it mildly, so didn't want to have to use a motor. Our apartment-block reception was within a few yards of our front door, where we could get meals or just have a quiet drink. To get to the port and beach we simply went through the back gate. It was ideal. Five minutes from the supermarket and five minutes from the shore. It was as perfect as we could have wished, with two bedrooms, a living room, a kitchen and a bathroom. We did a lot of work on it, installing a new bathroom, for instance, until it was exactly as I wanted it. But maybe it was too perfect, because it was an incentive to visit Tenerife at every opportunity, and we perhaps went there too often in the end.'

While the McGraws enjoyed their Atlantic sojourns, the Glasgow media began to speculate on who would take over the mantle from The Godfather following his death. A handful of names were tossed into the air, but one soon came to the fore: Tam McGraw. He was even given a nickname: 'The Licensee'. Suddenly, Margaret found her family in the spotlight. It was not something she welcomed.

21

BUNS AND PIES

POLICE WERE NEVER FAR AWAY FROM THE MCGRAWS, WHOSE underworld connections invited regular inspection. Tam and his reputation as a lawbreaker was always the cause. Margaret was never in trouble, but she had to bear an equal share, if not the lion's portion, of the pressure. Generally, she had a good relationship with the ordinary beat officers, lower-ranked police officers who had to work and even live in the East End and were therefore anxious not to unduly antagonise the community. It was most often the orders that constables and sergeants were given from on high that created bad feeling.

During the mid-1990s, the bus runs thrived. The only people grumbling were the youngsters, who moaned about the number of foreign holidays that their parents insisted on them taking and about the lack of variety in locations. From Disneyland Paris, the operation moved to the south of Spain and would ultimately transfer north to the Benidorm area.

The longer the scam continued and the more people involved, the higher the risk of exposure. But Tam was principally concerned about the extent of the 'expenses' being claimed by some of those recruited to run the Continental end of the operation. Eventually, he would take remedial steps to address the problem.

The holidays were said to be financed by a mysterious Irish benefactor, and there was inevitable gossip about his largesse and identity. It might have remained gossip had it not been for a police decision to target Paul Ferris, even though he was never involved in the cannabis runs. Ever since his acquittal over the shooting of Arty

Thompson, police had taken a greater than usual interest in him. In particular, the powers that be were keen to follow up information supplied by an associate of Ferris that he was heavily involved in the distribution of firearms. Police set up Operation Shillelagh to collate data about his movements and contacts. They listened in to his telephone conversations and noticed how often Manny McDonnell and cannabis trafficking were mentioned. At that time, detectives were conscious of a huge increase in the amount of the drug being imported into Scotland; it was readily available, and at £2,300 per kilo someone was clearly pocketing a fortune. Manny was wrongly believed to be masterminding the racket.

Despite their resources being stretched by Shillelagh, police decided to set up a second operation to catch the Irishman and his smugglers. It was called Operation Light Switch. According to some people, that name was chosen because one officer had said, 'Let's switch the lights out on this lot,' but according to others it was because a meeting of the traffickers at the Holiday Inn in Glasgow had been monitored using tiny bugging devices hidden in light switches.

Whatever the inspiration for its name, Operation Light Switch soon switched focus from Manny to Tam, who was known to be a top-rate organiser from his days leading the Barlanark Team. Police reasoned that if a crew was shipping huge amounts of hash to Glasgow, it would require someone capable of pulling together the various segments, including finance, collection and distribution. Intelligence specialists began reading through old reports from beat constables and traffic policemen detailing where they had seen Tam and who was with him. The telephone at Mount Vernon was tapped, teams of officers sitting in a basement room at police headquarters listening in to and recording conversations that were so trivial they were useless as evidence. Mobile-phone calls were monitored to ascertain with whom the McGraws talked and when. Finally, it was decided to go 'live', which meant not only listening in on the family, but watching and following their every movement.

The surveillance squad's efforts to remain undercover did not succeed. An attempt to secretly place a camera in a street lamp outside Margaret and Tam's front door was a bad start. When bemused neighbours asked why the technicians were busily carrying out repairs on the light and were told that the bulb was being replaced, they had to point out that it was actually the next one along that was faulty. The work continued regardless, and the broken light remained in the dark.

Margaret discovered that she could hardly move around the city without being accompanied by strangers: 'It was so obvious that they were police it was laughable at times. We knew right away whenever something was going on and that we had been put under surveillance. When I asked Tam if he had been bringing anything into the house that could cause us trouble, he assured me that the answer was no. And I believed him. No drugs or anything illegal came through my door. So as far as I was concerned, the police could sit out there in the street all day and all night – it didn't bother me. But it was impossible not to be aware of it. The police only have a limited number of motors, and they watched and followed us about for months, so it was inevitable that the same cars kept appearing over and over, stopping when we stopped and the people in them pretending to be taking an interest in something or somebody else.

'Just to let them know they weren't forgotten, I began giving them a wee wave. When I went shopping, they'd be in the street waiting, and they'd even go into the shops with me. One day, I went to the Forge Shopping Centre near Celtic Park. I was there for about five hours, and when I was ready to leave, I asked a friend to do me a favour. I pointed to the car with the police sitting in it and asked her if she'd nip over and let them know I was about to go home. When she did, the police looked so sheepish. Another time, they followed me into Thornton's, the chocolate shop, and I turned to a policewoman and said, "Go on, give me a sweet." She was so astonished that she just burst out laughing. They knew I knew they were there, and we kind of got to know each other, because it seemed to be the same team most of the time. I knew and they knew that they were wasting their time, but I suppose they were just following orders.

'Sometimes it was irritating. I was sitting having a coffee one morning at the Forge. The place was empty apart from a friend and me, but these two cunts came and sat at the very next table. I said to my companion, "Don't say a thing. They're coppers. They must like me, because they want to sit beside me." Then I said to them, "Join us if you want." They were clearly embarrassed and trying not to look, so I asked them again: "Come on. Your bosses aren't watching. Come over and join us." But, of course, they didn't. As we were leaving, I said to them, "Radio back to your pals waiting outside my house in Carrick Drive that I'm leaving now and will be back there in ten minutes." It was stupid. Even if I had known anything, there was no chance at all of me talking about it when they were sitting next to me. This sort of thing went on for months.

'I could never understand why they imagined they were invisible, because it was patently obvious who they were. It was a waste of time them watching me. The thing was, I'd gone through this sort of thing before when Tam was with the Barlanark Team. The boys used to tell me that when they were doing shops they would tune into police frequencies to find out what the coppers were up to, who they were chasing, who they were tailing, who they were eyeballing – it was normally Tam's team. Tam and the boys loved to manoeuvre themselves so that they ended up tailing the police. They'd have a right laugh when they heard comments such as "Fuck's sake, they're chasing us now" on the coppers' radios.

'That crowd, those in the Serious Crime Squad, were a total scream. They'd be on duty at night, and we'd listen in on them talking to each other. One of them was named Christina, and she seemed to favour an East End bakery called Greens. We'd hear them saying stuff like, "Christina's going for half a dozen hot-cross buns," or "We're going down to Greens for pies." For a laugh, I'd shoot down to Greens and ask them, "How many of you are there tonight?" Or when I was leaving the bakery as they were going in, I'd say, "I see there's six of you on this evening," because I'd heard them talking a few moments earlier about how many pies or buns Christina would need to buy. They took all of this as a joke, because it was just funny. The spoilsports then went and changed the waveband so that we couldn't listen in any longer. But being able to overhear them had given us years of laughs, and I genuinely liked a lot of the people in the crime squad.

'I'd turn up somewhere and tell them, "I'm watching you," and they'd say, "You're listening to the radio, aren't you?" I'd admit it, telling them, "Of course I am. I've got nothing else to do. I like to know what you're up to, because you're always sitting at my door watching me." When they drove past, I'd even give them a wee wave, and they'd wave back. When they sat watching, I'd go over and ask, "What's the script with you? We know you're here. He's not going to be out and about breaking into post offices when he knows you are watching, is he?" If they were sitting outside the house, I'd make a point of going over to them and saying, "Look, I'm going out to the butcher's to get a bone for the dog. Give me your order, and I'll get it when I'm there." There were even times when I'd ask, "When are you going to drop in for tea and toast?" But you couldn't joke with the Drugs Squad, even after they gave up trying to hide and just wandered about with me. In the end, I'd go over to them and tell them where I was going and how long I'd be.

'There had been a time when you could have a laugh with the police, but then new squads were introduced. These were usually specialist units, often staffed by men and women who didn't know or understand the East End or the people living there. These were only interested in making names for themselves, getting promotion, making lots of arrests. You couldn't stop and have a chat with them, because they were strangers with no sense of humour at all.'

The surveillance might have been indiscreet, but it was also intense, with the Serious Crime Squad and Drugs Squad officers joined by investigators from Customs and Excise. However, Margaret was able to move about freely and without fear of causing problems for Tam for the simple reason that she knew nothing of the bus team's arrangements. She continued meeting the same friends as before, but made sure that she was discreet, especially when talking on the phone, and that Tam was, too. Neither was to know it then, but her caution would pay rich dividends.

22

SAMURAI SWINDLE

MARGARET WAS DETERMINED THAT THE SURVEILLANCE WOULD NOT prevent her from carrying on with life as normal. And that included holidays. She realised that if she was being watched at home, it was odds on that the attention would continue wherever she was. But that was not her problem. If the police wanted to send their units to Tenerife, that was their business.

Extracts from police surveillance logs show just how intense their desire to trap Tam and how extensive the coverage of his and Margaret's movements were while detectives hunted for evidence that would expose him as the mastermind behind the racket that had cannabis flooding into central Scotland. On numerous occasions throughout 1995 to 1997, they were spotted coming and going from Glasgow to Belfast and Tenerife. Virtually every trip prompted some talking point or another. Margaret's visit to Belfast for a wedding in 1995, for instance, was hard to forget: 'Like everybody else, I'd read about the violence in Belfast – the bombs and shootings – and I'd seen television pictures of some of the terrible things that were going on. But when we booked into the Europa in the city centre, trouble seemed a million miles away. One of our friends knew a member of the hotel staff, and we invited him to join us for a drink when he was off duty. He was a really nice, quiet guy until he got into his stories. I asked him, "Have you worked here long?" and he said, "Oh no, not long, but I know the Europa very well indeed." I thought he must have been a frequent visitor. "Oh, you used to come in here for a drink or a meal?" I asked. I nearly fell off my seat when I heard his answer: "Oh no,

Margaret. I've bombed it three times. The commanders kept giving the job of blowing it up to me. Later, I was looking for work, and when I got a letter asking me to turn up at the labour exchange, I was told there was a job for me at the Europa. They even asked if I knew it or needed a map, and I had to tell them I knew the hotel very well." Later on, I found out the Europa was the most bombed hotel in the world. It had been blown up 70 times.

'I asked him what the IRA was like, and he told me stories about some of the activities that he and others had been involved in. He and some of the other members were eyeing up a bank job and wanted to make sure that everything went well when they did the robbery two weeks later. They spent a lot of time and took considerable care making sure they had planned every detail: what the exact layout of the bank was, how many people worked there, when and how it was opened and by whom, what the opening and closing hours were, how many people would be needed to switch off the alarm system when the doors were opened, what type of security system was in operation, what type of safe was installed, how many security men were usually on duty, and so on.

'The preparation was intensive, and the unit got together a whole load of equipment ready to bypass alarm systems and cut into the safe. Their plan was to break in one Friday night after the bank was closed and spend the best part of a weekend inside, taking their time to clean it out of every penny. Having done all the ground work, they stayed clear for a few days so as not to be spotted and arouse suspicions. Unfortunately for them, when they turned up on the Friday, they found that the bank was closed for refurbishment and everything had been removed earlier that day and taken somewhere else by the bank staff.'

During that visit to Ulster, Tam announced to Margaret that he wanted to visit Donegal. They took along a friend by the name of John Hughes. He and his wife Mary were long-time friends of the McGraws. Once in the town, Tam opened an account with the Allied Irish Bank, arranging to deposit a substantial amount of cash. British banks, including those in Northern Ireland, insisted on knowing the source of large cash deposits, a demand resulting from pressure not only by the London government, but by police determined to make life difficult for criminals wanting to launder money. Donegal, in the

Republic of Ireland, had no such restrictions on customers looking for a safe place to bank their loot with no questions asked.

Friends believed that Tam and the others involved in the bus runs had huge sums of loose cash wallowing about. Gordon Ross and Trevor Lawson, for example, confided to pals that they had stuffed massive amounts of high-denomination notes into paint tins, which they had then buried.

While in Donegal, Tam looked around the town, in particular at The Paradise Bar, a small pub that was in need of a lick of paint. Tam had heard that the pub was up for sale, and when he asked John Hughes for advice, he was told, 'Buy it.' Neither Tam nor Margaret went inside. The following January, The Paradise Bar was bought for £135,000 with money provided by Tam, a transaction that was noted by police in the Republic. It was reopened with a gala night. The drink flowed and the music rocked the little building. Television personalities, including cast members of various soaps, and a couple of football stars turned up, and the night was remembered for having raised thousands of pounds in aid of the town's football club. After that, Tam and some of the other smugglers paid an occasional visit, but it would turn out to be one of his less successful ventures.

Margaret had good cause to remember her visit to another wedding in Belfast a year later on 12 July. She and Tam had become good friends with Manny and his wife, who had relatives who lived on the notorious New Lodge estate, a scheme regarded as being out of bounds to the army and police. Strathclyde Police had arranged with the Royal Ulster Constabulary for checks to be made on him when he initially came under the spotlight during Operation Light Switch. Margaret and her party were shadowed all the way to the New Lodge estate because police in Glasgow wanted to know why they were going to trouble-ravaged Belfast. So did the Royal Ulster Constabulary.

It was hardly ideal to hold a wedding on 12 July. Rioters were running amok throughout the city, furious at a decision by the police to do a U-turn and allow a highly controversial Orange walk to go ahead at Drumcree near Portadown. Plastic bullets were flying, and at least three policemen were shot and injured. A bullet fired by a terrorist sniper pierced the door of a police Land Rover, ricocheting off an officer's helmet and into his arm.

Margaret had seen an East End rammy but nothing like this: 'I remember waking up, listening to the news and hearing that the whole of Belfast was on fire. There were cars ablaze everywhere. At breakfast, I said to Manny, "How are we going to get to the wedding? Everybody's motor's on fire. I really wouldn't like to go out in a car and come out of the wedding to find it in flames." Manny didn't seem at all worried. "Margaret, all the cars are burning so the owners can make insurance claims," he said. "The British government pays if your property is damaged or destroyed during civil disturbances. So, when trouble starts, everybody torches their car and then gets the money back from the government by claiming the IRA or Ulster Volunteer Force or one of the other mobs has torched it. One of the advantages of rioting is that if your motor is on its last legs, you can get a new one." That was a real eye-opener. The wedding went off without a hitch.'

Three months earlier, Tam had announced to Margaret that he needed to fly to Belfast with Gordon and Trevor for a meeting with Manny. He would not tell her the purpose. In fact, the get-together was to seek advice from the Irishman on recruiting an enforcer who would be based in Spain for the bus trips. Expenses had been spiralling out of control. Smugglers already making fortunes were getting greedy and charging astronomical sums for living expenses and accommodation. The task of the newest member of the team, in addition to keeping an eye on expenses, was to collect the cash brought over by couriers and buy the drugs, ensuring that the merchandise was loaded discreetly and safely the night before it was due to return. For each trip, depending on the load, he would receive around £10,000.

Margaret remembers one outcome of the visit: 'Tam liked browsing around second-hand and antique shops. He had a few hours to spare after his meeting, and while he was meandering in and out of shops with the others, he came across one with a pair of what were advertised as antique Samurai swords hanging in the window. Tam liked to give the impression that he was a bit of an expert on antiques and gave the swords a thorough examination before asking the price. The guy wanted something like £700 but eventually settled for £500. Tam also had his eye on a Second World War German soldier's helmet and bought that as well.

'He brought the lot back home and insisted on mounting the swords on a wall. Whenever he got wind of trouble, he'd take them with him, so they were off the wall more than they were on it. He decided to get them insured and was asked to have them valued. When the valuation came back, he was livid. They were worth £15 for the pair. Tam called Manny and demanded that the next time he came over to Glasgow he collect them, take them back to the shop in Belfast and get a refund. Manny returned with them, but it turned out that the shop was run by the IRA in aid of their funds and had a no-money-back rule. He thought better than to argue with them.'

Tam's visits to Belfast would result, some years later, in wild speculation in the media that he had struck up a friendship with terrorist leader Johnny 'Mad Dog' Adair and his wife Gina. One story claimed that Tam had taken Gina on a shopping trip through Glasgow. In fact, the McGraws never met either of them.

23

MALTESERS

IN EARLY SEPTEMBER 1997, MARGARET SENSED THAT SOMETHING WAS troubling her husband. Unusually, she decided to do a card reading to see what lay in store for her: 'The only time I do the cards for myself is if I want to know something, normally because I've had a feeling that something's not right. I don't sit and do the cards continually, every day. Sometimes I don't touch them for months at a time, but when I think there's a need to know something, that I sense all isn't right, then I will get the cards out.

'I didn't know what Tam was involved in, but if there was something terrible coming, I preferred to know about it. So I did a reading and turned over the tower card. I knew right away that something awful was in store. The tower tells you that after some significant and inevitable event, your life will never be the same, that you're frankly going to have a cunt of a life from then on. I said to Tam, "Look, I don't know what's going on, but whatever it is finish it now. If you're running something, don't run it any more. The tower card tells me that it's going to end in disaster and people, you included, will go to prison. I have a bad, bad feeling. Everybody concerned will end up in jail." Tam didn't want to listen, so that's how it was left, but I knew something terrible was coming.'

On 21 September, a coach carrying a party of youngsters and their mothers left Glasgow and headed for Spain. That same night, at eight o'clock, Margaret, Tam and a group of friends were spotted by police at Glasgow Airport taking a flight to Tenerife. A week later, having journeyed back through Spain and France and having crossed the English Channel to Dover, the bus was stopped by police as it was on the outskirts of Glasgow, and a search revealed a relatively small amount of cannabis, less than one-seventh of a full load. The arrests began.

Tam received a telephone call to his mobile in Tenerife that broke the news to him. Margaret knew straight away that something had happened. When she asked what was wrong, he had no alternative but to tell her about the bus trips and drug smuggling. She was furious and reminded him about their conversation a fortnight earlier: 'I shouted at him, "I told you something was going to happen and still you sent that bus, that fucking bus. Didn't I warn you? The tower card was there, and it meant as soon as that bus left, disaster was going to follow." He said, "Well there hasn't been any hassle up until now." I said, "Everything falls into place now. Just before we came out here, I did another reading. All the cards were court cards, which told me that whatever it was that was going wrong would involve people who are our friends. You're going to jail along with loads of your friends." I then said that nothing could be done to change what was about to happen.

'Tam said, "I think we'll just stay in Tenerife." But I refused, because our son William and his wife Mandy were with us, and like me they had absolutely nothing to do with the buses. I said, "Look, Tam, you stay for as long as you like, but I'm going home. You knew all of this was coming up, because I warned you. You have to understand that you and a whole load of others are going to jail." He thought about this and decided to return to Glasgow with the rest of us.'

The family flew back to Glasgow on 10 October. Their return was watched by the police, but Tam was not arrested, although others were. Margaret had demanded that he tell her the complete story of the buses and give her the names of all those involved. Some she knew, others were strangers. Then she took to an upstairs room of their home and laid out her cards.

A few minutes later, she returned. 'You're going to prison for a while Tam,' she said, 'but you won't be going to jail at the end of this. A lot of you will spend time in prison, but I think just three are going down.' Tam had mentioned John Healy, and after looking at her cards, she knew he was one of the three. She was not certain who the other two would be. Had she been on the same friendly and

familiar terms with them as she was with John Healy, she might have
been better able to discern who they were.

There was nothing anyone could do to halt the inevitable police
trawl as it netted more and more of their friends. Just over a week
later, Margaret and Tam returned to Tenerife, coming home on Guy
Fawkes Night. Still he was not arrested, but fireworks exploded in
Belfast when police from Glasgow travelled over there to haul Manny
McDonnell into their net. Six weeks after the bus had been stopped,
two detectives and a Customs and Excise investigator flew across the
Irish Sea to perform the task. Detailed surveillance and monitoring
of telephone calls had revealed where he was staying on the New
Lodge estate. It was a rough, tough, passionately republican area at
the best of times and hardly needed the inevitable fallout from one
of their own being dragged off to Scotland by the police.

The trio first made a courtesy call on the Royal Ulster Constabulary
at the heavily protected North Queen Street Police Station, where
they were shown into the office of a senior officer. They explained
that they were on their way to the New Lodge estate to detain
Manny and take him back to Scotland for questioning about a huge
hash-smuggling racket. A Royal Ulster Constabulary officer later
told Manny what happened next.

'Who's with you?' the senior officer wanted to know.

'Well, there's the three of us.'

'Yes, I can see that, but where are the others?'

'Others?'

'You've got others with you, surely?'

'No. What for?'

'You ever been to the New Lodge?'

'No. Why?'

'The three of you are going to New Lodge to arrest an Irishman
and take him back to Scotland?'

'That's the idea.'

'You're kidding. Three of you?'

'Yes. Is there a problem?'

'You could say that.'

The senior officer was finding it hard to hide his amazement.
Fighting the urge to burst into laughter, he told his visitors, 'Listen,
you'll need around 50 men if you're going in there. Who the fuck

sent three of you over here to do this?' Despite not getting an answer, he agreed to take the Scots to the New Lodge estate, where, with the help of the army, the contingent arrived in a fleet of armoured vehicles. The operation was not helped by the fact that the Scots initially went to the wrong address. Choice words from the occupant there directed them to Manny's door, where the plan to smash it down and snatch their quarry was immediately foiled because it was reinforced by a steel gate.

Following a series of discussions through the letterbox, the door was opened so that the callers could explain their presence. Despite protestations that those inside refused to recognise the authority of the British police, Manny was told he was being arrested and would be taken to Glasgow. He was seized, handcuffed and taken away, his head covered by a hood and his captors fleeing under a hail of stones, bottles, pots, pans and broken teacups. At another Belfast police station, his inquisitors told him that they would be tape recording the interview and asked him for his name and address and whether he had anything to say.

'I am being kidnapped by the British and taken to Britain against my will. I need help,' he later told me he replied. He was told he would be flown to Glasgow. 'If you put me on a plane, I'll attack any passenger within range and cause absolute havoc,' he warned.

'How do you think you'll do that?'

'Try it, mister, and see what happens.'

The Royal Ulster Constabulary knew from past experience that Manny was capable of creating mayhem. At the age of only seventeen, he had spent two years in the notorious Maze Prison after being convicted of possessing documents that would be of use to terrorists, and along with a group of other Irishmen had later been arrested in Cricklewood, north London, held for a week and deported under the Prevention of Terrorism Act.

After a hurried conference with the trio from Glasgow, he was driven 40 miles to Larne and taken by ferry to Stranraer, shackled to a bunk in a cabin for the duration of the crossing. It was a bizarre scene. Throughout the trip, he insisted upon singing republican songs while his captors pelted him with Maltesers.

Manny was held in the remand wing of Barlinnie Prison in Glasgow's East End. Meanwhile, Margaret waited for the knock on the door that would herald the start of Tam's ordeal. When nothing happened, her husband flew off to Spain to visit friends, returning late on 28 November. The police were again watching. At seven o'clock the next morning, loud knocks shook their front door. Margaret opened it to find a crowd of policemen and women standing there. One of them showed her a warrant, empowering them to search her home. Tam was roused from bed, arrested, handcuffed and immediately taken away, calling to Margaret over his shoulder, 'Mags, get my lawyer.'

'The police were mob-handed,' she remembers. 'They had video recorders and announced they would be filming everything, presumably so there would be no possibility of us disputing anything they said about the search later on. They filmed what they were doing and were in the house for around five hours. Whenever they did a search, they asked me to be in the room at the same time, and I wondered if this had anything to do with the letters I'd written to the Queen, telling her the police had fitted Tam up. They even took away all the correspondence I'd had with Buckingham Palace and all the letters that I had received as a result of my appeals to the Queen. What they wanted those for, I could never work out.

'After a while, I told them, "You'll need to stop recording. I need a cup of coffee. Your fucking getting me up at this time of the morning has meant I haven't had time for one, and I have to have my coffee." They were searching in one of the other rooms, and the coffee was in the kitchen. One of them said, "You'll have to wait until we are finished here." I said, "That'll be fucking right. You keep that fucking video tape going because I'm having coffee. This is my house. Charge me with something or let me get my kettle on. You had no right to get me up at seven o'clock in the morning when I've done nothing wrong." He said, "Oh, Mrs McGraw, don't get upset. Just go and make your coffee. We could be doing with a wee cup ourselves." I replied, "Well, you'll have to go to the Little Chef or somewhere else, won't you?" If they hadn't been so cheeky, I would have made them coffee. I then said, "You're wasting your time, because you'll find nothing here, and, in any case, Tam will not be done for anything. Remember what I've said."

'During the search, I noticed them hunting through my cupboards and saw one of the policewomen reading her horoscope in one of my books. She got a real jolt when she realised I'd spotted her. I said, "What right have you to come in here and waste my time and then start reading my books?" She said, "Could you do my cards sometime?" I said, "As soon as you leave here, I'll do them." She wanted to know how that was possible if she wasn't present, and I explained, "As long as I know what you look like, it's no problem. I'll just tuck your image away in my mind for when I do your cards." I knew her face anyway. She'd been on the surveillance team that had spent months following me around.

'Some days later, the police came back, and this same woman was with them. As well as the Royal letters, they'd gone off with photographs they'd found in books and albums they had searched through, presumably in case we'd been hiding anything in those. They wanted to know who were in the photographs, and I told them the were just of friends. When they asked again, I said, "You know the law of possession. You have them, so you figure out who they are." The police would try anything, but the thing was to just ignore them.

'The policewoman asked if I'd done her cards, and when I said that I had, she wanted to know what was going to happen. I said, "I'm not saying this just to be spiteful, but in this trial three women will give evidence. That's all the witnesses you've got. Of those three, two will be no use to you, and you'll be left with just one. My man's not going to jail." At that, she said, "So you think we're wasting our time?" I said, "I'm fucking telling you, you're wasting your time." She then said, "What about me? Did you do my cards?" and I told her a lot of personal information about herself and her family, stuff she clearly didn't want to know, because she said, "I don't want to hear any more." I said, "And I'm telling you, Tam's not going to jail." I'd seen this woman before but had never met her, yet she told me, "I believe you." I decided not to tell her the full extent of the considerable unhappiness the cards showed she was about to experience, so instead said, "You're going to be in for a hard time, hen. People are going to jail, but Tam's not going to be one of them."'

24

KNOWING THE FUTURE

DESPITE THE THOROUGHNESS OF THEIR SEARCH, THERE WAS ONE ITEM the police could not have found but which they would have loved to have got their hands on. Margaret is a skilled and experienced pupil of Tarot-card readings. But like any keen student, she is always keen to learn from others. Over the years she has come to discover which mediums are good and which are probably to be avoided. One whom she still enjoys visiting is uncannily accurate. It was to her that Margaret turned after Tam's arrest, some might say for a second opinion. This medium, called Anna, is so confident of the messages she receives and the information she imparts that she writes down her predictions on lined paper.

'I did the cards a few times then I went to see this medium who had a small shop in the East End of Glasgow,' Margaret says. 'I'd always thought she was brilliant, but even then I was amazed by what she told me. Although Tam and most of the others had been arrested, they had not been tried. As a result, nothing had been published about what it was the police were alleging they had been involved with. Yet when I asked how things were for us, she came up with buses, bars of hash, children and money. She wrote everything down, and I took the sheets home to read over again later. But after the first search, I decided to get rid of them, because if the police had come back and found them, I have no doubt they would have tried to make something of them and might even have used them against us. They weren't evidence, but we were not going to take a chance. After all, who was going to believe me if I said, "That's just what a fortune teller told me"? So I burned them. She knew who was going to prison. And like me, she knew that three women were involved.'

The police spent months gathering evidence in Scotland and Spain, and the homes of more than 40 suspects were searched. At the Pitt Street headquarters of Strathclyde Police, the force intelligence unit took over two spare rooms on the sixth floor. Computers were installed and a team of analysts sometimes ten strong worked for weeks going over the telephone bills of all the suspects. They were trying to establish that the suspects had been in regular contact but, more incriminatingly, that contact had been at its height at times when the buses were about to leave and then when they arrived. Much was made of mobile-phone calls between Tam and John Healy, and in the end they were accused of being the masterminds of the trafficking operation. Prosecutors decided to try the suspects in three groups, working on the assumption that if the first were found guilty it would be a pointer to the likely fate of the others. The first 11 were Tam, John Healy, Manny McDonnell, Gordon Ross, Margaret's old van boy Billy McPhee, Trevor Lawson, Graeme Mason, known as 'Del Boy' because he looked like the lead character in the television sitcom *Only Fools and Horses*, John Wood, Michael 'Benji' Bennett, who had been driving the coach when it was stopped by the police, John Burgon and Arthur Askey lookalike Paul Flynn from Rochdale in Lancashire.

Margaret visited Tam each day in Barlinnie, but they were both wary of being too forthcoming. The police were suspected of using dirty tricks to get evidence, and one firm of lawyers had even made an official complaint that bugging devices had been discovered in its offices. Margaret again wrote to the Queen, echoing her complaints from the past and telling her how sure she was that Tam was going to be fitted up once again. She received a reply that suggested she contact the secretary of state for Scotland, which she did only to be told that Buckingham Palace had forwarded him her letter and that he had sent it on to the Strathclyde Police. Taking no chances, Margaret wrote again, this time to Chief Constable John Orr, warning him that she believed his men would plant evidence on Tam, and she also sent a copy to the Scottish Office. Despite this, a number of the accused men would later claim that their telephone records were tampered with.

Tam had told her about the false floors in the buses and how the racket operated. 'I never knew if it was all Tam's idea,' she says. 'It seemed to begin with lorries carrying hashish from Spain to the Manchester area, and then someone had a brainwave and suggested using buses. From that developed a plan to fill the coaches with youngsters, which led to kids' football teams being given the chance to go abroad and play in tournaments for free.

'Tam was on remand for seven months. He always hated prison, and even though he was often inside, he always found it an ordeal. Quite simply, he missed home and my cooking. He lost a lot of weight and started to look drawn and gaunt.

'Whenever I went to see him, all I heard were moans and groans, with him constantly wondering if he needed an extra lawyer, telling me to see about this and that and wanting to know what the police were up to. He was the world's worst defendant, but he had been warned that if he was convicted, he should expect a sentence of not less than 14 years. Tam thought he'd end up getting 24. I was there every day except Sunday and spent most of my time trying to reassure him that everything was going to be OK. I told him, "Tam, as soon as you were arrested, I did a reading. It said you were going to prison, but I'd already told you that weeks before. Take it from me, you will get out. You're not going away for years and years. A few are going to have a bad time of it, but it will work out all right for you and most of them. But I don't think John Healy is going to be coming home when you do. The cards don't look good for him."

'The police set out to give Tam a bad time of it. They segregated him from the others in the "Barlinnie Wendy House" to try and make them believe that he was doing some sort of deal for himself, but it only gave Tam more time to study the evidence against him.'

With the start of the trial in April 1998 imminent, the accused who were still in custody were transferred to Saughton Prison to be nearer the High Court in Edinburgh. They had learned to be wary of strangers trying to make friends, although it was difficult not to like some of the remand inmates with whom they came into daily contact. One man had been warned by his advocate to expect 14 years for an armed bank robbery. 'I didn't do it,' he constantly protested in broad Glaswegian. 'Didn't do it, and I'm looking at 14 years.' His pleadings won sympathy until he added, 'I didn't do it. Didn't pull my fucking mask down far enough, and the security camera caught me full on.' The man's lawyer repeated his client's view of events in court and wondered whether the judge would appreciate his honesty. Whether or not the judge was influenced, the sentence passed down was not fourteen but seven years, much to the delight of the villain. They were also joined by a Finn by the name of Kari Paajolahti, who told them that he was awaiting deportation after having been caught stealing. In reality, Paajolahti was a plant who had been promised immunity from prosecution and had even been presented with a formal document by Customs investigators giving him permission to carry out petty crimes in exchange for infiltrating the smugglers and trying to worm their secrets from them. The ploy did not work.

Did knowing that her husband was going to walk free make Margaret any happier? 'No, because from the moment he was arrested and I did the cards, I knew I was going to have to go to the jail every day to visit him and listen to him greeting and moaning. And I mean greeting and moaning. Regardless of how many times I told him not to worry, he did.'

Margaret did not attend the trial. There was no point, because there was a possibility that the defence might call her as a witness, and, as such, she was not allowed to listen to evidence. Every day when court recessed, one of Tam's lawyers, Liam O'Donnell or Brian Geraghty, would telephone her with a progress report. 'They wanted to keep me up to date and give an idea how things were going,' she says. 'Sometimes Liam would admit to getting slightly nervous about the outcome, but I'd tell him, "Liam, I'm not the least apprehensive. Take my word for it: Tam's not getting the jail. Count on it." Brian would say, "What if we do this?" or "What do you think of that?" and I'd tell him, "Brian, it doesn't matter what you do. He's not getting jailed." He'd joke, "You got a judge somewhere who knows something?" and I'd say, "No, I don't need one. I know." I'd told them this throughout the time Tam was on remand. The cards said that he was not going to prison, so it didn't matter what Liam, Brian or Tam's QC, Donald Findlay, did or said, Tam was coming home. And the cards are never wrong.'

The cards also turned out to be right in their predictions about the three principal prosecution witnesses. Only one, they said, would be of any value. It had been expected that the evidence of policewoman

Kate Jackson and that of Hannah Martin and Caroline Dott would firmly hammer closed the cell doors on all of the accused men. Jackson said that she and another woman officer had overheard an incriminating conversation in a Chinese restaurant in Glasgow between Tam, John Healy and Manny. As the three men talked, she had written notes on a paper napkin. Crucially, she could not produce this vital piece of evidence. Unfortunately, a waiter had spilled water on the napkin, she said, and it had been lost. Even more unfortunate for the prosecution was a statement from the restaurant manager who pointed out that his napkins were made of cloth.

Caroline Dott and Gordon Ross had set up home after he had split up with his wife, Elizabeth. Caroline was the mother of one of his sons, and the couple had been passionate about one another. Although their relationship was on the wane by the time of the trial, she was a nervous wreck in the period leading up to it, knowing that she might have to give evidence that would sink the man she loved into a grave of concrete and iron bars. She didn't want to be called and was too distressed to be of any value to the prosecution.

Hannah Martin was selling catalogues around Glasgow housing schemes when she knocked on the door of Graeme Mason. That night, they made love, and he boasted that he was the mastermind behind a huge drug-smuggling plot. Hannah later fell in love with his friend John Healy after she and Mason fell out and parted in acrimony. In the witness box, she did her best to destroy Mason and Benji Bennett – in the case of one, she succeeded with a vengeance.

By the time the trial finished in July 1998, Margaret and the cards were once again proved uncannily accurate. Tam and seven others walked free. The news was not good for the others, though. Heartbroken Hannah Martin heard on the radio that John Healy had been jailed for ten years. She shed no tears over the eight years handed down to Mason, while Paul Flynn was sentenced to six years.

As Tam walked from the courthouse, his long-time friend John Malloy by his side, and headed to a waiting car to be driven home at last, he looked thin and tired to the point of being ill. Margaret was waiting for him. Liam O'Donnell had telephoned to tell her that the jury had returned a 'Not proven' verdict, but it was news she'd expected: 'I was already cooking Tam's favourite meal of mince and tatties when he walked through the door. Naturally, I was happy, but I'd known what the outcome would be for months. Some of Tam's friends arrived with him, and then well-wishers came around to congratulate him. I made enough mince and tatties for everybody.'

Although the trial had a happy outcome for them, it marked something of a watershed in the lives of the McGraws. Margaret and Tam's relationship was deteriorating. She had stood loyally by him, but close friends noticed that she had forced herself not to let him see her own worries after her husband's arrest.

During his trial, it was claimed that Tam had a healthy income but never paid income tax. Later, one section of the media would announce that Tam had stumped up £300,000 to appease the taxman. That was not the case. An examination of his affairs yielded nothing for the Exchequer. Officially, Tam had no assets. Had he been convicted, the family would have faced the prospect of Crown Office financial specialists trying to force Margaret to prove that the money that had paid for the Mount Vernon house had been genuinely earned by her. If she had failed, she would have been left homeless, something for which she would never have forgiven Tam.

A man who kept determinedly up to date with all the legal ploys and moves against criminals, particularly those suspected of being wealthy, Tam was already by that time aware of the consequences of assets seizures. Just weeks before the beginning of the trial, officials of the Irish Criminal Assets Board had ordered the closure of The Paradise Bar in Donegal, claiming that the McGraws had bought it with money resulting from drug trafficking. Significantly, they did not bother to wait for the outcome of the case but simply put the pub up for auction. Two months later, it was sold for £215,000, the money being held by the state. A long legal battle for the money ensued, the McGraws' legal team rightly pointing out that there was no justification for seizing the bar because he had been cleared by a jury of making illicit money through drugs. Eventually, the Irish government had to concede defeat in the face of human rights legislation, but by the time the various lawyers were paid, the family received just £23,000, a pittance of the original outlay.

'I thought buying the pub was a good idea and a great investment,' says Margaret. 'They were totally out of order to seize it, especially when Tam was declared innocent by the jury.'

Learning lessons from the loss of The Paradise Bar and the drugs trial, Tam was, from that moment on, more conscious of the risks that any lawlessness on his part could have for his wife. He was offered countless opportunities to invest in substantial criminal enterprises but consistently refused, invariably coming up with the excuse that he did not have funds available or that he could see problems with the venture. But the real reason was that he feared Margaret's wrath were he to be found out.

As her marriage crumbled, Margaret's friendship with Jim McMinimee strengthened. Jim's wife, Deborah, had died in 1997, a tragedy that caused heartbreak for Margaret. Later, the McGraws would become godparents to Jim's grandson, Liam, born to his son, Craig, and daughter-in-law, Claire. Jim would appear with increasing frequency at the McGraw home.

25

SELF-DESTRUCT

GORDON ROSS HAD USED HIS SAVINGS WELL. SMUGGLING DRUGS IN his car might have cost him his liberty for a while, but it had also earned him money. He sought advice from Margaret and Tam as to how to invest it. Margaret did not know where he got his money from, and as far as she was concerned that was his business, so she was happy to advise him. Margaret remembered the success and happy days she had spent on her ice-cream vans and suggested her friend follow suit. So he splashed out £23,000 on a van and began a round in East Kilbride in 1994. With the profits from this, he again called on Margaret for guidance and after listening to her bought a second van with a round in Cranhill. Eventually, he entered into a partnership with Chick Glackin. The pair had five vans, all of which earned well – sometimes as much as £3,000 a week – and allowed Gordon a comfortable lifestyle.

His green eyes, ready smile and dark hair never failed to impress women, and stories abounded about his bedroom exploits. However, in his younger days when he was short of money, he was something of a loner, sitting in corners at parties clutching a solitary drink. But taking that first step into drug trafficking and discovering the rewards that could result had changed him. He changed even more as the years passed and the money rolled in. Tam would sometimes give Gordon a friendly warning about the dangers of using drugs. And Gordon regularly turned to Margaret for help in overcoming his problems. But those close to him noticed that his personality changed with the onset of relative wealth. Problems following the break-up of his marriage to Elizabeth did not help, and wider family issues only made things worse.

Friends of Caroline Dott remember how he changed. One says, 'He used to be a very fun-loving guy, and to the end always tried to make a good impression with Margaret, because he valued her friendship so much. But Gordon became like so many of the young footballers of the modern era: nice guys when they are young and struggling to make a few bob but unable to discipline themselves once they have so much money that they don't know what to do with it. Caroline had to watch as he became impatient and moody. She was distraught when they broke up, but the only surprise to anyone who knew them was that the relationship had lasted so long. Gordon would often meet up with Billy McPhee. They'd be joined by Chick Glackin or George McCormack, and Gordon would disappear for days. When he met a pretty girl called Kellie Anne O'Neill and fell head over heels in love with her, he seemed to calm down, and perhaps if they'd had a child, Gordon might have changed. Sadly, that wasn't to be, and Gordon and Billy got themselves a bad reputation in the East End.'

On his farm in Stirlingshire, Trevor Lawson had splashed out his drug earnings on a series of extravagances, including a track on which he and his pals raced quad bikes and motorcycles, abandoning them if they had mechanical problems and simply buying a replacement. Gordon became a regular visitor, even moving into a caravan on the farm grounds and discussing with Trevor the possibility of building a holiday home nearby. He had plans, too, for the home he now shared in Coatbridge, Lanarkshire, with Kellie Anne. Although Gordon owned the property, the couple hit upon a problem when they decided they would like to extend it. For their extension to be a practical proposition, they would need to encroach into the garden of the adjoining house. They liked their home and rather than abandon any plans for enlarging it decided that the solution was simply to buy the next-door property. Gordon talked it over with Margaret.

'Margaret, I need £100,000 and haven't got it,' he said.

'I'll loan it to you,' she replied. 'We'll get everything drawn up legally, and I'll arrange for the money to be paid to your bank account.'

Gordon now had the means to push ahead, but, like so many

before and after him, he came up against the dreaded town planners, who placed a string of obstacles in the way of the extension. The resulting frustration did not help his moods.

When a young woman fell victim to a serious sexual assault by three young men, her family turned to Gordon, who knew one of the offenders, and demanded restitution. Such was the savagery of the attack that wind of it reached the ears of the police, who began making inquiries, and a long stretch in jail beckoned for the trio. However, Gordon approached some members of the woman's family, and a substantial sum of money was paid over to her on condition that she would refuse to make a complaint and ensure no charges were pressed in the event of police becoming seriously involved.

The arrangement upset another branch of her family, who had worked out that she could well make even more than the figure paid to her by Gordon simply by making a formal statement to the police and then approaching the Criminal Injuries Compensation Board. Admittedly, going down this route might mean her having to face the ordeal of giving evidence in court, but the girl's family reasoned that the difference between the two amounts would adequately compensate her for any distress. Their proposal meant, of course, that Gordon would have to be repaid his money, and the victim had already spent some of it. Nevertheless, she handed back the residue.

There was nothing Gordon could do. He was unlikely to accuse her of theft, considering that he had tried to bribe her. Overall, it was an uncomfortable and messy situation, and when the police heard rumours of what had happened, they decided not to proceed with their investigation. The episode caused ill feeling in the area, with a large number of people in the community upset at the attackers' apparent escape from justice. It resulted in comments being made to one of them one day by an elderly man, who was assaulted as a result. The victim had underworld connections, who assured his attacker that retribution would eventually follow, and it required all of Gordon's charm and a fulsome apology to avoid further bloodshed.

Worse was to follow, and this time Gordon was at the heart of the matter. He, Billy and a third man who still lives in the East End were accused of taking part in a brutal and vile sexual orgy with a young woman. The girl concerned was no angel and at one stage had worked as a prostitute. Nor was she an unwilling participant in the orgy, a description of which would have covered many pages of the Kama Sutra. However, when word of what had taken place reached the ears of a close relative, he was enraged and swore to avenge what he saw as the besmirching of her character.

Billy's path to self-destruction was as steep as that of Gordon's. Tough but not so dangerous as his appearance might have suggested, Billy had begun dating Elaine Gemmill, the former wife of Frankie 'Doughnuts' Donaldson. Frankie had been given the tag because it was said that in his younger days he sold doughnuts from a stall in the Barras. He had survived a harrowing but brief spell of imprisonment to become a highly successful and wealthy property developer. It was a dangerous liaison, even though Frankie and Elaine had divorced in 2001. Like her ex-husband, Elaine, likeable and attractive, popped into city-centre clubs from time to time, where there was every likelihood of a chance encounter between the two, a situation fraught with the possibility of an unseemly flare-up. She was besotted with Billy, but the bulk of the affection that existed between the two came from her.

Billy was warned by friends to think hard about what he was doing. He had a devoted wife and family, and there were many people in the East End who were unhappy at his sleeping with Elaine. Others simply disapproved of men who broke their marriage vows by committing adultery.

Margaret could only watch her friends' decline. It made her sad that two young men who were so close should encumber themselves with so many problems. She recalled fun-loving Joe Hanlon, who had been such a willing helper in the early days of The El Paso, but who, like Gordon and Billy, had allowed his life to take a turn for the worse. The outcome for him had been tragic. She did not want a similar ending for Gordon and Billy. 'Gordon worried incessantly about Stephen and Gordon junior,' she remembers. 'They did nasty things that frankly drove him bonkers at times, and he despaired of what he could or should do about them. Like any father, he'd had great hopes for them when they were young, and seeing them grow up into such troublemakers distressed him.

'My opinion of Gordon and Billy is different from that of others who perhaps remember them for the wrong reasons, thinking only about the nasty things for which they came to be blamed. I was their friend. I knew the good and the bad, and they might have hurt others, but they never harmed me. True, I heard about the things they got up to, and they did some really awful fucking things for no reason whatsoever. But never to me.'

Watching the clouds of trouble envelop them dismayed her, but this was not the only cause of darkness in her and Tam's lives. Likeable Paul Flynn, from Rochdale but with strong connections in the Liverpool area, died suddenly in prison from a heart attack. He was in his late 30s, and Tam went to his funeral, where he made many friends with the Liverpudlians who were grateful to all the Glaswegians who had shown such affection for the little man. In the early days after the arrests, Paul had offered to plead guilty in the hope that this would relieve the pressure on others. His job had been to drive a Transit van carrying bales of hash, double covered in polythene using a machine normally used to wrap sausages, from the delivery point at Benalmádena in the south of Spain to Benidorm in the north after the traffickers had decided to alter their route and shorten the journey for the coaches. Unfortunately, he made the mistake of removing a glove while transferring one of the bales to the coach as it was about to set off on its final journey, one that ended in a police pound in Glasgow. The result was that when forensic specialists set about dusting down the packages, they found a fingerprint that was traced back to Paul. No one knew if he had salted away any savings for the day when he was released from prison. What was certain was that Paul would not be there to claim his money.

And another death, this time sudden and violent, would intrude on the world of Tam and Margaret. In 2000, as he was passing The New Movern Bar, owned by his family, a gunman walked up to Tony McGovern, believed by many to be the real brains behind a successful East End crime family, and assassinated him. The young father died wearing a bulletproof vest supplied by Tam, who had nonetheless warned him that this was no guarantee of safety. Once again, it brought murder close to their home. But, as they were to discover, violence was never far from their doorstep.

26

BOTTOM UP

Margaret had never met Paul Flynn, the first of the smugglers to die, but the second was a friend who had frequently sought her guidance and advice. Trevor Lawson, who owed his life to Tam and William, had been drinking with friends one evening at a bar named The Pines when a fight started. Since the trial, he had been obsessed with the thought that strangers were after the money he had made from his share of the hashish scam. The farm was worth £400,000, and he had invested in flats in Glasgow, but the word was that Trevor had buried his tins of money somewhere on his property.

Fearing the brawl might be an excuse to kidnap him, he took to his heels and headed for Broomhill Farm on the other side of the M80 motorway from the pub, determined not to get involved and simply get home unscathed. It was a short cut – albeit an illegal one – that he had used dozens of times previously without mischance. However, on this occasion he ran into the path of an oncoming car. He was thrown into the air and run over by other following vehicles. None of the drivers had any chance of avoiding him, and Trevor was killed.

The news shattered the McGraws. Only the cards could have foretold something so unexpected, but Trevor had not asked Margaret for a reading since the trial. Now it would seem as though his violent death had triggered a tide of fury. On 26 April 2002, Tam was driving through Barlanark in his familiar green jeep when he realised that a car was heading towards him. The road was narrow and interspersed with humps to slow traffic, and parked cars meant that there was insufficient room for the two vehicles to pass. One would have to pull in behind a parked vehicle to let the other through. It was at this point that Tam realised that there were two men in the other car. One was Paul Ferris. Tam did not recognise the other man.

There are varying versions of what happened next, but there is general agreement that the two principals opened their doors and approached one another. There was then a brief conversation that resulted in the men exploding into a rage.

Ferris's passenger was Mark Clinton, a friend of Manny McDonnell. Clinton was literally there for the ride, having been offered a lift to an East End destination. Tam would later tell friends, 'Ferris had been calling me names for a long time, and I asked him if he wanted to repeat them to my face. When he didn't, I went to the back of the jeep, where I had my golf clubs, took out a seven iron and started to leather him. He went down, and I was trying to gouge his eyes when the passenger jumped on my back.'

Clinton has confirmed several times that he went to the aid of his friend, who was clearly getting the worst of the encounter. A thin-bladed knife was produced, and he used it to hack at Tam. The fight ended when local residents shouted that the police had been told and were on their way. This was untrue, but it had the effect of breaking up the melee.

Tam discovered that he was unable to raise his right arm and drove to Victoria Infirmary, where doctors found 14 wounds. Their patient told them that they were the outcome of an accident while carrying out a DIY job. After treatment, he telephoned William, who drove him home where Margaret warned him, 'You watch. You'll be all over the papers tomorrow.' And she was right. The next morning and in the days that followed, newspapers variously reported that Tam was 'fighting for his life', was 'critically ill in hospital' and had been 'stabbed six times in the stomach'. In fact, but for the injury to his arm, he was, like Ferris, unscathed.

Clinton later apologised for getting involved, claiming that while he knew Tam, he had not recognised him. For sound reasons, Paul Ferris said nothing. He was still on licence, having been released from a seven-year jail sentence imposed in London in 1998 for gun running. If the authorities got wind that he had been involved in violence, they would certainly revoke his licence and haul him back to prison.

Three days later, Tam was once again in Barlanark, driving his jeep in the vicinity of the Ferris incident, this time with a passenger, Billy McPhee. At the same time, T.C. Campbell, finally released from his life sentence after appeal-court judges accepted that he and Joe Steele had been the victims of miscarriages of justice, was at the entrance to the local community centre, having just collected some medicine for his four-year-old daughter, Shannon. The jeep stopped, Billy, apparently carrying a knife, approached T.C. and a vicious and bloody fight followed. T.C. was a noted street fighter of his day, and he had lost none of his wits during his long imprisonment. It was quickly evident that he was gaining the upper hand over Billy, who was no slouch himself, when Tam intervened with his trusty seven iron.

Eyewitnesses said they heard a 'thunk', and T.C. staggered back as his assailants vanished. It seemed only seconds before police and paramedics arrived to take him to Glasgow Royal Infirmary, where he was treated for cuts to his head, neck and body and an indentation in his skull before being allowed home. Police questioned Billy, who said nothing, while T.C. refused to name his attackers. As a result, the matter was dropped. T.C. did, however, tell a journalist, 'I've read reports that the people who tried to kill me were McGraw and McPhee. I am not naming names, but those reports are accurate.' There would be further fallout from the two incidents.

Margaret found her home besieged by journalists, many anxious for a medical bulletin on her husband, others simply trying to work out what, if anything, had happened. The police had denied any knowledge of the incident with Ferris, and if either man had been treated at any of the local hospitals, they must have given false names, because there was no record of either having been treated.

For Margaret, an episode of her married life that could easily have ended in tragedy instead concluded in laughter: 'The incident with Ferris was just an accident. It was a complete coincidence that both happened to be on the same road with no room to pass unless one pulled over. In the circumstances, it was impossible not to notice who the other driver happened to be. Tam saw Ferris, even though it was years since they had last met.

'Tam thought nothing of the episode, and we laughed when we read how the newspapers were talking about him being close to death and that we were preparing to flee for our lives to Tenerife and would never again return to Glasgow. It was much the same with the T.C. incident, an accidental meeting. Billy was being given a lift in the jeep, and as he and Tam drove through Barlanark, he suddenly said to Tam, 'Stop a minute. I'm just going to see somebody.' Tam didn't have a clue who that was or that Billy was going over with the intention of fighting. Had he known, he wouldn't have stopped the jeep.

'When he saw Billy was getting a beating, he knew he had to do something. We might not have agreed with a lot of the things that Billy was up to at that time, but he was a friend, and we'd known him and his family from the days when they lived above us in Burnett Road. You just can't watch as a friend takes a hiding, so Tam opened up the back door, got out his seven iron again, and went over and sorted it. Tam was tickled pink by an imaginary account in one of the papers of a golf match between him and Tiger Woods in which Tiger ran off as soon as Tam pulled out his seven iron. The newspapers kept coming up with increasingly exaggerated accounts of what took place, and one of Ferris's minions kept shouting his mouth off about how badly injured Tam was.

'In the middle of all this, Tam went out with Gordon Ross one day, and when they returned to the house, Carrick Drive seemed to be filled with reporters and photographers. It felt like we were under siege. They were everywhere. When Tam came in, I said to him, "Fucking hell. Look at that lot out there. There are hordes of them." Tam said we should just ignore them, but I told him, "They are not going to go away unless we do something." I then said to Gordon, "You get out to the front of the house and tell a couple of them to come in." Gordon wanted to know why, but I told him just to do as I'd asked. Then I said to Tam, "They're printing all this rubbish about you being stabbed. When Gordon brings them in, strip off so they can see you haven't been marked and definitely don't have any stab wounds. Once they've seen for themselves, they'll leave, and we'll get them off the street."

'Gordon shouted to some of the reporters to come forward, but one of them must have thought he was going to be kidnapped and wouldn't move. One of the guys with a camera stepped forward, but Gordon told him, "You with the camera, just stay where you are." He then brought a couple of the reporters in. They came into the living room, and I said, "Now just take note of what you are going to see." At that, Tam dropped his pants, turned around and told them, "You can see for yourself that there's nothing wrong with me." We didn't know at the time that one of the reporters was the same guy who had been writing most of the stories claiming that Tam was at death's door. This same guy was speechless. He obviously couldn't believe what had happened. We were amazed that for a reporter who claimed to know so much, he never asked Tam to remove his top. Had he done so, he would have seen the marks on Tam's arm and shoulder that were still not fully healed. But we had counted on the reporters being so terrified and shocked that they would only want to get out and tell their editors what they had seen without wondering why Tam had dropped his pants so willingly.

'Gordon then escorted them back out onto the street. There were a few of us there at the time, and we just could not stop laughing, because it was so fucking funny. When he came back, Gordon was in stitches and said, "Surely to fuck that will put a stop to all of this." I told him, "I expect we can now look forward to reading a story about how he's running around the house naked." And that's more or less what appeared the next day. Tam's strip made headlines.'

Paul Ferris's supporters claimed that the man who had been the star performer in the impromptu strip show was not in fact Tam but his brother William and that the deceit was laid on to cover up the reality that Tam was still carrying the scars of being attacked by Ferris. 'That caused more laughter when we were told about it,' says Margaret. 'But there was nothing else we could do to prove what we had been saying about Tam having not been injured.'

While Tam was baring his body, Strathclyde Police were claiming to the Home Office that they had uncovered a guilty secret about Paul Ferris. Press reports of the fight had stirred police interest, and they claimed that he had been seen in the company of a drug dealer, sufficient grounds to revoke his licence. He was recalled to prison, but ever suspicious of the Strathclyde force, he asked the *News of the World* to take him over the border to Durham, where he would hand himself into the police and be returned to the high-security

Frankland Prison. On the journey south from Glasgow, he insisted upon stripping to the waist to show he too was unmarked and that the fight with Tam had left no physical signs. He would spend several weeks behind bars before being allowed to return to Glasgow after his lawyers established that police could not justify their claims.

Having acted as master of ceremonies for Tam's impromptu strip show, Gordon Ross left the McGraws and returned home to Kellie Anne O'Neill. But Margaret continually worried about him. After the wild days of the cannabis runs, when money seemed to grow on trees, she sensed that he had settled down and was maturing, and he and Kellie Anne were hoping for a baby, but he often encountered problems that were not of his making. Billy was also a concern. His friends wondered at the wisdom of his continued relationship with Elaine, reminding him of his obligations to his wife Tricia and their two children. On their own, Gordon and Billy were easy to handle. It was when they paired up that bad things happened.

27

PREGNANCY TEST

WHEN MARGARET DREW BACK THE CURTAINS ON THE MORNING OF 24 September 2002, she knew a busy day lay ahead. It would also be one that would haunt her for the remainder of her life. That morning she was meeting up with a close friend called Rose and Kellie Anne O'Neill.

Tam and Margaret both had a soft spot for Gordon. He had four sons. His wife Elizabeth bore him Gordon junior and Stephen. When the marriage collapsed, his relationship with a woman called Kim produced Mark. Then, in the late 1980s, he fell head over heels for Caroline Dott. He loved taking her for high-speed spins in his flash cars, the windows open to allow her long flowing blonde tresses to stream out behind her. Caroline and Gordon had a son called Bradley, on whom Gordon doted, but Tam would occasionally call in to satisfy himself that his protégé was looking after mother and son after the couple split. It was obvious to him that pretty Caroline still held a torch for her one-time lover, while Gordon would often reminisce with friends about the good times they had spent together.

However, his heart now lay with Kellie Anne, who had good reason to be excited that morning. She thought she might be pregnant to Gordon and was eager to learn whether she should consult her doctor by taking a home pregnancy test. If the test was positive, she would book an appointment with her GP and break the news to her lover.

Margaret liked Kellie Anne, not just because Gordon loved her, but because she brought a breath of youthful and enthusiastic excitement into her and Tam's lives. In short, Kellie Anne loved life and wanted all those around to share in her happiness.

The previous night had seen the spacious rooms of the Mount Vernon house rocking with laughter and the sound of music. Margaret had invited a few of her pals around for a women-only gathering. The drink had flowed and the shortcomings of the various menfolk had been discussed. It had gone well, lasting long into the early hours – in fact, too late, Margaret announced, for Kellie Anne to return home. So she had stayed overnight, and because Rose's partner had gone off on a fishing trip, she had also remained.

Margaret and Kellie Anne had booked an appointment with a local beautician and looked forward to spending some time being pampered. Rose had left her mobile telephone at home. She told the others, 'I'll dive up the road to the house, pick up my phone in case there have been any calls, pop into one of the shops and collect some morning rolls then come back here so we can have breakfast.'

'All right, brand new,' Margaret replied. 'We'll see you when we come out of the beautician's.'

And there it was: nothing to get excited about – just three women going about their day. Only somewhere along the line things went wrong, and the events of the day would become imprinted on Margaret's mind for ever: 'When we left the house, we were probably still half pished from the night before. Certainly, all three of us were giggling, laughing and joking, and passers-by must have thought we didn't have a care in the world. And we didn't.

'When we came out of the beautician's, I called Rose and could immediately sense from the tone of her voice and reluctance to talk that something was wrong. I'd known her for a long time and realised she was holding something back. I asked her, "What's the matter?" but she would only say, "Nothing," even when I repeated the question. So I said, "Have you got the rolls?" and she said, "No, I'm on my way to get them now." I said, "Not to worry. We'll get them." I then mentioned the name of the shop where Kellie Anne and I would go. It was run by a friend, and Rose said she would meet us there.

'Before leaving my house, Kellie Anne had said she would get a pregnancy test from a local chemist. I thought there might be one near the beautician's, but there wasn't. However, it turned out there was a pharmacy near our friend's shop. By the time Kellie Anne and I reached it, Rose was already there with the rolls. But the laughter from earlier that morning had gone. She looked very sombre and serious, and, again, I was certain something had happened to cause her change of mood. I asked what was wrong and wondered if her partner was unwell or something had gone wrong with the fishing trip, but she just replied, "No, he's fine." At that point, Kellie Anne came out from the pharmacy clutching a package.

'She was a dead jolly, lovely wee person who made you feel full of energy. I asked her, "Well? Did you get it?" referring to the kit, and she said, "Aye, it's here. Come on. You make the breakfast, and I'll do the pregnancy test." So we jumped into the two motors, mine and Rose's, and came back to my house. She went off to do the test while I started the breakfast. Rose said nothing, and in a few minutes Kellie Anne was back. She said that she wasn't sure if she was pregnant or not. I said, "What do you mean you're not sure? Doesn't it tell you in the instructions how to be sure?" And she said, "I think it's OK, but I don't know for certain." I knew nothing about pregnancy tests, because they weren't on the market when I was young. Kellie Anne said, "Maybe it's too soon. I'll get another one next week and try again then." She had to go off to meet a pal who worked as a secretary in a lawyer's office in Glasgow. The two had arranged to have lunch.

'Now there was just me and Rose. I said, "Come on, Rose. What's the matter?" She replied, "Nothing," but I said, "What do you mean, nothing? We were having a laugh, and now your face is tripping you." For a second or two, she said nothing. Then she looked at me hard and said, "Margaret, I didn't want to tell you in front of Kellie Anne, but when I went to my house to collect my phone, I knew I'd have a few minutes to spare, because you were in the beautician's. So, I thought I'd do a wee hand of the cards for Kellie Anne to see if she is pregnant. Then when she was going off to do the test, I could say to her, "No need to do that. I can tell you're pregnant, because I've read it in the cards. But what came out was the last thing I expected or wanted."

'I asked her what she meant, and she said, "Gordon Ross is going to die." I was totally shocked. All I could say was, "What?" She said, "Definitely. He is going to die. I know he is." She knew what she was talking about, I realised that, but it was incredibly difficult to take in. However, when you lay the cards down and they come out a particular way and tell you someone is going to die, then they are going to die. Yet I was still finding it hard to accept, and all I could blurt out was, "Fucking joking." And she replied, "No, no joke."

'So I got out my cards, and there it was. No doubt. Death. The two queens were there – of wands and cups. I was the queen of wands, which is interpreted as representing work and communication, and the queen of cups means a loving and affectionate woman, which clearly meant Kellie Anne. The final two cards to emerge were the ace of swords, which can represent a medical investigation, such as an injection, but can also mean a stabbing, and the ten of swords, which indicated an outcome of ruin or the disintegration of a life. It was plainly obvious. As the communicator, I was being told of an event relating to Kellie Anne in which there would be a fatal stabbing. And that could only refer to Gordon. Also, I would be the one who broke the news of that stabbing to Kellie Anne. There could be no reprieve from the chain of events that were to take place. The only uncertainty was whether the tragedy would happen that day.

'Kellie Anne had gone without knowing what Rose and I had foreseen. But, in any case, there was nothing we could do. You cannot change the inevitable. So we just sat outside. It was a beautiful day, but I was finding it hard to think. Images of Gordon kept appearing. We sat and waited. Sat. Waited. Waited to hear the sound of a car or the noise of footsteps and somebody coming up the drive to tell me Gordon had gone.

'At first, I did not know whether it would be that day, but as the hours passed I sensed not just that it would be, but that it would be soon. The day went so slowly, and I tried to be busy, but it was impossible. I sat and smoked. And waited. The hours dragged on, and I thought I'd better prepare dinner.

'Kellie Anne and Gordon were due to join us and some of our other friends for a meal, but Gordon didn't show up. Kellie Ann arrived, but I couldn't tell her what I knew. What would have been the point? She decided she ought to look for Gordon and found him in a pub in Edinburgh Road. He was with Billy McPhee and had not wanted to bring Billy with him to our house, so had decided to have a couple of drinks with him and then send him home. Gordon suggested to Kellie

Anne that she should head home to Coatbridge. He said that he and Billy would move on to The Brackley, a pub in Shettleston, where they would watch the start of a televised football match. Manchester United were playing that night. It was a big match, and although Tam didn't watch much football, he liked Manchester United and had stayed in to watch the game. Kellie Anne went off home to wait for Gordon, who asked her to order a takeaway meal.

'Gordon and Billy then went to The Brackley. From that moment, nothing went right. I was at home when the telephone rang, and as soon as I heard it, I knew what the call was about. It was a friend asking for Tam. He said, "Mags, Gordon's just been stabbed at The Sheiling Bar in Shettleston." The bar was only a mile and a half away. I said, "Tam will be there in a couple of minutes. He's on his way." I rushed in to where Tam was watching television. "Better get your shoes on. Gordon's just been stabbed at The Sheiling." He was out of the house in a jiffy, and by the time he reached the bar, the emergency services were already there.

'Tam rang and said, "They're giving Gordon medical assistance." He could see into the ambulance and said, "They're fucking jumping on his chest. I think he's dead." I said, "Oh, he'll be fine. He'll be OK." But I knew he wasn't going to be fine. I knew he was going to die. It wasn't just trying to give Tam hope. I was trying to calm him down. Then he said, "They're going to the hospital. I'm going to shoot up after them." When he reached the hospital, he rang me again. He was upset and said, "I don't know what's happened. I can't find out what's going on."

'In the meantime, I telephoned Kellie Anne and asked her, "Did you find Gordon?" When she told me she was waiting for him, I found myself lost for words. All I could think to ask was, "What are you doing?" She said, "Margaret, I've had a couple of drinks." I'd been going to say to her to come over, but she couldn't drive if she'd been drinking. Instead, I said, "Look, hen, Gordon's been stabbed, and he's on his way to the Glasgow Royal Infirmary. Do you want me to come and pick you up and take you in?" She said, "No, Margaret. I'll just jump in a taxi."

'I knew before anyone told me what she would learn when she reached the hospital – that Gordon was dead. I'd known all day that he was going to die. When he'd called back, Tam had said, "He might be all right," and I just couldn't bring myself to say to him, "No, Tam, he's not. He's not going to be all right.' Because I knew. I knew as soon as I looked at the cards.'

Gordon Ross died that night. No one could have known that he would be at The Sheiling Bar. He had certainly not planned to be there. Instead, fate had decreed that the manageress of The Brackley, who held the key to a cupboard in which the television controls were kept, had been late for work. Staff were unable to switch channels to the match, so the two men had moved to The Sheiling.

There are a number of theories as to why Gordon was murdered. The most likely is that he met and swapped insults with the relative of an individual he disliked in The Sheiling. A telephone call was made, and the individual who turned out to be the killer went to a house in the East End of Glasgow, where he procured a kitchen knife and wrapped it in the pages of the previous Sunday's *News of the World*. He called some of his acquaintances, one of whom drove the murderer to The Sheiling. A message was passed to Gordon, sitting inside watching television, that someone wanted to speak with him. When he went outside, the killer held out his hand in a gesture of friendship. As it was clasped, he plunged the knife into Gordon's chest with his other hand. 'You're down. Fucking stay down,' was his assassin's message. Horrified witnesses watched the knifing, and the killer had to dodge angry locals as he fled to the waiting car, also pursued by Gordon, who staggered a few yards before collapsing, blood soaking his clothes, into a gutter, where he lay helpless as his life ebbed away.

The names of the killer and his assistants are well known in the East End of Glasgow, as is that of their driver, who remains scared, protesting that he did not know what his passengers' intentions were. Needless to say, no one has ever been charged with Gordon's murder.

The two card readings had been chillingly correct. But there would be more. Kellie Anne has since gone on to begin a new life with another man, and the couple have started the family she and Gordon had hoped for before his murder. A few days after he died, she found out she had not been pregnant by him.

28

COVERED IN BLOOD

THE MEMORY OF THE BRUTAL MURDER OF HER FRIEND GORDON ROSS was never far from Margaret's thoughts. 'We were really good friends,' she recalls. 'In a sense, Gordon and I were partners. We trusted one another, and he knew I was always there for him when he needed advice. Gordon was getting his life back on track, but then his sons began getting into trouble. He was dragged into the problems they caused, often getting the blame for what they did, and, as a result, he went off the straight and narrow. It was desperately sad to see.

'I didn't cry when I knew he was going to die or when I was told he was dead. I'm not a crying person, but I was dreadfully upset. The night of his murder, I remember sitting alone at home while Tam was at the hospital, going over the many happy memories and laughs I'd shared with Gordon. I thought, "I never want to endure this again."' But she would.

After Gordon's death, Billy McPhee became even more of a loose cannon, although he had always been unpredictable. In 1994, for example, he went on the run when police said they wanted to question him about the fatal stabbing in a Glasgow nightclub of Graeme Thomson, aged 23. Luckily, he was able to turn to Jim McMinimee, who was then living on a farm in Strathaven, Lanarkshire. Jim remembers Billy's stay with fondness: 'He turned up out of the blue, desperate for help. All he would say was that the police were looking for him. He did not say why, and I never asked. It was Billy's business and up to him whether to tell me. We had been friends for years, and I would never desert a friend in need.

'He was good fun to have around and helped on the farm in ways that I would not have expected. For example, some local neds were causing my family a lot of trouble. I explained what had been going on, and Billy suggested that we put it around the local community that not only were we going to go after them with knives, but that the knives would be coated with cow dung so any cuts would be infected. The rumour about Billy and his cow-crap blades was enough to scare the yobs away.

'He stayed with us for six or eight weeks, and when he left, he thanked us for looking after him. It was only later that I discovered he was a murder suspect, but that would have made no difference. Billy was still my friend. He went to the police, who had arrested two other men by that time. When Billy was questioned and asked where he had been, he just said he couldn't remember, and the police knew better than to waste their time by pressing the matter.'

Now the shoe was on the other foot. Instead of being a suspected murderer, Billy was a potential victim, but he ignored warnings that there was a price on his head resulting from the orgy he'd been involved in. Friends warned him to take care, but he appeared oblivious to their appeals for him to pay more attention to his security.

'Billy was a daftie – a big, mad drug machine,' says Margaret. 'He was in and out of my house all the time. He'd drive by and suddenly decide to call in and have a meal. Sometimes when he had a disagreement at home, he would stick all his clothes in his car, drop in on us and say, "I need my wardrobe washed." It was a favourite saying of his, and I knew it meant he was using our machine to do his washing. When it was done, he would iron everything, put his belongings back into his car and then head off.

'After Gordon's death, he used drugs even more heavily. For much of the time, he was full of them, and it was no use trying to explain to him the harm he was doing to himself. Yet I liked Billy. I thought he was a great guy, but I understand that others saw a side of him that made him seem a not very nice person. When he was on drugs, he'd go about leathering this person and that person, yet the Billy I knew was brand new – likeable. He and I got on fine. But although he behaved himself around me, he made himself unpopular with others.' Just how unpopular, she would soon discover.

Just as she had known in advance that Gordon would die, so Margaret learned that a similar fate lay in store for Billy. The circumstances are remarkable. Many of those people who believe in spiritualism, who think that messages are passed from the dead to loved ones through mediums, also believe in the existence of spirit guides. These guides frequently appear to believers in the form of dead friends. They act as guardians, guiding those they are tasked to protect and help through life, much as guardian angels are said to do.

Few might regard Joe Hanlon as an angel, but following his murder in 1991, he had been Margaret's spirit guide. Two months after the killing of Gordon Ross in September 2002, Margaret visited a fortune teller named Ellen. There was no particular reason for the rendezvous. She called upon Ellen each year, and it happened to be the occasion of her annual visit. Snads' partner Violet was with her. 'Ellen was a really nice, ordinary wee woman,' remembers Margaret. 'She was very popular, because her predictions were usually so accurate. When I went to see her, she often told me that she saw someone beside me, and I'd tell her, "I bet it's a wee guy with a cheeky, round face." When she said it was, I'd say, "That's Joe. He's probably wanting to give me a cuddle."

'But this time she said, "There's a guy standing behind you, Margaret. He's one real handsome bastard, and he has his arms around you. He has black hair, Brylcreemed back." Right away, I knew who it was. It wasn't Joe. If she had said gel or something else, I might not have known the identity of this man, but the only person I knew who used Brylcreem was Gordon. And he had black hair and was handsome. I told Ellen, "I know there's somebody there, because I can feel him." And she said, as if to confirm it was Gordon, "He's right handsome. He is here to tell you that he misses you. He misses having a blether with you and getting advice." I said, "He knows I miss him." I had a feeling that something wasn't right, but I could not work out what was causing the sensation.

'I knew Ellen would have the answer, but mediums are not supposed to give the name of someone who is going to die. She hesitated for a while and then said, "Margaret, do you know a Tricia McPhee?" I said, "Aye, I do," and Ellen said that Tricia stayed close to her own daughter. There had to be a reason for Ellen to make that remark, and I was thinking furiously, "What the fuck does that have to do with Gordon?" Then she said, "It's not finished yet, Margaret. There's another one. Another young man is going down." I knew right away what she meant without her actually saying it. Gordon was there to tell her that Billy was going to be next – that Billy would be joining him. Ellen couldn't mention him, but she gave me a hint by asking if I knew Billy's wife. I knew then for certain that Billy would definitely be the next to die. Apart from Tam and Violet, I told nobody what was going to happen to Billy. And Tam, I know, did not tell Billy, who was becoming paranoid about his safety anyway.'

So Margaret had to carry a deathly secret, the knowledge that another friend was doomed, for the second time. And Billy had every right to worry. Not long after the grim news of his future was imparted by the fortune teller, he was drinking in the bar of Shettleston Juniors Social Club in the East End of Glasgow when he began arguing with another customer. The dispute became heated. Suddenly, a shot rang out, Billy staggered back, blood pouring from his face, and the gunman, the man he'd been arguing with, fled through the bar door. An ambulance was called and the victim taken to hospital, where prompt and skilled work by emergency staff saved his life. Police announced the attack was being treated as attempted murder and appealed for anyone who knew the gunman – described as being white, in his 40s, stocky and with dark, receding hair – to come forward. Nobody did.

Billy recovered, but Margaret knew that his days were numbered. She visited another fortune teller, who told her, 'There are two guys here, and they're covered in blood.'

On a cold morning in February 2003, Gordon was buried. The turnout was massive. Expressions of sorrow and despair are to be expected on such occasions, but fellow mourners could not avoid commenting on the unusually grim expression on the face of Billy. Some there knew the reason. There was an increasing expectancy that retribution for the attack on the girl was coming. The third of the trio was present, too, noticeably peering about for signs of a stranger. 'Billy knew that after Gordon, he was next,' said Margaret. 'He should never, ever have had any doubts that he was next.'

Early in March, Tam announced that he was going to Sweden to take delivery of a hand-made bulletproof jacket. Ever since

Gordon's murder, friends had advised him to wear protection. Tam often scoffed at their suggestions, but, nevertheless, his crumpled, faded blue denim jacket that sometimes bore the look of being worn around the clock had a bulletproof lining, as did a black bomber jacket that hung in his wardrobe, although this was only known to a handful of the people who were closest to him. He would only wear one of the jackets when keeping a rendezvous at which he suspected trouble. Friends who lived in Sweden but who had met Margaret and Tam when they holidayed in Benidorm had invited them over. The would-be hosts had been extolling the merits of a new, lighter-than-ever protective vest, and Tam, always keen to try out the latest gadgetry or indeed anything even vaguely linked to the world of spies or spying, decided to test one out and have it fitted to a new jacket. The trip would last just four days, but Margaret decided that she preferred the comfort and warmth of Glasgow. 'There's no way I am going anywhere where it snows. I hate snow,' she told her husband.

She was sceptical of the value of bulletproof outfits in whatever form, reminding him, 'What use are these jackets anyway, Tam? If you wear one, they simply get you down and then finish you off. Remember Tony McGovern? He wore one that a friend brought over for you from America that was said to be absolutely guaranteed to stop anything, but he was hit in the chest a couple of times, the impact knocked him over and he was killed while he was on the ground. They're a waste of time. If somebody is going to do you, they'll just put one in your head.'

Undeterred, Tam asked if Billy wanted to join him, but the younger man declined. 'There's an Old Firm game on at Celtic Park, Tam,' he said. 'I don't want to miss it.'

'OK, I'll bring you a vest back,' Tam said.

'I have one,' Billy replied.

'Well, be sure you wear it, Billy.'

On Saturday, 8 March, Billy headed for The Springcroft Tavern, not far from his home, to watch the match, which Celtic won, scoring the only goal of the game. He then decided to watch a televised rugby match while drinking with a handful of regulars. It was one of his regular habits to visit the Tavern late on a Saturday afternoon, and a stranger looking for him at that time on that day of the week could be pretty certain where he would be.

The bar's restaurant was packed with families enjoying an early supper or late tea. Mothers chided noisy children, while fathers craned their necks for a sight of the television screen. Billy had been warned to vary his movements, friends pointing out that he was in danger, but he ignored their advice, wandered in, ordered a drink and waited. One of the drinkers moved away and dialled a number on his mobile.

Margaret was in her local Safeway, gathering shopping for the weekend, when Kellie Anne called to tell her that one of Billy's sisters had telephoned her asking to speak to Tam. 'Tam's in Sweden getting a bulletproof jacket made,' said Margaret.

'Oh no,' said Kellie Anne. 'Billy just got stabbed in the Springcroft.'

'I'll get Tam,' Margaret said and immediately remembered the words of Ellen the fortune teller. She had difficulty contacting Tam, a prolific user of mobile phones, but finally got in touch with him to tell him that Billy had been stabbed.

'I don't know how he is,' Margaret said, but she sensed that Tam, like her, realised the prediction of Billy's murder had just come true.

The killer had walked through the main doors and up to Billy, plunging a knife into his neck to paralyse his victim and then repeatedly stabbing him in the face, head and body. Then he walked out to a waiting getaway car and disappeared as Billy bled to death. Steven McVey was questioned by murder-squad detectives, but it was Mark Clinton who the police would ultimately charge with murder. He denied being the killer, and his subsequent trial at the High Court in Glasgow in April 2004 collapsed almost as soon as it got under way due to a lack of evidence.

Now the paranoia that had haunted Billy fell on the shoulders of their surviving companion from that vile night when a young woman was humiliated. Many of those who had mourned Gordon now took out their dark suits and ties to say farewell to Billy. Two months later, some of them were saying prayers for the dead once again. Elaine, distraught at the death of her lover, hanged herself.

For much of the drugs trial in Edinburgh in 1998, Paul Flynn, Trevor Lawson, Gordon Ross and Billy McPhee had sat beside one another. Tam had sat next to them, and now all four were dead. Was he next?

29

KICKED OUT

OVER THE YEARS, MARGARET HAD GROWN CLOSE TO JIM MCMINIMEE. Inevitably, the relationship caused strains on her marriage. Margaret and Jim both say that Tam was aware of their feelings for one another but did nothing to sever the cord of romance that bound them with increasing tightness. Jim frequently visited the house, one time arriving with flowers, causing Margaret to ask Tam, who was present, 'How come somebody else has to send me flowers?' From that day, Jim would arrange for flowers to be delivered to her almost daily.

On one occasion, Jim sent a proposal of marriage to Margaret from his mobile phone but deliberately made sure it arrived on Tam's number. 'Tam didn't speak to me for six months, but I wanted her to know how I felt about her – that I genuinely wanted us to marry – and I wanted Tam to know, too,' says Jim. So why did a man with the reputation for ruthlessness that Tam had acquired over the decades permit the situation to continue? According to Margaret, the truth was that the marriage had begun to disintegrate. She still loved Tam, but it was a love based on loyalty rather than passion.

Loyalty and affection shore up many failing unions, but Margaret had lost much of her respect for her husband. Two principal factors were the cause: drugs and Tam's choice of friends. He had been prescribed the controversial antidepressant Prozac but now began dabbling in drugs – most likely another antidepressant, Valium – and had, probably as a consequence, allowed his halo of invincibility to fade. Publicly, Tam had always denigrated drugs, a curious stance considering that he was thought to be the mastermind behind a hash-smuggling racket that lasted for at least half a decade and earned the participants somewhere in the region of £40 million. It was well known that over the years many of those closest to him, including Billy and Gordon, were heavy users not just of hash but of the harder and more addictive cocaine. He had resisted temptation, but their deaths robbed him of the friendships that mattered most.

Margaret despised some of those with whom he now associated: 'After Gordon died, Tam didn't have anybody he could really rely upon. He started going about with people he should not have bothered with. The trouble is, once you've been with trash, you can't double back to the good people. I knew that if he had any problems, Drew Drummond and Snads would always be there for him, that they'd never let him down, but he kept associating with so-called toughies who just weren't tough. And Tam was not the guy many people thought he was. Frankly, he could be an arsehole. He began using something. I don't know if it was Valium, but whatever it was it changed him.

'Tam and one of his pals always seemed to be full of drugs. There might have been a time when nothing could scare Tam, but I saw how he lost his fearlessness. The pair of them were chasing weans about Barlanark – wee boys they were to Tam. He would be told that somebody was causing trouble in a pub, some daft boy of 18 maybe, and Tam and his pal would go threatening him, not thinking that the boy's dad might have been an old friend of ours. The only effect was to make a pure arse of himself. One of our friends rang me one day and said, "Tam's running about after these boys, and they're going, 'Come on, auld yin. Come on, auld yin,' taunting him, and he can do nothing about it." The drugs turned him into nothing. He went around threatening people for his pals, and I kept saying to myself, "One of these days, somebody is going to leather you, Tam," because you only needed to look at him to know that Tam couldn't stand there and fight with a boy of 19. It was his name that carried him, and it was Paul Ferris who had made his name by going to the newspapers years earlier and telling them stories about "The Licensee". Of course, he'd leathered Ferris.

'But now he had to be full of drink and Valium in order to make him feel tough and as though he was Superman. In the end, I threw him out because I didn't want drugs in my house.'

The couple split up in August 2004, Tam moving in with friends. During his enforced absence, a letter arrived in mid-September informing him of a hearing at the Court of Session in Edinburgh to inquire into his tax affairs. It remained unopened, and as a consequence Tam was declared technically bankrupt, a situation that was swiftly repealed when he called at the house to check for mail and immediately contacted his lawyers on opening the letter.

Tam begged Margaret to take him back, and she relented when he turned up on Christmas Eve that year. That she agreed to let him return to her home was a sign of her loyalty, but her disappointment in Tam remained. Much of this could be attributed to his apparent inability to carry out retribution on Paul Ferris, who had infuriated the McGraws and their friends with cheap attacks on Margaret in newspaper articles: 'Tam would sometimes sit reading a newspaper, then he'd throw it down, furious, saying, "Look what he's saying now," or, "This just isn't on." I'd say to him, "A few years ago you wouldn't have let him get away with that. Go and do something about him." Tam could have, had he bothered to. But, as he grew older, he seemed to get used to the lies and insults and just let them go by, as though he wasn't bothered by them.'

According to Tam, Ferris had gone into hiding, but Margaret didn't think that was an excuse for retribution not being exacted: 'It was all very well Tam saying, "Well, I'm here. I'm not running away or hiding. He can come and get me any time he wants," but I felt that if Tam really wanted to get Ferris, there was no reason for him not to do so. There had been times when he and others had hidden out in long grass in the soaking rain, night after night, waiting for somebody until they succeeded. There's no way Ferris would have been allowed to survive for all those years if Tam had really wanted to do something about him, not after the rubbish and lies he spread about us. Tam could have taken Ferris any time if he'd really wanted to, but he seemed to get sidetracked.

'Everybody was coming to him with their problems, and as a result he would go off threatening this one and that one. I'd ask, "Why are you doing this, Tam? You never used to have any enemies. Now, see that fucker you've just threatened? He's got two brothers, three sisters, three brothers-in-law, sons, daughters, friends and you've just made enemies of them all – twenty or thirty of them – and for nothing. And it went on and on until people stopped liking Tam.

'He used to greet about some of the things that were said about him. He would say to me, "People are going to think I've done this and I've done that." I'd say, "Well, did you?" and he'd reply, "You know I never did that." I'd then have to say, "Well then. Get fucking dressed, get out of here, go to the pub and act normally. You've done nothing wrong." The reality was that, to my knowledge, Tam never shot or stabbed anybody, but whenever there was a murder in Glasgow, he'd be blamed for setting it up. It was pure rubbish.

'Things have been written about me that I've never done. But you don't have to have done anything for that to happen, and you don't have to harm anyone for these stories to appear. Too often, all that is needed for nasty things to be said and written about you, to experience jealousy and envy, is for you to achieve a comfortable lifestyle. Those behind the nastiness could have had what we did, but they didn't because they didn't make the effort. And because we did and had succeeded, they hated us for it. We were constantly on the receiving end.

'It was said that Tam never went out without Eastern European minders. Utter rubbish. Then we were supposed to have been so scared of being attacked that we ran off to live in Tenerife. The neighbours would joke, "Was the weather bad, Margaret? You didn't get a tan," because they'd read the stories and knew we'd never left the house.'

Another of the stories circulated by enemies of the McGraws concerned an incident in The Royal Oak public house in Nitshill in February 2004. Tam had arranged to meet with two friends: John 'Joker' McCartney and Craig Devlin. Numerous versions of what happened have been put forward, but Margaret knows the truth, because Tam was caught up in the drama. 'One of them was buying a motor from the car dealer Tommy Wallace, a long-time associate of Tam's,' she says. 'When they arrived, they were told the vehicle wasn't quite ready and were asked to return in an hour. The Royal Oak was nearby, so they went in for a pint and a game of pool. But hardly had they begun playing when two young men carrying guns burst in and began shooting. They were spraying bullets around, and most of the customers dived for cover. Some others threw bottles and glasses at the gunmen, but Tam, who had been about to take his shot, set about the leader with his pool cue. When the second gunman saw what a leathering Tam was giving his mate, he ran off. Others joined Tam in trying to yank the gun off the remaining shooter, but he had it tied to his wrist. He then managed to wriggle free and run off. It was then Tam saw that Craig and Joker had been hit. Blood was pouring from Joker.

'Tam shoved the pair of them into his jeep and headed for hospital. When he saw a police car, he stopped and asked for help, and they gave him an escort. On the way, he telephoned and said, "Margaret, there's been a shooting. Joker and Craig have been hit. I'm taking them to hospital." I asked how they were, and he said, "They're bad, Margaret. It doesn't look good for Joker. I'm trying to keep him awake, because I have the feeling that if he goes to sleep, he'll never wake up." When I asked what had happened, Tam said he'd been playing pool and had heard a bang. He said nothing about having whacked one of the gunmen with his pool cue. He called me again when he got to the hospital, but then the police took him away, arrested him and gave him a breath test, because he'd been in a pub. It was negative, but they kept him in for six hours before letting him go to meet up with me.'

Both victims survived, but doctors would later admit that Joker had come close to death and that it was only Tam's quick thinking that had saved his life. Tam was rewarded for his efforts by having his mobile phone taken from him, doubtless so that the police could take note of his numbers.

Some accounts of the shooting claimed that Tam had cowered under the pool table. Astonishingly, one was written in clear contempt of court before the trial of one of the alleged gunmen. But who was to be believed? Was Tam a hero or a coward? The answer was provided at the High Court in Edinburgh in February 2006 when Ross Boyd, aged 21, was cleared of being the gunman who shot Joker and Craig. Advocate Depute Alan Mackay said a 'grey haired man in his 50s' had hit the gunman with a pool cue. 'You may think that accords with the description you have heard of Mr McGraw,' he continued. 'Tam McGraw certainly seems to have played a significant part in the events which unfolded. He drove the victims at high speed to hospital and even commandeered a police escort.'

Other wives might have been infuriated at the attempts to twist the facts, undermining a simple act of bravery and quick thinking by her husband, but Margaret had spent years sorting fact from fiction. And she could never forget that Tam had a reputation for exaggeration and was on occasion referred to as 'Tam Addabit'. Sometimes she found it difficult to know precisely what to believe, and her advice to him had always been to keep a low profile and say as little as possible or nothing at all. His failure to follow the golden rule of silence was an irritant.

Tensions between them were not helped by the discovery that the police, still smarting after failing to net Tam and the other alleged smugglers in 1998, had continued their surveillance on the couple. They were returning home after meeting a friend when the car they were driving was stopped. They had £6,000 in cash with them. Under legislation covering seizures of assets suspected of being accrued as the result of criminal activity, police could demand an explanation of the source of such a sum and take the money if a satisfactory one was not forthcoming. It would then be up to the owner to fight for its recovery.

'We had been in the car, and Tam was talking on his mobile phone to our friend, who asked to speak with me,' Margaret remembers. 'I took the phone, and he simply asked me to call in because he had something he wanted to give to me. I said, "Fine," and handed the phone back to Tam. Nothing else – just "fine". But when the call ended, I told Tam, "He should never have mentioned anything on the telephone. You just never know who might be listening." I had an uncomfortable feeling about that call.

'We had been on our way to buy a dance machine for the house. Tam was crazy about karaoke and dance, and we thought we'd see if it would be possible to install one. In case we liked it and wanted to buy it, we'd taken sufficient money to pay for it. After meeting our friend, we then went and inspected the machine, but it wasn't what we were looking for, so we drove home. That's when we were stopped and taken to a police station, where the money was taken from me. It was obvious the police knew we had it. From the outset, I told them, "I've got fuck all to say. You know you're going to have to give me the money back." Tam had gone into a spiel about buying the dance machine, but the police said, "We know what this is all about." To which I said, "Well, if that's the case, why are you annoying me? If you are going to charge me, charge me, and if not, get to fuck. Ring my lawyer."

'About half an hour later, they returned, and I said, "You're having a laugh. This is a joke, and you're wasting our time. There's no way I'm going to sit here and talk to you." They said, "Well, it's like this. Were you going to buy a dance machine?" I said, "That's none of your business. Charge me or let me out of here." They claimed they could hold us for six hours without access to our lawyer but added, "Of course, we won't hold you that long if you tell us where the money came from and what it was for." So I said, "I'm telling you fuck all. Charge me, let me out of here or come back in six hours with my lawyer." Eventually, they had to let us go, but they held onto our money.

'When we'd left, I said to Tam, "You should have said fuck all about a dance machine. Did you tell them who we were meeting?" He said that he had not, but the police must have known, because they had been listening to our telephone conversations. How do I know that? Because our motor was in the garage for repair, and we'd been given a courtesy car. The only way the police could have known which car to stop was by having overheard our telephone calls to the garage and the short call with our friend.

'We learned a lesson that day, and it was never to hold a private or important conversation on the phone. Tam was forever using his mobile phone, but I was very wary of what I said during any calls I made, and I never used the house landline for anything other than to order groceries.'

After intervention by the family lawyer, the money was repaid and asset-seizure officials had the embarrassing task of working out how much interest they would have to pay Margaret. They eventually settled for £26.

30

SEEING DEATH

MARGARET HAD ALWAYS KNOWN THAT THE CARDS COULD PLAY cruel tricks in the wrong hands. Poor interpretation of their meaning is a common fault, which is why she always prefers to form her own judgement of fortune tellers, rather than accepting the word of others as to their ability: 'There have been times when I've been out socialising with friends when someone has asked me to do a reading for them and I've turned them down for the simple reason that I hate doing just anyone's cards in case the prediction turns out to be wrong. And if something bad comes up, you really don't want to have to pass that on. On the other hand, I can sit at home and remember meeting someone earlier in the day and think, "He was looking a bit weird. I'll do his cards and see what the fucker's up to."

'If I meet a friend who tells me, "My ma's in hospital, and I'm really worried about her," I'll think to myself, "What a shame. I'll go home and maybe do a wee hand for her." Then the cards tell you, for example, that her ma is going to have an operation but will be all right. As a result, the next time you come across your friend you can say to her, "Look, I think she's going to be OK," and she'll say, "Did you do the cards, Margaret? Are you sure she's going to get well?" I'll say, "Well, I'm not 100 per cent sure," when really I am or else I wouldn't have told her. My friend might ask, "She's definitely not going to die?" and I'll tell her, "No, she's definitely not going to die. She'll maybe be in hospital for a wee while and might have to have some surgery, but at the end of the day she is going to be fine."

'I'd only tell her if I knew her mother was going to get well. If the cards said she was going to die, I just wouldn't say anything, because how can you say to a friend, "Your ma's going to die"? And what if you were wrong? If I did a reading and it told me personal information about someone close, I might get in touch and say, "Look, I'd get your credit card sorted," or, "I think you should get your finances fixed." But I'd say nothing if the cards told me someone was going to die.

'Trevor Lawson got in touch one day to say he had discovered a fortune teller who, according to him, was great, and he insisted I should see her. I eventually did, and there were a whole load of people present, including Gordon Ross, Chick Glackin and the father of one of guys in the group. He was a nice wee man who had been ill for years and years, having to be fed through a machine that pumped liquid straight into his stomach. So the fortune teller did a reading and then asked the sick man's son if she could have a private word with him. She told him she thought there was going to be a death soon and that the victim would be his dad. She also told Trevor, Gordon and Chick that they would be attending a funeral and automatically assumed it would be for the father.

'When Trevor told me what the woman had said, I wasn't happy. I already had my doubts about her, because she'd drunk wine during the readings. Water is fine, but definitely not wine. He asked me to do the cards to check what she had said, but I refused. I said, "I'm not going to do the cards just to tell this man's son his father is going to die, because that's something you should never, ever do." Needless to say, when I returned home, I did a reading. I then telephoned the son and said, "Your dad is not going to die soon. Honest to God, trust me. I realise you think the woman who gave you the news is really, really good, but I've had doubts. Somebody close to the group that was there is going to die, but it's not your father. I have no doubt from what I read that although you are going to a funeral, it will not be for him, because the king of cups, the card necessary to confirm what the fortune teller predicted about your dad, was not there."

'So, this woman got it badly wrong, and can you imagine what it might have been like for the old man's wife had she been told her husband was about to die? In fact, he lived on for another six years. She got the most crucial part of the reading badly wrong. There was a funeral all right, but not that of the man she predicted would die.

It was for a relative of Gordon who died very tragically after a fall in Glasgow. Gordon, Chick and Trevor all attended the funeral.'

One morning in late 2004, Margaret awoke with a sensation that something was wrong, but she couldn't put her finger on what, and there was no visible or obvious reason for the feeling of unease that would not leave her. When it persisted, she wondered if it might concern Tam, so she took out her cards and did a reading for her husband. The cards foretold a death: 'It was Tam's cards I was doing and when a death came up, I wondered to myself, "Is this him? Is he going to die?" I telephoned a friend and said, "I think Tam's going to die," but she told me, "Margaret, don't be daft." Then she called back to say, "I've just done the cards, and it does look that way." I said, "I have this bad, bad feeling."

'It was as though there had to be a death for the feeling that something terrible was going to happen to go away. And then there was one. My nephew John from Shettleston died of natural causes in January the following year aged just 22. I thought that would mean the awful nagging feeling I had would go away. But it did not. It carried on and on. I told my friend, "It's not gone away. I'm telling you, Tam is going to die." The cards did not say how. They did not predict a heart attack or how his life would end, but I knew that what they had told me was inevitable. Should I have told Tam? No, you cannot tell someone they are going to die. And what if I was wrong? I had no doubts I was right, but I'd thought that Tam would die when in fact it was John. And it was only when that sense of foreboding persisted that I knew there would be another death.

'A Tarot reading begins with a situation. It might start with the death card. Although that can mean there is to be a death, it is really telling you there are going to be major changes. What those changes are and how they will affect the person for whom the reading is being done depends on what cards follow. It could be a wands card, telling you the change is that you are moving house. Or if you follow death with cards showing swords, it means your health is going to be affected. The three of swords, for example, tells you that it is your heart that is going to be affected. So those were the cards I did not want to turn up.'

Her presentiment continued, and she struggled not to let her fears show. Each day her routine continued, with the same friends calling,

Jim visiting with flowers and a kiss, and Tam continuing to chain smoke. For more than two years, Margaret continued to hide her dreadful secret, and then in the spring of 2007 she once again took out her pack.

Those closest to Margaret were conscious that she was unusually sombre, and when she began her reading that March morning she hoped the bad omens of a year ago might have changed, allowing the heavy and depressing atmosphere around her to lift. It was not to be. The ten and three of swords, the very cards that she had not wanted to appear, turned up as though an evil genie had manipulated them into place. 'I knew right away what this meant,' Margaret says. 'The cards were telling me that Tam was going to have a heart attack and that it would kill him. It was not a matter of if but when, and nothing I or anyone else could do or say would change the inevitable, including Tam. It made no difference that he was fit and healthy. Friends even commented on how well he looked, although everyone was forever urging him to quit smoking. He kept promising but never did.

'I did other readings with the same cards, and also with the Russian gypsy pack, but the outcome was always the same. Tam was going to die. When using the gypsy pack, the first complete picture I was able to form by moving the cards around was that of the hearse. While doing one reading, I remembered that about three years earlier Tam had come home from a meeting and was doing his nut about something or other and I'd said, "You had better calm down or you'll have a heart attack." The cards even showed that he would die without reaching a hospital. The only uncertainty was when, although I was sure it would be before the end of July.

'I tried putting it out of my mind, because there was simply nothing I could do. But each time I looked at him, I would ask myself, "I wonder how long you've got, Tam." I felt sad, and then I would think, "Well, he's going to a better place, isn't he?" Because I firmly believe that when we die we go to a world far happier and more loving than the one in which we live.

'It was not long after this that Tam started to complain of always feeling tired. That was out of character. He'd always been a livewire, constantly on the move, but now I noticed he seemed to be getting stressed much more easily than before. I was forever telling him to calm down and take things easy. In the end, we arranged a check-up with the family GP, who got in touch a few days later to say they could find nothing wrong. Despite that, Tam insisted there was something wrong with him, because he constantly suffered from diarrhoea, so we arranged for further tests, including an examination of his bowel.

'While he waited for a second opinion, I also decided to double check my findings from the cards. The fortune teller who had told me about the buses, money and drugs when it was impossible for her to have known anything of what was going on came to the house to give me a reading. She said that Tam would suffer from pains in his arms, chest and stomach but thought that these would result from his being shot twice. I said nothing but did not go along with the shooting, because I never had any doubts that he would suffer a fatal heart attack.

'When Tam suggested we take a week-long caravan holiday with friends in Cornwall in June, I hesitated, thinking that it might be his last month on earth. I didn't want him dying hundreds of miles from home. But I went along with it. It was so cold in Cornwall that the birds were hiding to keep warm. Tam loved it and wanted to stay on, but it was freezing, and he eventually agreed he was missing home.

'By the time we returned to Glasgow, it was July, and I was sure he would be gone before the month was out. He certainly began to take on the look of an old man. There was the usual pile of mail waiting, including a letter making an appointment for his second check-up. We had missed it through being away but rang up and rearranged the examination. Tam was asked to report to the Glasgow Royal Infirmary early on Monday, 30 July 2007. I knew he had only days to live.'

Curiously, in the two weeks leading up to the appointment, Tam barely ventured out of the house, which was unusual for him. Close friends remarked on this fact, and privately Margaret wondered whether he had had some premonition of gloom and wanted to stay around her to share as much time as possible with her. It would be almost six months before she received an answer, and in that time she would attend a funeral.

31

BEAM ME UP

I T WAS NOT JUST MARGARET WHO WORRIED ABOUT TAM. AT THE beginning of July, in The Black Bear, one of his regular drinking spots a couple of miles from his home, he had told a casual acquaintance with whom he sometimes shared a chat, 'I'm not feeling too good. If anything happens, you're invited.' A few days later, and out of the blue, he had suddenly hugged a long-time associate and told him, 'Thanks for being my friend.' The man was bemused. Such behaviour in Tam was bizarre.

No one can really know what was in his mind when he awoke, unusually early for him, on the morning of 30 July 2007. Traditionally a man who preferred going to bed two or even three hours after midnight and rising shortly before lunch, he was out of his bed at 7 a.m., Margaret having risen an hour earlier. He had worried about the bowel examination for days, particularly after being told it involved a tiny camera being inserted into his anus. A family member who had experienced the procedure twice previously did her best to reassure him: 'Tam, there's nothing to worry about. They stick a needle in your backside, take a look inside you and then tell you to go home.' Indeed, she had even been able to drive herself home immediately afterwards. Having heard this, Tam announced he would do the same.

Following a motoring ban after failing a breath test in 2005, Tam had sold his jeep and had not yet got around to buying a replacement. He therefore borrowed Margaret's car and set off on the short journey, his confidence boosted by hearing how simple the procedure would be.

These were hours that will be for ever imprinted on Margaret's memory. 'He did not look too well, and I was certain something was going to happen to him. In the middle of the morning, he rang to complain nothing was happening and said other patients who had arrived after him had been given their consultations and check-ups and sent home. I said, "Tam, that's probably because you got there early and they turned up right on time. Calm down and wait. The hospital staff know you are there." I was anxious, too, because of what I already knew through the card readings. I waited for the phone to ring and for him to tell me it had all gone well and he was on his way back, but it was as if every time I looked at it, the telephone was saying, "I'm not going to buzz while you stare at me."

'There was only one thing I knew I could do to try and ease the tension. I took out the cards and did another reading. I was telling myself, "It's definitely today. Tam is going to die today." Out came the ten and three of swords, the cards that told me he was going to suffer a heart attack. Then I realised for certain there was no hope, although I had known all along what was going to happen. Finally, the telephone rang, and it was Tam to say the checks had been done but he wasn't feeling well enough to drive himself back. He said his stomach didn't feel right, so I told him I would ask Violet to give me a lift in order that I could collect the car and fetch him. But almost immediately he called back telling me he had bumped into an old friend in the hospital waiting room who had offered to ferry him home.

'They arrived a few minutes later, but his friend didn't have time to stop. Tam came in and complained that he had a splitting headache. I told him, "Take a couple of pills and get to your bed," and off he went.'

Anxious and apprehensive, Margaret telephoned Jim, who was astonished to receive her call. He, too, remembers that day with unswerving clarity: 'When I answered, she said, "Where are you?" and I told her, "I'm on my way." She asked, "When will you be here?" and I told her, "In about half an hour." When the exchange ended, I thought it was strange that she had called, because she never telephoned to ask when I was arriving. Whenever I said I would be seeing her, I was always there, and I'd been with Margaret the previous evening and had told her I'd be at her home at half past one the next day. She even knew in advance when I'd arrive, because I'd walk through the door just as she was placing a plate filled with fresh toast and a cup of tea on the table for me.'

As Jim prepared to set off, Margaret was checking on Tam, who said, 'Can I have some tea and toast? I have dreadful pains in my stomach.' She tried to reassure him: 'It's just wind, Tam. You've had nothing to eat since last night. Once you've had a bite, you'll probably feel better.' After taking him his snack, she returned downstairs to await the arrival of Jim and arrange a lift to collect her car from the hospital park.

Just under half an hour later, she went back to see Tam, who asked for more tea and toast. 'He said he felt a little better, but his stomach was still painful, and he asked me to rub his back in the way you'd pat a baby to get rid of wind,' Margaret remembers. 'Although I did that, he said it made no difference, so I thought more tea and toast would help and went off to get them. When I returned upstairs, he was still complaining of being in pain. While I sat on the end of the bed tying the laces of my trainers, he said, "I would rather be dead than put up with this." And those were the last words he ever spoke.

'He slumped over and hit his head on a small bedside table. I jumped up to hold him, but he was a dead weight, and I screamed for Connor, my grandson, who was in the house with us, to help. When Tam had gone to bed, he had unplugged the phone in order to charge up his mobile, and I couldn't get it to work.'

Around the time when Margaret had taken up Tam's second portion of tea and toast, Jim had pulled into the driveway at the front of the house: 'I did what I always did and walked around the side of the building and in through the back door. The table was empty, except for Margaret's phone, which I thought was odd, because she always took her mobile wherever she went. What was even more unusual was that there was no sign of my tea and toast. Normally, when I said "half one", that's when my tea and toast appeared on the table. I stood at the door without entering and shouted, "Margaret," but there was no answer. Then I remembered I had to make a telephone call from the car, so I walked back, all the time telling myself, "That's funny: her phone on the table and my toast not there." I got into the car and picked up the phone to make the call but thought, "Nah, there's something not right here." I decided to ring Violet: "Violet, I'm going into the house because something's not right. Margaret's phone's lying there, and when I shouted, nobody answered . . .' At that moment, I became aware of a loud banging on one of the windows at the front of the house.

'When I looked up, Connor was there. He was chalk white and shouting at me through the glass. I thought I heard him say, "My gran's dead." And I just felt the blood leaving me, draining right down to my feet. It seemed to take me for ever to get from the car to the house, even though I was running. All sorts of things were going through my head. I shouted, "Where are you? Where are you?" and headed upstairs. As I climbed, I heard Margaret's voice shouting, but I couldn't make out the words. "What the fuck's going on here? Is this him winding me up?" I said. When I got to the bedroom, Tam was lying on the bed, with Margaret pleading, "Do something, Jim. Do something." I said, "What is it?" And she said, "He's dead, he's dead." I immediately gave him the kiss of life.

'Margaret then said, "Phone the ambulance," and I said, "You phone the fucking ambulance. I can't do both." I gave her my phone, and she dialled 999. The ambulance controller told her what to do, and she relayed the instructions to me. I said, "Tell them I'm already doing that. Tell them just to fucking get here." The paramedics arrived incredibly quickly. There were two of them, but they couldn't get Tam off the bed. I said, "You want him on the floor then?" One of them replied, "Aye," and I said, "Right, out the fucking road then." I picked Tam up and laid him on the floor. They were working on him and appeared to be about to inject adrenalin right into his heart. They pointed to the toilet and asked Margaret to wait inside. So while they tried to save Tam, we sat in the toilet.

'Margaret was hysterical, shouting, "Do something, do something." Then the ambulance arrived. We were still sitting in the toilet. Margaret asked me what had happened, and I said, "You've lost him, hen. He's dead. He's not coming back." She knew it anyway.

'That is the only time I've seen Margaret hysterical. I'm used to death, because my father-in-law worked in the mortuary, and in any case dying is part of life. That's why I was able to give Tam the kiss of life without panicking.

'Connor was absolutely brilliant through all of this, doing

exactly what was asked of him. It was a terrible experience for a boy of 12.'

The ambulance took Tam to the Glasgow Royal Infirmary. At nine minutes to three in the afternoon, he was officially declared dead, the cause later being attributed to Ischaemic heart disease and coronary artery atheroma. The cards had foretold that Tam would die before the end of July. His end had come with less than a day and a half to spare.

'The waiting was the worst,' says Margaret. 'Watching him day by day, knowing there was nothing I could do to change what was in the cards. I would look at him and wonder, "Does he look worse today than he did yesterday? Is he looking better?" We did everything possible to check on Tam's health, to ensure there was nothing wrong, and still he died. Would I have preferred not to have known? No, because having that knowledge made it easier to cope. When he died, it was not a shock. I would rather know if I was going to die, so that I could see all my loved ones before it happens and tell them how much I love them. Then they'd know how I felt about them when I was gone. Too often after someone departs, those left behind say, "I wish I'd said this," or, "If only I could have told him or her that," but because death has come suddenly, there was never the chance.

'It was a burden carrying around what I had read. And it is sometimes a burden being able to understand what the cards say. I'm sure a lot of people have the gift, but they don't realise it or don't think about it. Surely everyone wakes up in the morning sometimes and says to themselves, "I don't feel right today," and something happens to them.'

In August, Margaret and William led the mourners to Daldowie Crematorium for Tam's funeral. His coffin had lain open at home for friends to say their goodbyes, and before the lid was closed, Margaret had placed Tam's mobile phone in his hands, because he went nowhere in life without it, and it might come in useful in the hereafter.

Inevitably, the usual crackpots tried to get in on the act. One sent a congratulations card. Pasted inside was a photograph of Margaret cut out from a newspaper. And police called to say they had been tipped off that her home might be firebombed. 'They said they'd need to be around to make sure nothing happened, but I told them I didn't want police cars or vans sitting outside all night,' Margaret says. 'So they agreed to make their surveillance discreet. But what sort of person wants to have a go at a house with a dead man inside?'

Margaret had arranged for the playing of Tam's favourite song, the Robbie Williams hit 'Angels', at his funeral. The Reverend David Locke, who conducted the service, said, 'Everybody makes mistakes, and I don't know what Tam got up to. It is not for us to judge the actions of others. God shall be the judge.' As the red curtains closed around the coffin, in a reference to Tam's passion for *Star Trek*, the minister added, 'I wonder if Tam, if he was able, would now say, "Beam me up, Scotty."'

32

MESSAGE FROM THE DEAD

I T IS A CURIOUS FACT — ALTHOUGH SOME PEOPLE MIGHT THINK IT ENTIRELY appropriate – that the Jocelyn Spiritualist Church in Glasgow sits only a few yards from the city mortuary. The dead could almost shout out their messages of affection and guidance to their loved ones, instead of relying upon one of the friendly and dedicated mediums who act as go-betweens each week. Unlike those at many traditionalist churches, spiritualist congregations tend to hop between venues, often following a particular or favourite medium, craving news of those in the better world.

Spiritualists believe the dead can talk, and to them it is difficult to otherwise account for strangers being able to pass intimate secrets to family members: the location of a hidden piece of jewellery, the words written on the back of a photograph, the colour of a pair of shoes tucked away unseen since the death of their owner. To spiritualists, there is no other explanation for a medium to possess such detailed and personal information.

Margaret has attended spiritualist meetings for three decades. Following Tam's death, she never doubted that her husband would want to make contact with her, just as had Gordon and Joe Hanlon. Shortly before Christmas, less than five months after being cremated, he did just that. Most of those present would not have been aware of the identity of the sender or the recipient of the message. And spiritualists, accepting the privacy of grief, would not seek to make capital from such knowledge; instead, they would just be happy that a mind had been eased, a memory in turmoil made glad.

Margaret says she knew Tam was there even before the medium

indicated that someone had come through with a message for her. 'I have two men and a woman for you,' she was told. 'One of the men has not long passed over.' The men were, of course, Tam and Joe Hanlon. Of the woman, Margaret heard no more. Perhaps she was overlooked by a medium anxious to satisfy as many demands for contact as possible in a short period of time.

Margaret was so overwhelmed that she found it difficult to recall what had been said to her. Fortunately, she was accompanied by a companion, who recalled almost word for word what the medium said: 'The message was mainly from one man, and we knew right away that it was Tam. He never stopped talking in life, and he was obviously burdened with matters that he wanted to get off his chest, things he needed to say to Margaret. The message came through very clearly, the medium only now and then having to put a finger to an ear as though the words were being spoken very quickly. But, then, that was Tam.

'To begin with, he asked for her forgiveness. He said he was very, very sorry. He said that he would have loved to have been able to go back to the point at which he and Margaret had shared a home in the sunshine. We knew immediately that he was referring to the many good times they had shared in Tenerife, because those were his very happiest memories: sitting in the sun, enjoying a drink, being with friends and loved ones, and hearing the sounds of laughter. He missed those experiences so much and begged for forgiveness.

'Tam knew he needed to clear away all the hurtful things he had done to Margaret in order that he could rest in peace. He said, "I have hurt the one I loved the most. She was my rock." He said he was floundering, unable to rest until he received a sign of forgiveness, because Margaret was his one and only love. The medium said to Margaret, "You have the same abilities as us. He is seeking a release that only you can grant him." Tam also said that without Margaret he would have been nothing.'

At the end of the meeting, the medium approached Margaret and said, 'The man who came through for you tonight said he had never believed in this or the cards.'

'Well, of course,' Margaret replied. 'He didn't believe in anything.'

'He believes now.'

'Well, he must do if he's been standing talking to you.' The two women broke into laughter.

Margaret had also expected to be contacted by Joe and knew that he would have a message for her. Some days earlier, she had been socialising with friends in a Glasgow bar called By The Way when she had been approached by Joe's widow, Sharon. Within days of Tam's death, a newspaper had reported that Sharon had celebrated by sipping champagne as she sat next to Joe's grave in the cemetery at Dalbeth in the East End of Glasgow. The article quoted a 'close friend' as saying that Sharon blamed Tam for the deaths of Joe and Bobby Glover. Just over a week later, the same newspaper claimed Joe's headstone had been 'ripped from the ground' and a note left: 'One more celebration of McGraw's death, Sharon, and you will be joining your beloved Joe sooner than you think. Take the fucking warning. P.S. Nice stone.'

Margaret had read neither article and most of her friends had forgotten about them as Sharon approached the group. Margaret's friends recall Sharon shouting, 'Your man was a grass.'

Margaret calmly replied, 'I don't think he'd be interested to know this. He's dead. You've left it a bit late to tell us, Sharon.'

Margaret remembers what happened: 'We were sitting there, minding our own business, when Sharon came over. Apparently, I was supposed to sit quietly and just say, "Well that's all right, Sharon. Just say what you like." Instead, I said, "Look, you're talking about 16 years ago. You could have come to see me any time in that 16 years. So, why do it now?"'

Margaret's companions that evening were incensed by Sharon's outburst in a public place and advised Mags not to return to the same venue, but she refused to be intimidated, and her next visit passed peacefully. The incident, she knew, accounted for Joe's brief message passed to her at the spiritualist meeting. 'Sorry, hen,' he had said. 'The past is past.'

Tam's desperate quest for absolution from Margaret would explain his rarely leaving her side in the two weeks prior to his death. His appeals to her through the medium suggest that during that short period he was convinced he was on the verge of death or had a premonition that his time with her was short. She, of course, knew he was dying. It appears that he, too, knew but, like her, decided not to pass on the awful knowledge. She also knew why he sought forgiveness and for what, but that will remain a secret.

Margaret was not surprised by Tam's presence at the spiritualist church, a church in which he had no belief, because within days of his death she had been conscious that he had rejoined her in the home that had brought them so much pleasure. Tam, she knew, had initially been with her dad William but had struggled to find peace in the afterlife. A sympathiser calling to offer words of comfort had been told, 'I know Tam is with me because I feel his presence. The hairs on my arms stand up. I talk to him and have the sensation he is not happy. He is suffering badly.'

Other people were anxious to help Margaret, but while their motives might have been admirable, their timing was not, as she remembers: 'One Sunday evening, I went to the pub with some friends to wind down and relax when a wee guy approached me and started talking about Tarot and messages from Tam. I had to tell him, "Please, don't even think about going on any further. I don't want to know. I'm here for different spirits tonight. I'm here for a laugh." But that didn't stop him, and I said, "Go to the spiritualist church. Talk to them, and they'll teach you how to control what you believe you have and how to deal with all the messages you receive. You can't just sit in the pub and irritate everybody." At that, he said, "You think I'm daft – that I don't know what I'm talking about." I said, "I know you're not daft, but there are others who believe you are."

'When he persisted, I said, "Oh, please don't, because I can't be bothered. If you want, come down to the house and we'll talk about these messages there." He replied, "I'm not coming to your house. I'll get shot." I said, "You'll have nothing to worry about. I've got rid of all my guns." I don't know whether or not he believed me. Other people have approached my friends to say they think I ought to visit them because they've been receiving messages from Tam. But when I don't know them, I'm wary, because who is to say that what they tell me hasn't been gleaned from newspapers?'

33

LOST HEART

MARGARET SAYS SHE FELL IN LOVE WITH JIM MCMINIMEE 25 YEARS before Tam died. Who can say what attracts a woman to a man or him to her? It may be looks, a smile, a joke, an act of kindness or a thousand other trivialities. Just as all human beings look different, so no two couples fall in love for precisely the same reasons.

Margaret is a woman not normally given to uncertainty. She has guided herself through a sometimes turbulent and difficult life, and she offered Tam guidance so he could follow a route to safety and prosperity, although he chose not always to follow her, usually to his cost. However, in this matter of the heart, she is unsure as to the motive but certain about the outcome: 'I fell in love with Jim when I met him, but don't ask me what it was about him that I liked, because I cannot explain what drew me to him. I just knew Jim was different. I love him.'

Over the years, their love had to remain underground, away from prying eyes. Inevitably, Tam realised that his wife had fallen for another man, and during a trip to Tenerife in 2005 he admitted to me that he and his wife had effectively lived separate lives for a decade. While that is an honourable outcome for a relationship made increasingly difficult over the years, it is also true that Tam and Margaret remained, to Tam's dying day, fiercely protective of one another.

Tam was a man of enormous generosity of spirit. At his funeral, Margaret was approached by a total stranger, the mother of a child with a physical disability. She explained that Tam had been openly moved by her boy and one day had had words with an onlooker staring at the youngster. To Margaret, Tam displayed a huge amount of trust, placing every facet of his life in her hands, and not once was he failed. It is an indication of the strength of that trust that Tam continued to have unswerving faith in his wife's judgement despite being aware that he had lost her heart to Jim.

After the death of his wife Deborah, Jim became an ever more frequent visitor to the McGraws. He still looked upon Tam as being one of his closest friends. 'But if I needed to talk to anyone, I'd always turn to Margaret, and while I was telling her my problems, she would share hers,' he says. 'As time passed, we found we had total trust in one another and could tell one another anything. Tam knew I saw her and kept trying to throw me out of the house. He'd pick an argument, and when I refused to give in, would say, "Right, I'm away to my bed until you go." I'd say, "You might be there for a while, Tam." I made no secret of my feelings by sending Margaret flowers every day, knowing Tam would realise who they were from. When we met, we'd kiss on the lips, no matter who was there, and when we spoke on the telephone, we'd always end up with the words "I love you". Margaret knew I wanted to marry her, and so did Tam. I proposed to her one day, and she said, "Jim, I'm not divorced." But I said, "Not to worry. I'll wait."'

Around Christmas 2007, Margaret received a dozen red roses from Jim. They arrived as she was talking with me, and I noted the sparkle in her eyes as she carefully arranged them, standing in her kitchen gently handling each of the beautiful blossoms as though she feared it might crumple or break. It was at that moment that she decided she wanted to share the remainder of her life with Jim. He, meanwhile, had determined to ask her again to wed. One evening as they sat quietly watching television, he went down on one knee and proposed. 'It was a total spur of the moment thing,' he recalls. 'I hadn't planned it. I looked at Margaret and knew I didn't want to lose her. She said, "Yes, Jim. You know I will." And that was that.'

They were conscious of being seen together, aware that the gossips would have a field day at their expense should they attempt a furtive relationship. So they simply and publicly declared their joint feelings, and on Valentine's Day 2008 were formally engaged, exchanging specially made diamond rings supplied through a long-time jeweller friend. They named the day and immediately began to arrange to make their wedding vows in February 2009.

34

GOOD AND BAD

Early in 1995, as the curtain was beginning to fall over The El Paso, Margaret began to suspect that her husband was up to no good. Not long afterwards, the police had the same feeling – and they were right: Tam's drug-smuggling scam was building up into a multimillion-pound racket. In Margaret's case, her concerns stemmed from being aware of Tam making furtive telephone calls, of hearing whispered conversations between her husband and his closest associates, and noticing mutual friends exchanging knowing looks when they might have thought she could not see their expressions.

'I knew something was up but couldn't work out what it could be,' she says. 'Something wasn't right, and try as I might I could not find out what the explanation was, so I asked my brother John what was going on. He didn't want to tell me, but I almost pleaded with him, and finally he said, "Look, Margaret, I'll tell you, but you must never tell Tam how you found out. He's planning a surprise 25th-wedding-anniversary party for you." I was astonished. "Well, I hope it's next year," I said. "It's our 24th anniversary this year, not our 25th. We were married in 1971." John was flabbergasted. "You'd better let Tam know," he said.

'Tam had got the wrong year. But he was never the sharpest when it came to domestic life. He did absolutely nothing about the house and didn't even change a plug. I used to say to him, "I'll do it, because at least I know what I'm doing." Tam made up for his lethargy. He always bought me a present when he went away. Never once did he come back from a business trip without a gift for me.

If he had money, he wasn't the sort who bought things for himself – he always bought for others. He bought one relative a house and another a car, and the decisions to get both were made on the spur of the moment.

'At one stage, he was making so much money that he didn't know what to do with it. But it was his money, and I had nothing to do with how he came by it or where it came from. If Tam had £50,000, he wouldn't go out and buy himself an expensive Rolex watch, as so many of the others he had known over the years had done. That just wasn't him. He might go and buy somebody else a Rolex, but he wore a very modest watch, just as he drove an old and nondescript jeep. He didn't wear jewellery because he didn't think it was manly. At the same time, he knew that I collected dolls and would never feel embarrassed flying back up from London carrying a doll for me. My mother might have doubted the wisdom of my marrying him, but over the years she, like the rest of my family, came to think he was brilliant.'

Was it that generosity that resulted in Tam, a man said to have amassed a fortune during his lifetime, leaving just £621 in a solitary bank account and a life-insurance policy worth just £33,508? Death came so unexpectedly that he left no will, so Margaret, his next of kin, was his executor.

Drew Drummond was one of Tam's most trusted friends, and his sister Meg has been close to Margaret since they were in their teens. 'We were first introduced when Tam brought Margaret to our house to see Drew,' says Meg. It turned out to be a confusing beginning. 'It was some time before we discovered Margaret thought she was at Tam's ma's house, not mine. After that initial meeting, we saw a lot of one another and had lots of fun. This was in the days when attitudes were different. There was a great community spirit and everyone looked after everybody else. Odd, isn't it, that so many of the Barlanark Team lived in the same area and yet everyone felt safe? We loved to go out, get drunk and have a dance and a few laughs, and we watched each other grow up. Before Margaret could drive, we used to take taxis everywhere. If she thought the driver was going too fast, she'd have a fit. She'd then ring up the taxi office and tell them, "Don't send that guy back again." Eventually, she'd banned them from sending so many drivers that there was only the boss left. He used to come for us himself and would say, "Now, how slowly must I go?"'

Margaret was also close to Snads' partner, Violet. About four years ago, Tam and Margaret took fifteen members of the family and six other friends to Florida on a two-week holiday. 'They paid for everything, and it was one of the best times we ever spent together,' says Violet. 'As you grow older, you wonder if every time might be the last time you are together, and in this case it was true. At least our final time as a crowd with Tam present will always be remembered as a happy time.

'Not long before Tam died, Margaret and I were messing about with the karaoke machine at her home. We'd had a few drinks, and Tam, who had been upstairs in bed watching television, came down for a last cup of tea before going to sleep. He was stone-cold sober and wearing his tartan housecoat, which I called his "braveheart coat". Possibly because we were pretty close to being sloshed, we could not get the karaoke machine to work and wanted Tam to sing instead. He kept telling us, "The pair of you are crazy," but he ended up taking the microphone and singing "Angels", his favourite song, to us. Tam wasn't a great drinker – two pints and he was half drunk – but he loved singing, and especially loved it when others asked him to sing. When he'd finished, he made his tea and went off to bed. That memory will stay with me for ever. The first time we met, I thought how clever and kind Margaret was, and more than 20 years on I still feel exactly the same about her now.'

What does the future hold for Margaret McGraw? She had hoped for a new life with Jim McMinimee but their marriage ended in 2011. Now, surrounded by close family and friends she has no plans to move from the house that was her and Tam's home. And in addition to sorting out her husband's estate, she started legal action against the family members who had responsibility for the estate of her long-time friend Gordon Ross. The proceedings were intended to recover the loan she made to Gordon to help with the improvements he planned to the home he shared with Kellie Anne. After a protracted series of court hearings, the matter was resolved in Margaret's favour in August 2008, with an award to her totalling £125,000, made up of the loan plus interest and some legal expenses. At the same reading when she predicted Tam would be shot, the medium told Margaret that Gordon had come through with a message. It was simply 'Sorry for the hassle.' Most people assumed this was a reference to the upset Gordon caused to his friends through his activities in the time leading up to his murder. In fact, it was an apology for passing on and leaving her to recover the £100,000 he had owed to her. Freed from the stresses of living with a man whose reputation inevitably attracted controversy and threats, Margaret has a simple wish for herself: to live quietly and happily. Many people might think it odd that she has no regrets about her life thus far. 'Even if I could live my life over again, I would not, because it might be worse second time round,' she says. 'I believe that you do not know the good times unless you've lived the bad.'

POSTSCRIPT

F OR ALMOST THE FIRST 25 YEARS OF THEIR MARRIAGE, MARGARET
and Tam McGraw stayed out of the limelight. Margaret was
well known in the East End of Glasgow thanks to her thriving
commercial enterprises, while her husband's name frequently
appeared in police-station logs. But the media was largely unaware
that they existed. It was a situation they, and everyone else they
knew, preferred. Publicity meant attention, and attention brought
curiosity. No one wanted outsiders poking about in their affairs,
because those outsiders might include the police. So, the less the
media knew, the better.

The first hint of change came in the mid-1990s when Tam was
labelled the new godfather of crime in Glasgow. Convicted armed
robber Thomas Bagan made the accusation during his trial at the
High Court in Glasgow, creating inevitable, if initially lukewarm,
newspaper interest. Against the advice of his wife, Tam agreed to an
interview with a Sunday newspaper, but the experience determined
him never to speak to the media again and left Margaret with a
sense of disgust and revulsion.

A short conversation took place in their Mount Vernon home
against the background of Zoltan's death, a distressing occurrence
that appeared to interest the interviewer more than Tam's denials of
being a major criminal. If he had hoped to eradicate further interest
in his activities and dispel rumours that he was a major force in the
underworld by going public for the first time, he soon discovered
that the reverse was the case. As a result, neither Margaret nor Tam
would willingly speak to any journalist for the next ten years.

There were exceptions. Freed following his lengthy High Court trial in Edinburgh in 1998, Tam advised the waiting media crowd as he left to return home to Margaret to 'Fuck off'. The amazing dropped-pants incident happened in 2002, and a couple of years later Margaret was in the midst of decorating when a reporter knocked on her door and surprised her by asking for Tam. She answered truthfully and briefly that he did not live there – the couple were separated at the time.

Throughout these years, the name of Tam McGraw appeared with increasing frequency in the media. The stories were remarkably varied. Most were fantasy, some were vicious and others were cruel, but all had two common factors: not one included a comment from the McGraws, and none of the authors had ever met Margaret or her husband. This could have been put down to the fact that the family, on sound advice from friends and lawyers, had chosen to remain silent and ignore requests for interviews. But there was a simpler explanation: apart from a handful of exceptions, no one bothered to knock and ask for a brief word . . .

In April 2002, a friend telephoned and asked me to join him at a bar in Woodlands Road in Glasgow. I arrived to find myself shaking hands with Tam and most of his closest friends. Gordon Ross was there, Billy McPhee bought me a drink and Eddie McCreadie was cracking jokes.

A couple of days earlier, Tam had been fighting with Paul Ferris in Barlanark, and he was anxious to let me see at first hand how inaccurate the reports were that the encounter had, as one newspaper claimed, left him fighting for his life in hospital. I sounded him out about an interview. 'Not now. I promise to talk some day and I promise it will only be with you,' he said. He kept his word, but it was two and a half years before Tam finally agreed to tell me his life story.

While researching and writing *Crimelord*, I had regular meetings with Tam at his home, where I was introduced to Margaret. She always welcomed me with friendliness and kindness, and I was treated to an endless supply of tea and coffee. I met many family friends, most of them surprised by the presence of a journalist. 'You're privileged,' I recall being told by one. 'They must like you, so don't let them down.'

'There's been so much crap written and talked about them over the years that they've learned not to react.'

'The only opinions that matter to Margaret and Tam are those of people close to them.'

Tam's death in July 2007 gave the usual suspects a chance to cash in on a trade of unchecked and frequently untrue stories – one received six thousand pounds from a single newspaper. But with Tam's passing, Margaret now became the chief target. Since the McGraw name first became synonymous with criminality and the underworld, there have been countless cases of the family name appearing in the media.

Until Margaret agreed to collaborate with this book, she has never publicly talked about her life or that of her and Tam or, commented on articles about her family.

In this respect, Tam's death has changed nothing. Mags is a strong woman who says her only concerns over claims of this nature are not any potential effects upon her personally but on those close to her.

So, what of the future? Will she continue to suffer from the fallout of Tam's activities? Yes, probably, is the answer. Will she spend the remainder of her life looking over her shoulder, waiting and worrying for the next wild insinuation?

Definitely not.